FINANCE KNIGHTS
PUBLICATIONS

ACCOUNTING FOR BEGINNERS
[ALL-IN-ONE]

Everything You Need to Understand Financial & Managerial Accounting Without Prior Experience. Master Financial Statements, Business Performance, and Taxes.

Copyright © 2025 by Finance Knights Publications. All rights reserved.

"Accounting for Beginners [All-in-One]" and all of its contents, including but not limited to text, graphics, images, and other materials, are protected by copyright law and international treaties. Finance Knights Publications is the sole owner of the copyright for this work.

The content in this book, including all text and illustrations, is for informational purposes only and does not constitute financial, accounting, or legal advice. The authors and publishers of this book shall not be liable for any errors or omissions, nor for any actions taken based on its content.

Finance Knights Publications explicitly states that it is not responsible for the activities, operations, or services of any companies or services mentioned within *"Accounting for Beginners"*. The inclusion of any company or service name in this book is for informational purposes only and does not imply endorsement or affiliation. Finance Knights Publications will not receive any commission or compensation if a reader decides to purchase a product or engage with any of the named companies or services. Readers are encouraged to conduct their own research and due diligence before opting to use any products or services mentioned within this book.

Any unauthorized reproduction, distribution, or public display of this book, in whole or in part, is strictly prohibited by law. This includes, but is not limited to, photocopying, scanning, uploading, sharing, or any other means of copying or disseminating the contents of this book without the explicit written permission of Finance Knights Publications. All rights reserved.

By accessing, reading, or otherwise using this book, you acknowledge and agree that the information contained herein is for personal use and informational purposes only. You may not use this book for any commercial or promotional purposes without obtaining prior written consent from Finance Knights Publications.

In the event of any unauthorized use or infringement of our copyright, Finance Knights Publications reserves the right to pursue legal remedies available under applicable copyright laws. This may include seeking damages, injunctive relief, and legal fees.

What the Experts Say About This Book

Gregory Davis – *CPA, CMA, CFM, CTP, CGMA, Author of the book "Checkmate"*

"Accounting for Beginners (All-in-One)" is an outstanding resource for anyone looking to gain a better understanding of accounting and related topics. As an accountancy professor for over 15 years, accounting can be difficult to understand, but the author does an excellent job of breaking down the key concepts into manageable, actionable steps.

Jordan Jasper – *CPA*

Finance Knights Publications has accomplished something remarkable with "Accounting for Beginners (All-in-One)", it has made accounting simple, digestible, and engaging, all in under 300 pages. For a subject that's often regarded as dry and complex, what has been done here is truly impressive. Having spent nearly a decade studying at universities, working in consulting and accounting, and enduring rigorous exams to become a Certified Public Accountant, I've seen my fair share of accounting books. Most are dense and difficult for beginners to absorb. That's why I can say with confidence that this book should be required reading for every entry-level accountant.

Rodney Roque – *CPA, PFS*

Whether you're an educator seeking the perfect teaching tool, a student navigating the often-confusing world of debits and credits, or simply a curious mind eager to explore the language of finance, this book delivers on every front. In the world of accounting books, few manage to strike the perfect balance between clarity, engagement, and depth. But this book has done just that, earning my wholehearted recommendation for educators, students, and even those who know nothing about accounting. Highly recommended for anyone who values learning resources that truly empower.

Michelle Payne – *CPA*

This accounting book serves as an invaluable resource for newcomers to the field, offering clear and concise explanations that help readers establish a solid foundation. Beyond the basics, it delves into some of the more complex aspects of accounting, providing practical insights and advanced techniques. Whether you're just starting out or looking to deepen your understanding, this book is a fantastic tool to navigate the challenging elements of accounting with confidence.

Lyndsey Reed – *Financial Analyst, Accountant*

Whether you're a small business owner, a college student, or simply someone looking to get a handle on the numbers, it offers clear, practical insights into accounting and bookkeeping fundamentals. The chapters are thoughtfully organized and break down complex concepts into manageable, easy-to-understand sections, complete with real-world examples. One of the book's biggest strengths is its accessibility, it's written in plain, approachable language without dumbing things down. You'll be introduced to key terminology in a way that feels natural, not overwhelming.

Rory Lynch – *Financial Analyst, Accountant*

If you new to accounting, or just want to strengthen your financial knowledge, this is the book for you. It breaks down fundamental concepts into clear, easy-to-follow steps, making even complex topics accessible. This guide provides practical explanations that will build your confidence and set you up for success in managing accounts and financial records

INTRODUCTION

For many people, the thought of diving into accounting can seem daunting or even a bit boring. It's easy to imagine accounting as nothing more than a maze of numbers, spreadsheets, and tax forms. But the truth is, accounting is much more than just crunching numbers; it's the *language of business,* as world-renowned investor Warren Buffett once said on the subject. Whether you're a small business owner, a student, or someone just curious about how money moves, understanding accounting can unlock doors to better financial decision-making and clarity in both personal and professional finance.

At first glance, accounting might seem like a mountain to climb. Some students even compare their first accounting course to learning a foreign language. However, just like any new skill, once you grasp the basics, the pieces start to fit together, and the concepts that seemed confusing at the start suddenly make sense.

Here's a little secret: accounting is not as hard as it seems. In fact, many people discover that it's a bit like solving puzzles. You take the information available, whether it's about sales, expenses, or profits, and piece it together to create a clear financial picture. It's a rewarding process that can even become *enjoyable* once you get the hang of it.

Imagine this: you're running a small business selling handmade products online. Sales are going well, but at the end of the month, you're not quite sure where all your money went. Bills are paid, yet the profits don't seem to add up. This is where accounting comes in to save the day. By keeping track of every dollar coming in and going out, you gain control over your finances and can make better decisions for the future of your business.

Or think about managing personal finances. Have you ever wondered why your bank account seems emptier than expected at the end of each month? By applying basic accounting principles, you can *pinpoint* where your money is going and make adjustments to improve your financial situation.

This guide is designed for those with **little to no knowledge of accounting**, whether you're a student, business owner, or professional seeking a clearer understanding of the basics. We'll start from the very basics, and build from there, whether you're looking to manage a business, study for an exam, or just learn the ropes, this guide will walk you through everything you need to know

Many newcomers to accounting need encouragement. For students, introductory courses are often seen as a "trial by fire," designed to filter out those not up for the challenge. In the professional world, accounting is often viewed as confusing and tedious, reserved for humorless "number crunchers." However, learning even the basics of accounting can make a significant difference in managing your business or personal finances.

I've seen firsthand the cost of ignoring accounting. There was a small business owner who didn't track her rental property finances correctly. She ended up paying over $15,000 more in taxes than necessary! Another entrepreneur lost a potential multi-million-dollar sale because his accounting records were such a mess that the buyer didn't trust the numbers. It's clear, **accounting matters**.

One of the most common reasons people avoid learning accounting is the fear of math. But here's a surprise: **accounting isn't about advanced math.** It's about organizing and interpreting financial data. Most of the challenges are conceptual, not numerical. With a bit of independent study, you can build a strong foundation without needing to be a math whiz.

Why You Need Accounting Skills

Accounting is useful in so many situations. Here are just a few examples:

Getting a loan – If you're seeking funding, well-organized financial statements help you communicate clearly with banks and investors, increasing your chances of approval.

Tax planning – Accurate accounting ensures businesses pay the right taxes on time, without overpaying or facing penalties.

Self-employment – If you're a freelancer or run your own business, understanding accounting helps you manage income, expenses, and taxes effectively.

Everyday business decisions – Whether you run an Etsy shop or a local café, accounting helps you make more informed decisions. With clear financial data, you can confidently assess how much money you have, how much you can reinvest, or how much you can safely take out of the business.

New job or career growth – Understanding accounting basics can make you more effective at your job. Whether you're a bookkeeper or a manager, it gives you the confidence to take on more responsibility.

Solving cash flow issues – Many businesses seem to be running fine, but their bank balance keeps shrinking. Accounting helps pinpoint where the money is going and how to resolve these issues before their cash reserves run dry.

Preventing fraud – Small businesses are especially vulnerable to fraud. A strong grasp of accounting helps owners and managers spot irregularities and prevent losses.

If you're a student, I encourage you to use this book as a **primer** for your accounting courses. By studying the basics here, you'll be better prepared and ready to dive deep into advanced topics in your educational studies.

So, grab a cup of coffee and get comfortable. You might just discover accounting is a lot more interesting and useful than you imagined!

Support & Feedback

FINANCE KNIGHTS
P U B L I C A T I O N S

Before we dive in, we want to thank you for choosing to explore the world of accounting with us. This book is packed with everything you need to learn the basics of accounting, and we're holding nothing back because we genuinely want to see you succeed. You'll find a lot of detailed information ahead, some of it may seem quite technical or even a bit tedious, but we assure you it's all necessary and will prove invaluable as you move forward.

Before moving on, here's a quick reminder:

1. Access Your Bonus Content

Head over to the section at the end of the book to learn how to download additional resources. These extras were created to help you get even more value out of your reading experience.

2. Share How Excited You Are to Begin This Adventure

We'd love to hear your initial impressions and see how you're preparing to tackle the world of accounting. Choose whichever option feels most comfortable for you:

> - **Option A: Create a short video**
>   Record a quick clip showing off your new book and sharing your thoughts or expectations for the journey ahead.
>
> - **Option B: Post a photo (or photos)**
>   Snap a picture of your copy in a creative setting and tell us what excites you the most about starting this process.
>
> - **Option C: Just Write**
>   If you would rather share your thoughts in writing, we would love to read a few sentences about your early impressions and hopes.

Scan the QR code or click the link (if you're on Kindle):

https://www.amazon.com/review/create-review/?ie=UTF8&channel=glance-detail&asin=B0DRTNJ419

Your feedback **costs you nothing** and **takes less than a minute**. It encourages us to keep creating valuable resources and helps others discover the guidance they need to start their accounting journey.

All of this is *completely optional*, there's no obligation whatsoever, but if you do decide to post:

Pat yourself on the back for making a positive difference in someone else's life. Remember, what goes around comes around.

Thank you from the bottom of our hearts for your support. It truly means so much to us.

If you don't find the book useful or encounter any other issues, please let us know at **info@financeknightspublications.com**. We genuinely appreciate your input, and if we integrate your suggestions, we'll gladly email you our updated digital copy as a small token of thanks.

So let's begin. Together, we'll lay the foundation for your business and set you up for long-term success, without the costly mistakes or sleepless nights worrying about what you might have missed. Let's get started!

TABLE OF CONTENTS

What the Experts Say About This Book	3
INTRODUCTION	5
Support & Feedback	8
CHAPTER 1 Accounting: The Language of Business	13
The Core Functions of Every Business	14
Branches of Accounting	17
Bookkeeping	17
Financial Accounting	18
Managerial Accounting	19
Tax Accounting	20
The Accounting Cycle	21
Accounting Principles	25
Chapter 1 Assessment Test	29
CHAPTER 2 Financial Accounting	33
The Income Statement	34
Statement of Owner's Equity	35
Balance Sheet	37
Statement of Cash Flows	41
Cash Basis vs Accrual Basis	47
Chapter 2 Assessment Test	49
CHAPTER 3 The Accounting Equation	53
Double-Entry Accounting	53
Assets	55
Intangible Assets	56
Liabilities	63
Debits & Credits	65
Equity	72
Example of Accounting for Leo's Pet Supplies	74

Creating the Income Statement, balance sheet, and a cash flow statement	79
Understanding Equity in a Corporation	85
Chapter 3 Assessment Test	91

CHAPTER 4 Recording Transactions — **95**

What is an Invoice?	97
What is a T-Account?	98
Journal Entries and General Ledgers	99
Chart of Accounts	103
Subsidiary Ledger (Subledger)	105
Trial Balance	106
Prepaid Expenses & Unearned Revenues	109
Cehapter 4 Assessment Test	112

CHAPTER 5 Financial Statements — **117**

Breaking Down the Income Statement	118
Earnings Per Share (EPS)	122
Understanding the Balance Sheet	124
Understanding Liquidity Through the Liquidity Ratios	127
Solvency Ratios	129
Equity Differences: Corporations vs. Small Business	129
Depreciation and Asset Valuation	130
Analyzing Cash Flow Statements	138
Capital Expenditure vs. Revenue Expenditure	141
Example of Financial Statements	143
Chapter 5 Assessment Test	144

CHAPTER 6 Managerial Accounting — **149**

The Purpose of Managerial Accounting	149
Cost-Volume-Profit (CVP) Analysis	150
Making Managerial Accounting Work for You	155
Setting Target Income Goals	159
Marginal Costing vs. Absorption Costing	162

Multi-Product Analysis	164
Variance Analysis	167
Inventory Accounting	169
Inventory Management	172
Budgeting	180
Top Budgeting Software for Small and Medium Businesses	185
More on Managerial Accounting: Tools and Techniques for Precision	186
Decision-Making Scenarios	188
Chapter 6 Assessment Test	197
CHAPTER 7 Income Tax Accounting	**201**
Marginal Tax Rate versus Average Tax Rate	202
Accrual or Cash Accounting for Income Tax Purposes?	204
Tax Deductions vs. Tax Credits	207
Long-Term Capital Gains vs. Ordinary Income	209
Why Business Entity Type Matters: A Tax Perspective	211
Chapter 7 Assessment Test	214
CHAPTER 8 Accounting for Investors	**219**
GAAP	219
The Four Accounting Principles	222
The Four Accounting Assumptions	223
The Two Accounting Constraints	225
What investors are really looking for	226
Choosing Investments	228
Chapter 8 Assessment Test	231
Conclusion	**235**
Glossary	**237**
Bonus Chapter and Tools	**239**
About Us	**241**

CHAPTER 1

Accounting:
The Language of Business

> *Accounting is the language of business.*
>
> — *Warren Buffett,*
> *Investor and Philanthropist*

Imagine you run a thriving online store, selling eco-friendly skincare products. Business is booming, and you've just moved your operations from the spare bedroom of your apartment to a rented studio in a trendy part of town. You're considering hiring a few employees to help with production and customer service, but you're unsure if your budget can handle the extra salaries. You've got rent to pay, inventory to manage, and now you're wondering: **Can I afford to hire more help without putting my business at risk?**

Meanwhile, down the street, a café owner named Sarah has been feeling the pinch. She's noticed that certain menu items aren't selling, and the cost of keeping them on the menu is cutting into her profits. After speaking with other café owners, Sarah is ready to make some tough decisions. She's reviewing her financials to figure out what needs to go and what's helping her stay afloat.

At the same time, a well-known regional grocery chain is preparing to distribute dividends to its shareholders after a successful quarter. But before doing so, the company's executives need to ensure they're keeping enough cash on hand to cover operations and potential expansion.

From small startups to large corporations, **accounting is the key** to making smart, informed decisions. Whether you're figuring out if you can afford to hire new staff, streamlining your product offerings, or planning to distribute profits, understanding your financial situation gives you the power to act confidently.

Good accounting practices also help maintain the financial health of your business. Balancing the books regularly, producing financial statements, and reviewing profits and losses keep you in control. Even if you don't have a full-time accountant, **accounting software** can help you manage your finances effectively, something we'll explore later in this guide. But for now, let's start with the basics!

The Core Functions of Every Business

Here's something surprising: no matter how complex a business might seem, all companies essentially perform three key functions. Whether you're running a small bakery or managing a tech startup, the basic activities of any business can be grouped into **financing**, **operating**, and **investing**. While this might sound like an oversimplification, these categories form the foundation of every business's accounting system.

Financing

Financing activities focus on **raising money** to support business operations. Owners can use their own savings or seek external funding, such as loans or investments. I remember when I first started my consulting business, I used a combination of personal savings and a small loan from the bank. At the time, getting that loan felt risky, but with the right financial planning, it allowed me to invest in my business early and grow faster.

Debt financing involves borrowing money (like loans), while **equity financing** involves selling ownership shares (stock) to investors. Even as businesses grow, managing debt wisely is crucial to maintaining strong relationships with lenders and ensuring future access to capital at lower costs. Another option between debt and equity financing is to seek funding from a venture capitalist (VC). While this is still technically equity financing, as the VC now owns a portion of the company, and will have some say in they decision making, you can limit the overall percentage owned by this outside entity and thus their influence. It is a way to help get your business off the ground if you don't have enough capital, without the repayment obligation of debt.

Operating

Operating activities involve the **day-to-day work** of the business, generating revenue and covering expenses. This includes selling products or services and paying for things like rent, utilities, and wages. When I ran my first business, one of the biggest operating expenses I had to manage was marketing. It was a constant balancing act to figure out how much I should spend on ads versus the return I was getting in new sales.

Unlike investments, operating expenses are usually **short-term** and recurring, like rent or payroll. Understanding the difference between an *expense* and an *asset* is key to making sound financial decisions, something we'll dive into further as we explore accounting principles.

Investing

Investing activities are about **acquiring assets** to help the business operate. This could mean purchasing equipment, property, or technology. I once worked with a client who decided to buy a new delivery van for his bakery. While it was a large upfront expense, it allowed him to expand his delivery area and increase sales significantly. That purchase was an *investment* in his business's future.

Businesses also invest in other assets like real estate, machinery, or software, anything that helps them grow or run more efficiently. Investments are typically **long-term** and represent significant commitments to the company's future operations.

How Accounts Help Track Business Finances

An **account** is essentially a record that tracks specific financial transactions. Every account falls into one of five major categories: **assets**, **liabilities**, **equities**, **revenues**, or **expenses**.

Asset Accounts	Liability Accounts	Equity Accounts	Revenue Accounts	Expense Accounts
Cash on Hand	Loan Obligations	Shareholder's Equity	ProdLKt Sales	Office Rent
Customer Receivables	Bills Payable	Owner's Investments	Service Income	Operating Supplies
Real Estate	Employee Salaries Payable	Profit Distributions	Interest Income	Inventory Costs
Buildings	Vendor Payables	Capital Contributions	Royalty Income	License Fees
Machinery	Debts Payable	Retained Profits	Other Revenue	Utilities
Stock Inventory	Other Payables	Other Equity Accounts		Insurance Premiums
Patents and Trademarks				Miscellaneous Expenses

No matter the industry or size of the business, these five categories form the foundation of financial tracking. Whether you own a local bakery or run a consulting firm, accounting is all about managing these types of accounts. For example, if a café owner wants to track the sales of coffee separately from pastries, they can create a specific account for coffee revenue. This flexibility is what makes accounting adaptable to any type of business. There are also many options for adding additional categorizations for future reporting. For example, if you want to know how profitable pastries are, you can use classifications on the expenses related to making pastries specifically.

At this stage, it's not necessary to fully understand how all the different accounts work together, that will come later. For now, let's focus on the five **main account types** and how they connect to the three key business activities: financing, investing, and operating.

While there isn't a strict rule tying each account type to specific activities, using these business activities as a reference can help clarify how different accounts function.

Financing activities are closely tied to **liability accounts**, which record debts or obligations that the business must repay. For instance, if you take out a loan to help finance your business, that loan is logged as a **liability**. When you make payments on the loan, the liability account decreases, and your **cash account** (an asset account) reduces to reflect the money paid out.

I recall financing some new office equipment when I started out. I initially feared how it would impact my books, because I was uncertain about debt in my financials. Once I understood how to mark down the liability as I paid it off, it was no longer a source of stress but became about strategic calculation in my business.

Financing also involves **equity accounts**. When a business owner puts personal money into their business, it's recorded as an increase in equity. Likewise, when a company raises money by selling shares, **shareholder equity** goes up.

Operating activities focus on **revenue** and **expense accounts**, which track the money flowing in and out of the business from day-to-day operations. Revenue accounts log sales and service income, while expense accounts handle the costs of running the business, such as rent, wages, and utilities.

I remember advising a small shop owner who initially tracked all her sales in one lump sum. Once she started separating revenue into different categories, product sales and services, she could quickly see which part of the business was generating the most income, allowing her to make smarter decisions.

Revenue and expense accounts are central to creating an **income statement**, one of the key financial statements used to measure a company's performance. We'll dive deeper into financial statements in the following chapters.

Investing activities are tied to **assets**. Assets include anything the business owns that is expected to bring an economic benefit to the company in the future, like cash, property, or equipment. When a company purchases new equipment, that adds to its asset accounts.

A photographer friend of mine invested in a high-end camera system, which increased the value of her **equipment account**. Since she paid in cash, her **cash account** decreased. Had she financed the purchase, her **accounts payable** (a liability account) would have increased instead of the cash account decreasing.

Branches of Accounting

Let's consider a small business owner who runs a successful coffee shop. She needs accounting to ensure her sales cover her expenses, to keep enough cash on hand for supplies and employee wages, and to plan for the future growth of her business. Accounting helps her spot areas that need improvement and prepares her for tax season without any unwelcome surprises.

Now, compare her needs to those of a large construction company managing multiple projects, or a non-profit organization making sure donations are spent effectively on their programs. Or think about a multinational corporation planning a merger, its accounting needs are far more complex. In each case, accounting plays a critical role, but the *type* of accounting needed varies significantly.

There are many specialized branches of accounting, including **auditing**, **forensic accounting**, and **government accounting**. However, we'll focus on the four **core branches** that are most commonly used: **bookkeeping**, **financial accounting**, **managerial accounting**, and **tax accounting**. These branches form the foundation of financial management for businesses large and small.

Bookkeeping

Bookkeeping is one of the simplest yet most **fundamental** aspects of accounting. The primary role of a bookkeeper is to accurately **collect and record data**. While accountants focus on organizing and presenting financial information, the collection of data goes far beyond just the accountant's responsibilities. Cashiers, assistants, and even warehouse workers all contribute data in various forms.

Take, for example, a retail store. The cashier logs each sale, while the stockroom manager tracks inventory levels. The information collected by these employees is essential for the bookkeeper to compile into a coherent financial picture. Bookkeepers act as the **central hub**, consolidating this scattered data into reports and maintaining key financial documents.

To put it another way, if accounting were a ship navigating the financial seas, the bookkeeper would be the one constantly ensuring the **ship's supplies** (financial data), are well-stocked and organized. This allows the accountant to steer the ship in the right direction by performing detailed financial analysis and making informed decisions.

With the rise of **accounting software**, much of the manual work once handled by bookkeepers has been streamlined. These tools are **user-friendly** and capable of generating financial reports with just a few clicks, making them indispensable in modern bookkeeping practices. The automation provided by these programs makes it easier than ever for anyone to be able to organize and analyze financial data. Most also have built in controls to prevent some common user errors when manually tracking data. This is why you will very rarely see manual "paper" books in today's business world.

One of the most popular bookkeeping tools today is **QuickBooks Online**, known for its versatility and ease of use. For those looking to master this powerful tool, we have a **specific guide** available on Amazon that covers everything you need to know about using QuickBooks effectively.

You can find it at this link: **https://www.amazon.com/dp/B0CP6N1_WY8** or using this QR code:

Financial Accounting

Financial accounting is centered on preparing financial reports and data for individuals or organizations outside the business. Whether it's a company reporting its financial performance to investors, or a small business owner sharing financial records with a potential lender, financial accounting is crucial in these situations.

Other external users of financial data include potential investors or business partners. Imagine a tech startup considering an investment from a venture capital firm. Before committing any funds, the firm would thoroughly review the startup's financial statements to assess the company's value and potential risks. This is an example of financial accounting aiding in an important business decision.

Consider another scenario: a manufacturing company, **TechParts**, is looking to acquire smaller businesses that own valuable machinery. They target companies with modest profits but significant physical assets. TechParts aims to purchase these businesses at competitive prices to acquire their equipment and expand their production capabilities.

Which financial statements would TechParts need to evaluate potential acquisitions?

In this case, the companies under consideration would provide several years of **balance sheets and income statements.** TechParts would analyze the income statements to understand profitability, while the balance sheets would give insight into the overall equity (or value) of the business, along with liabilities and the assets, especially the machinery and equipment that TechParts is most interested in. This demonstrates the critical role of financial accounting in **mergers and acquisitions**.

Compared to managerial accounting, financial accounting shows more information that's directly related to reporting. When a business shares its financial information with external parties, it must be transparent about its overall performance but can choose to withhold sensitive internal details, such as specific vendor agreements or payment terms. Additionally, financial accounting reports are often prepared less frequently, focusing on periodic reports such as quarterly or annual statements.

We will explore financial accounting further throughout this book, especially in chapter 8, where we discuss its role in **selecting and monitoring investments**.

Managerial Accounting

Managerial accounting is, in many ways, the opposite of financial accounting. It involves operational, strategic, and more frequent reporting tailored for internal use within a company. For instance, think about a restaurant owner who notices a decline in profits. By using managerial accounting, she can analyze the cost and sales data of each menu item. She might discover that some dishes are not generating enough revenue to cover their ingredient costs. With this information, she can decide to either adjust the prices, change the ingredients, or remove the items from the menu altogether.

Another example could be a small clothing manufacturer that is trying to decide which products to feature in their upcoming summer collection. By using managerial accounting, the company can analyze sales data from previous seasons, production costs, and current fashion trends to make informed decisions about which designs to prioritize.

Managerial accounting is all about using detailed financial data to inform **internal business decisions**. This can range from determining the effectiveness of marketing campaigns to setting employee compensation. It starts with accurate **bookkeeping**, without reliable data, any conclusions drawn from managerial accounting would be flawed.

Managerial accounting is used for a variety of purposes beyond making decisions on product lines or menu items, such as:

- Designing promotions or discounts
- Analyzing customer purchasing patterns
- Planning product packaging and presentation
- Setting salaries and compensation packages
- Creating and maintaining budgets
- Evaluating employee performance
- Making investment choices
- Assessing creditworthiness of clients

One of the great aspects of managerial accounting is that it allows for a lot of **creativity**. A CFO or business manager can design custom reports, systems, and strategies that cater to the specific needs of their company. Some businesses develop proprietary managerial accounting methods that are considered valuable intellectual property.

While many of the reports used in managerial accounting resemble those in financial accounting, they are typically generated more frequently, contain more detail, and are often customized for particular decision-making needs. For example, in addition to standard **profit and loss statements**, a manager might request reports on individual employee performance, the success rate of a new product launch, or even the progress of a long-term construction project.

A unique feature of managerial accounting is that it often involves **non-monetary data**. Reports might be based on inventory counts, customer feedback surveys, or employee performance evaluations. This data, while not financial in nature, can provide invaluable insights into the operational aspects of a business.

Tax Accounting

One of the biggest reasons small business owners and managers strive to maintain organized books is to stay on top of **tax compliance**.

The goal of **tax accounting** is simple: pay as little as possible in taxes, while still remaining compliant.

Tax accounting methodology differs significantly from financial or managerial accounting, particularly when it comes to the specific laws and regulations. In many countries, financial accounting follows a standard set of principles, such as **GAAP** (Generally Accepted Accounting Principles) in the U.S. designed to ensure consistency and transparency in financial reporting. Publicly traded companies are required by law to follow GAAP, while many private companies voluntarily adhere to these guidelines to give their financial statements credibility.

For instance, imagine you're an investor considering buying shares in a company. You would want to feel confident that the company's financial reports are accurate and follow consistent rules. This is what adherence to GAAP ensures, it prevents companies from manipulating their financial data to present a misleadingly positive picture.

However, **tax accounting** has its own set of rules, often dictated by the government or tax authorities. In this case, the focus shifts from providing information to investors or shareholders to ensuring that all taxable income is reported correctly and that any potential deductions are taken in line with tax laws. While it sounds confusing and a bit deceptive, a business may show one set of financial results to investors, based on GAAP, and another to the tax authorities, based on tax regulations.

While we'll explore **tax accounting** further in this guide, it's important to remember that staying compliant with tax rules is just one side of the coin. Many businesses also engage in **tax strategies** using legitimate methods to minimize their tax burdens through careful planning and deductions.

The Accounting Cycle

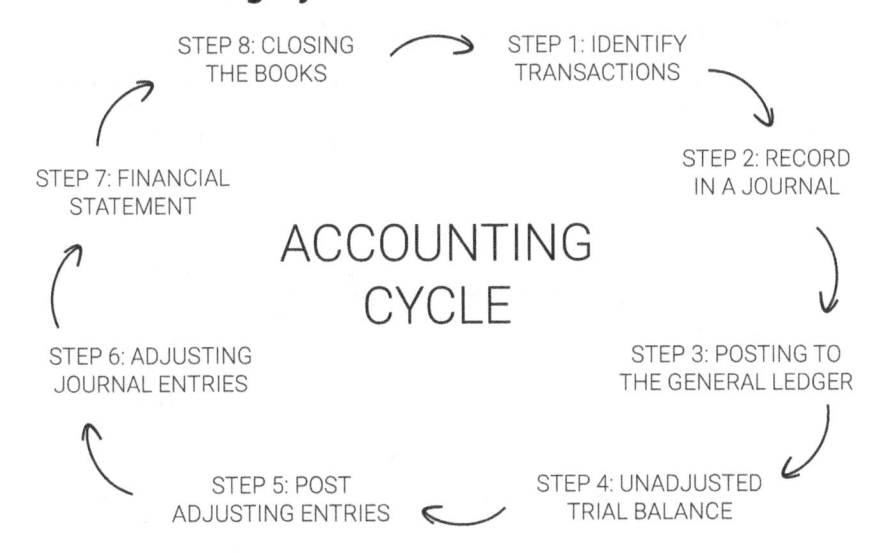

ACCOUNTING CYCLE

- STEP 1: IDENTIFY TRANSACTIONS
- STEP 2: RECORD IN A JOURNAL
- STEP 3: POSTING TO THE GENERAL LEDGER
- STEP 4: UNADJUSTED TRIAL BALANCE
- STEP 5: POST ADJUSTING ENTRIES
- STEP 6: ADJUSTING JOURNAL ENTRIES
- STEP 7: FINANCIAL STATEMENT
- STEP 8: CLOSING THE BOOKS

Before we dive into the details, let's take a moment to get familiar with the **accounting cycle** as a whole. This cycle is the backbone of financial accounting, a systematic process that transforms raw financial data into clear, accurate reports.

In this section, we'll provide a brief **overview of each key step** in the cycle—from identifying transactions to creating financial statements and closing the books. Think of it as your roadmap to understanding how businesses maintain their financial records.

Let's say you own Bean Bliss, a specialty coffee shop known for its unique blends and engaging customer service. In March, you decide to run a promotional offer: customers can purchase a "Coffee Club" subscription for $500 upfront, which gives them unlimited coffee for the next 12 months starting April 1st.

Your promotion is a success, and you collect $30,000 in cash from eager coffee lovers. This event marks the beginning of the **accounting cycle**. The first task is to identify the transactions as they happen.

Step 1: Identifying the Transaction

The first step is to recognize each transaction. In this case, the $30,000 is the amount paid for coffee subscriptions, it involves money and represents an inflow of cash.

Proper identification is critical because every financial event, whether it's a sale, an expense, or a loan, needs to be recognized before it can be recorded. Missing a transaction can lead to inaccurate financial records, which may result in poor decision-making or even legal complications.

Step 2: Recording the Transaction in a Journal

After identifying the transaction, the next step is to **record it in a journal**, often referred to as the "book of original entry." A journal provides a chronological log of all financial transactions, capturing details like the date, description, and the accounts affected.

For this transaction, your journal entry might look something like this:

JOURNAL ENTRY			
J/E NUMBER: 1052			
DATE	ACCOUNT	DEBIT	CREDIT
March 31, 20X5	Cash	$30,000	
	Deferred Revenue		$30,000

> - Date: March 31st
> - Description: Coffee Club subscription payments
> - Accounts: **Cash** and **Deferred Revenue**
> - Amounts: Debit Cash for $30,000, Credit Deferred Revenue for $30,000

This is where **double-entry accounting** comes into play. Every transaction affects at least two accounts, one is debited and one is credited. Whether the account increases or decreases depends on its normal balance type: some accounts increase with a debit, others with a credit.

Step 3: Posting to the General Ledger

Once the transaction is recorded in the journal, the next step is to **post it to the general ledger**. The ledger is the central repository of all your financial data, organized by the five major categories of accounts such as assets, liabilities, equities, revenues, and expenses. Think of it as the master book that holds the entire history of your financial transactions.

Historically, businesses relied on large, physical ledgers that required manual updates. Today, digital systems make this process faster and less prone to human error. These systems also tend to record the transaction in the journal and post it to the ledger at the same time, further streamlining the process. Once posted, the ledger provides a detailed, organized view of your business's financial activity, making it easier to analyze and prepare reports.

Step 4: Unadjusted Trial Balance

At the end of an accounting period, typically December 31st, you'll need to prepare a **trial balance**. This is an internal report that lists the closing balances of all your accounts, ensuring that the total debits equal the total credits.

For *Bean Bliss*, the trial balance will include accounts like:

> - **Cash**: Reflecting the money collected from customers.
> - **Deferred Revenue**: Showing the amount of service still owed to customers.
> - **Expenses**: Tracking costs like supplies, rent, and employee wages.

The purpose of the trial balance is twofold:

> 1. To check for errors in the recording and posting process.
> 2. To lay the groundwork for preparing financial statements.

One of the key rules of accounting is that debits must equal credits when you record a transaction in Step 2. If the debits and credits don't match, it indicates an error that needs to be corrected before moving forward.

Step 5: Post Adjusting Entries

This step involves bringing your records in line with the **accrual basis of accounting**, which requires recognizing revenue when it's earned and expenses when they're incurred, regardless of when cash is received or paid.

Step 6: Adjusting Journal Entries

After identifying the necessary adjustments, the **adjusting journal entries** are recorded in the journal and posted to the general ledger. These adjustments update the account balances so they reflect the correct financial position before preparing financial statements.

Step 7: Creating Financial Statements

Once the adjusting entries are posted, the next step is to prepare the **financial statements**. These reports are the cornerstone of financial accounting, providing a clear summary of your business's activities and financial position over a specific period or at a specific point in time. There are three primary financial statements:

- The Balance Sheet
- The Income Statement
- Statement of Cash Flows

Together, these three statements provide a comprehensive view of your business's financial performance and position. We will discuss these statements further in the next chapter.

Step 8: Closing Entries

Once the financial statements are prepared and shared with stakeholders, the final step in the accounting cycle is to **close the books**. This involves posting **closing entries**, which reset the balances of temporary accounts—like revenues, expenses, and dividends, to zero, transferring their totals to permanent accounts such as **retained earnings**.

After the closing entries are posted, your temporary accounts are cleared, and your business is ready to start the new financial year with a clean slate.

The Accounting Cycle: Bringing It All Together

Together, these steps form the **accounting cycle**, the foundation of **financial accounting**. This process involves identifying, recording, summarizing, and analyzing your business's financial transactions, culminating in the preparation of financial statements. These statements provide a clear and accurate picture of your business's financial health and performance, serving as a vital tool for decision-making and transparency.

While this overview might feel like a lot to take in, it's essential to see the **big picture** before diving into the details. In the following sections, we'll take a closer, more relaxed look at each step of the cycle. This step-by-step approach will help you build a solid understanding of how the accounting cycle works and why it's so important.

Accounting Principles

When studying a financial report, you want to be able to rely on the statements presented. How do you know the profits shown aren't exaggerated or that important costs aren't hidden in another period? Understanding the fundamental accounting principles can give you that confidence: the **Matching Principle**, the **Conservatism Principle** and the **Materiality Concept** – which work behind the scenes to ensure financial statements are accurate, consistent, and useful. These concepts are crucial because they help ensure the numbers in a financial report truly reflect a company's performance and financial health. Let's take a look at how they work.

Matching Principle

This **principle** is an accounting guideline that tells companies *when* to record their revenues and expenses. In simple terms, it means recording expenses in the same period as the revenues they helped to generate. You pair up (or *match*) the income earned with the costs incurred to earn it, so that each accounting period shows *the real profit* made during that time. By doing this, businesses avoid painting a misleading picture of their profitability – you can't boost your profits by recording revenue now and pushing related expenses to a later period (or vice versa). This principle is a core part of **accrual accounting**, which is all about timing transactions to the period they actually belong to, rather than just when cash changes hands.

The matching principle ensures companies report expenses in the same period as the related revenue, aligning costs with benefits for an accurate picture of profit.

For example, suppose a company sells $10,000 worth of goods in December, but only pays $5,000 to the supplier for those goods in January. According to the matching principle, the company will **record that $5,000 expense in December**, and the same month it records the $10,000 revenue. This way, December's income statement reflects the true profit ($5,000) from that sale, rather than showing $10,000 profit in December and a sudden $5,000 expense in January with no revenue against it. Similarly, if a local shop buys inventory in August but doesn't sell it until September, the cost of that inventory is reported as an expense in September, matching the timing of the sale.

The impact of the matching principle on financial reporting is significant: it makes earnings **more consistent and meaningful** from period to period. Without matching, financial results could swing wildly – one month might look very profitable (if revenue is recorded now but expenses are pushed off), followed by another month that looks terrible (when the expenses finally hit with no revenue). By matching them together, the income statement isn't "lumpy" or misleading; it shows a smoother, more **normalized view of the business's performance**. Investors and managers get a better sense of the company's true economics, because all the costs related to earning the revenue are shown alongside that revenue. Another common example of matching in action is **depreciation**: if a company buys a machine for $100,000 that will be used for 10 years, it doesn't expense all $100k in year one. Instead, it spreads the cost over the machine's 10-year life (about $10,000 per year). This way, each year's profit reflects one-tenth of the machine's cost, appropriately matching the machine's expense to the revenues it's helping produce each year. In short, the matching principle helps ensure we're looking at *real profitability* for each period – revenues and the related expenses side by side – which is invaluable for judging performance and making informed decisions.

Conservatism Principles

The Conservatism Principle (or Prudence Concept) is all about **playing it safe and being cautious** when reporting finances. The Prudence Concept essentially means that when using judgement in accounting, an accountant should be conservative with their revenues but liberal with their expenses. Accountants often summarize this with the saying: *"Do not anticipate profits, but provide for all possible losses."*. In other words, you only count your gains when you're sure of them, but you recognize expenses or losses as soon as they are foreseeable. This conservative approach ensures that the financial statements **aren't too optimistic**, they give a realistic (or even slightly cautious) view of the company's financial position. The goal is to avoid unpleasant surprises for the users of the financial statements by preparing for the worst and not assuming the best without evidence.

Conservatism in accounting ensures assets and income aren't overstated, while all likely losses or expenses are recognized – essentially erring on the side of caution.

For a practical example, imagine a business is closing its books for the year and learns two pieces of news: (1) there's a chance it will earn a **$1 million profit** from a contract that's still under negotiation, and (2) there's a possibility of a **$500,000 loss** from a lawsuit claim. Under the prudence concept, how do they handle this? The company will **not record the $1 million gain yet (because it's not guaranteed to happen), **but it will record the $500,000 as a potential expense** or provision. In some cases, businesses will use a probability threshold to decide if something should be included. For example, if you are over 75% certain you include an accrual, and if it is less you do not.

By doing so, the financial statements don't show profits that might never materialize, but they do account for a loss that could be coming.

In everyday business, prudence appears in several ways, **one common application is making provisions for doubtful debts:** if a company has customers who owe money, and there's a risk some customers won't pay, the company creates an **allowance (expense) account on the balance sheet** to reflect potential losses. The **actual expense only appears on the income statement** if and when the debt is officially written off. This means **expected losses from bad debts are recognized in advance**, rather than waiting until a customer actually defaults (which could be too late for readers of the financial report to know the risk). Another example is **inventory valuation**: under prudent accounting, inventory is reported at the lower of its cost or its market value. If some stock in the warehouse is worth less now than what the company originally paid (i.e. due to damage or obsolescence), the company writes down the inventory value to that lower amount . This way, the assets aren't overstated on the balance sheet, and any expected loss in value is recognized as an expense immediately.

The prudence concept is crucial for building **trust in financial statements**. By being conservative, it prevents companies from inflating their profits or assets in good times and then shocking investors with losses later on. Stakeholders (like investors, lenders, or owners) can take comfort that the company has **prepared for potential losses and isn't prematurely counting on gains**. After all, it's better to be surprised by realized gains than to be misled by overly optimistic reports.

Materiality Concept

Not every line item or transaction in accounting needs the same level of detail, this is where the **Materiality Concept** comes in. Materiality is about **determining what's important enough to matter** in financial reporting. Information is considered "material" if omitting it or misstating it could influence the decisions of someone reading the financial statements.

In other words, if something is big enough or significant enough that it would change how an investor, creditor, or owner views the company, then it must be reported clearly and in detail. If it's *too small or insignificant* to meaningfully affect judgment, it may be reported with less detail or scrutiny. Importantly, this doesn't mean the item is ignored, **every transaction must be recorded**, but the organization can set internal policies for how to handle immaterial items in reports. The materiality concept acts like a filter or threshold: it helps accountants decide *what merits attention* and what can be considered negligible. This keeps financial reports focused on the key information without getting bogged down in minutiae. Importantly, materiality isn't a hard-and-fast number – it requires judgment. What material for a small startup might be immaterial for a giant multinational company, and vice versa.

To understand materiality, consider that **"importance" is relative to the size and context of the business**. For example, a **$25,000** expense is major for a small business that earns **$500,000** a year, could have a noticeable impact on profits, so it should be reported and discussed in the financial statements. But that **same $25,000** might be just a drop in the bucket for a corporation with **$500 million** in annual revenue; in the larger company's financials, $25k might be considered *immaterial* (not significant enough to detail). This doesn't mean the $25k won't be recorded in some way, it just may be rolled up to a broader account with less detail.

Each company often sets its own guidelines (sometimes called a **materiality threshold**) for this. For instance, a company might decide that any transaction under $1,000 is too minor to separately report and can be lumped into some miscellaneous expenses. This policy helps streamline reporting, focusing on big-ticket items, without losing meaningful information. However, **materiality isn't just about the raw dollar amount; context matters too**. Sometimes an item can be material *because of its nature or effect*, even if the amount seems small. For instance, if a tiny accounting error of just a few thousand dollars is the difference between a company reporting a net profit versus a net loss for the year, that error is definitely material, it can change how stakeholders perceive the company's performance. Similarly, a relatively small expense might be material if it causes a company to violate a loan agreement or a regulatory requirement. In such cases, accountants will report the detail despite the amount being small, because it's important to the users of the financial statements.

This principle prevents financial reports from becoming overwhelming lists of trivial data, focusing instead on what truly matters to investors and decision-makers. For readers of financial statements, knowing about materiality is empowering: it reminds us that statements are a communication tool, highlighting the significant events and figures that one should pay attention to. It also means that if something *isn't* mentioned in detail, it was likely judged not significant enough to affect the overall picture (or it's bundled into aggregate numbers). In practice, auditors and accountants use materiality as a guiding light, they ask, "Would the average person making a financial decision care about this number or error?" If yes, it's material and must be correct and clearly shown; if not, it can be handled in a simplified way. This ensures that the financial statements provide a fair, decision-useful view of the business without unnecessary complexity, which is exactly what someone making important financial decisions needs.

Chapter 1 Assessment Test

Welcome to the Chapter 1 Assessment test, this is designed to help you evaluate your understanding of the key concepts covered.

It is recommended that you achieve at least **6 correct answers out of 10** before moving on to the next chapter. If you don't reach this target, take some time to review the chapter before trying again. Good luck!

1. **Why is accounting often referred to as the "language of business"?**

   a. Because it involves complex terminology that only accountants understand.

   b. Because it provides a structured way to record, analyze, and communicate financial information.

   c. Because businesses use it primarily to calculate tax obligations.

2. **Which of the following is NOT one of the three core business activities?**

   a. Financing

   b. Advertising

   c. Investing

3. **What is the main purpose of financing activities in a business?**

   a. To secure funding through loans or investments.

   b. To manage daily operations like rent and wages.

   c. To track customer transactions.

4. **Which of the following is an example of an investing activity?**

   a. Paying employee salaries.

   b. Purchasing new machinery for the company.

   c. Selling products to customers.

5. **What are the five main types of accounts in accounting?**

   a. Assets, Liabilities, Equity, Revenue, and Expenses.

   b. Income, Assets, Debts, Liabilities, and Equity.

   c. Cash, Wages, Inventory, Expenses, and Profits.

6. If a business takes out a loan to purchase equipment, how does it impact the accounts?

   a. Assets increase and liabilities increase.
   b. Expenses increase and revenue decreases.
   c. Cash decreases and equity increases.

7. Which statement best describes the role of bookkeeping in accounting?

   a. Bookkeeping involves analyzing financial statements for decision-making.
   b. Bookkeeping focuses on accurately recording financial transactions.
   c. Bookkeeping is primarily used for preparing tax reports.

8. How does financial accounting differ from managerial accounting?

   a. Financial accounting focuses on external reporting, while managerial accounting is for internal decision-making.
   b. Managerial accounting follows strict external regulations, while financial accounting does not
   c. Financial accounting is primarily used for tax reporting, while managerial accounting is used for profit calculation.

9. According to the matching principle, when should a business record expenses?

   a. In the same period as the revenue they help generate.\
   b. Only when cash is paid out.
   c. When the company decides it is convenient.

10. What is the main purpose of the conservatism principle in accounting?

    a. To ensure companies do not overstate profits or assets and recognize potential losses as soon as they are likely.
    b. To allow businesses to report their financials in a way that makes them look as strong as possible.
    c. To encourage businesses to record profits even before they are fully realized.

Answers

1. Why is accounting often referred to as the "language of business"?

Correct Answer: (b) Because it provides a structured way to record, analyze, and communicate financial information.
Accounting helps businesses track and understand their financial performance, making it a universal tool for decision-making.

2. Which of the following is NOT one of the three core business activities?

Correct Answer: (b) Advertising
While advertising is important, the three core business functions are **financing, operating, and investing**.

3. What is the main purpose of financing activities in a business?

Correct Answer: (a) To secure funding through loans or investments.
Financing activities involve raising capital through debt (loans) or equity (investors) to support business growth.

4. Which of the following is an example of an investing activity?

Correct Answer: (b) Purchasing new machinery for the company.
Investing activities involve acquiring long-term assets like equipment, real estate, or intellectual property.

5. What are the five main types of accounts in accounting?

Correct Answer: (a) Assets, Liabilities, Equity, Revenue, and Expenses.
These five categories form the foundation of accounting and are used to classify financial transactions.

6. If a business takes out a loan to purchase equipment, how does it impact the accounts?

Correct Answer: (a) Assets increase and liabilities increase.
The new equipment increases assets, while the loan increases liabilities since it must be repaid.

7. Which statement best describes the role of bookkeeping in accounting?

Correct Answer: (b) Bookkeeping focuses on accurately recording financial transactions.
Bookkeeping ensures that all transactions are recorded systematically, providing accurate financial data for decision-making.

8. How does financial accounting differ from managerial accounting?

Correct Answer: (a) Financial accounting focuses on external reporting, while managerial accounting is for internal decision-making.
Financial accounting prepares reports for external users (e.g., investors), while managerial accounting helps business owners make internal strategic decisions.

9. According to the matching principle, when should a business record expenses?

Correct Answer: (a) In the same period as the revenue they help generate.
The matching principle ensures that costs are recorded in the same period as the revenue they contribute to, preventing misleading profit calculations.

10. What is the main purpose of the conservatism principle in accounting?

Correct Answer: (a) To ensure companies do not overstate profits or assets and recognize potential losses as soon as they are likely.
The conservatism principle helps businesses take a cautious approach to financial reporting, preventing overestimation of profits and assets.

CHAPTER 2

FINANCIAL ACCOUNTING

Behind every good business is a great accountant.

– Patti Fortune,
CPA and Author

Accounting has been a vital part of businesses for centuries, evolving into various branches such as financial accounting, managerial accounting, tax accounting, auditing, and bookkeeping. While these fields have their unique focuses, when people mention "accounting," they're often referring to **financial accounting**. But what exactly is it?

Financial accounting is the process of identifying, recording, summarizing, and analyzing a business's financial transactions to report them in **financial statements**. These statements serve as tools to communicate the financial health and performance of the organization to stakeholders like investors, lenders, and creditors.

If accounting is the **language of business**, then **financial statements** are the translation tool that turns complex financial data into actionable insights. Whether you're a small business owner or a CEO of a large corporation, understanding these statements is crucial for making informed decisions. The good news? You don't have to be an accountant to use them effectively.

When I first started managing my own business, I remember feeling overwhelmed by the amount of financial data I had to deal with. But once

I learned how to read my financial statements, it felt like unlocking a hidden code. Suddenly, I could see exactly where my money was going, what was working, and where I needed to make changes. It was a game changer.

While CFOs and bookkeepers are often hired (and compensated well) to prepare these reports, **anyone**, from business owners to managers and shareholders, can use them to make intelligent decisions based on clear financial information.

Here are the four most **important** and commonly used financial statements:

- Income Statement
- Statement of Owner's Equity
- Balance Sheet
- Statement of Cash Flows

In this chapter, we'll walk through each of these statements and explore how they are interconnected. Understanding these documents will help you navigate the financial health of your business with confidence.

The Income Statement

Often referred to as the **earnings report** or **profit and loss statement (P&L)**, the income statement outlines a business's **revenues** and **expenses** over a particular time period. Its key function is to reveal the company's **net profit** (or loss), which is simply total revenues minus total expenses. This bottom-line figure may also be called **profit**, **income**, **net income**, or **earnings**.

In an income statement, revenues and expenses are categorized by type. For example, you might have *product sales* or *service income* as revenue accounts, while expense categories might include *utilities* or *advertising costs*. Expense categories are also often separated between Cost of Goods sold, and SG&A (Sales, General, and Administrative) sometimes also called operating expenses.

Let's say you own a small gym, and you want to review your income statement for December. The gym generated **$7,500** from membership sales and **$2,800** from personal training sessions, bringing your total revenue to **$10,300**. After adding up your expenses, things like rent (**$2,200**), employee wages (**$3,100**), and utilities (**$350**), equipment Maintenance (**$900**), and marketing costs of (**$600**), your total expenses amount to **$7,150**. By subtracting the expenses from your revenue, you find that your **net income** for the month is **$3,150**.

Revenues	
Membership Sales	$7,500
Personal Training Sessions	$2,800
Total Revenues	**$10,300**

Expenses	
Rent	$2,200
Employee Wages	$3,100
Equipment Maintenance	$900
Marketing Costs	$600
Utilities	$350
Total Expenses	**$7,150**

Net Income $3,150

For businesses that operate through multiple channels, it's common to separate income sources. For instance, if you own a café that also sells merchandise online, you might want to track **in-store sales** and **online sales** separately. This helps you see which part of your business is performing better and where improvements can be made.

Let's say, in this case, the gym's income statement for December shows a **net profit of $3,150**. That figure will later be used in the **owner's equity report** to determine how the profits impact the owner's share of the business.

Statement of Owner's Equity

Let's imagine you own a small café that has been in operation for several years. Like most business owners, you take a regular **owner's withdrawal** each month as personal income, transferring money from the business account to your personal account. But to ensure the café continues to grow and increase its value, you aim to pay yourself less than what the business earns in net profit.

For instance, in December, your café made a **net profit of $3,150**. Instead of paying yourself the full amount, you decide to withdraw **$2,500**, leaving **$650** in the business as part of your **owner's equity**. This amount, while still in the business's bank account, technically belongs to you and is tracked separately as part of your personal share of the company's wealth.

Description	Amount ($)
Net Profit for December	$3,150
Owner's Withdrawal	$2,500
Increase in Owner's Equity	$650

Owner's equity is simply the owner's stake in the business after all liabilities have been paid off. In other words, it's what you, as the owner, truly "own" once all debts are cleared. This section is often separated between the owner's investments and withdrawals, retained earnings, and net income. This better illustrates how much of the profits are being reinvested compared to how much the owner is taking out. The **statement of owner's equity** is a financial report that shows how this equity changes over a specific period, whether a month, quarter, or year.

This statement typically includes four main sections:

1. **Beginning equity balance** – This is the amount of equity you had at the start of the period.
2. **Net income** – The profit your business earned during the period, as reported on the **income statement**.
3. **Owner contributions** – Any additional money you've invested in the business during that period.
4. **Owner withdrawals** – The amount of money you've taken out for personal use.

Let's say at the beginning of December, the **starting equity balance** for your café was **$20,350**. After adding the **$3,150** of net income for the month and subtracting your **$2,500** withdrawal, your **end-of-period equity balance** would be **$21,000**. This final figure represents the owner's claim on the assets of the café as of December 31st, which will carry over as the **starting balance** for the next month.

Description	Amount ($)
Starting Equity Balance (Dec 1)	$20,350
Add: Net Income for December	$3,150
Subtract: Owner's Withdrawal	$2,500
End-of-Period Equity Balance (Dec 31)	**$21,000**

The statement of owner's equity helps track how your ownership share in the business changes due to profits, losses, and withdrawals. It's a useful tool to measure how much value has been retained in the business over time. If you were to invest more personal funds into the café, those would be recorded as **owner contributions**, which would also increase your equity.

In a larger company or corporation, where there are **shareholders** instead of a single owner, the process becomes more complex. Instead of a simple **statement of owner's equity**, corporations use **shareholders' equity** accounts and typically prepare a **retained earnings statement**. This statement shows how much of the profits are kept in the business after paying out **dividends** to shareholders.

It's important to align all your financial statements with the same time frame. If your **income statement** covers December, the **statement of owner's equity** should also reflect December. This ensures that the **net income** figure from the income statement can be directly added to your equity.

By the end of the month, the café's end-of-period balance of **$21,000** will be the **opening balance** for January. This fluidity between periods helps you trace the growth of your equity over time, providing a clear view of how much value you're building within the business.

If your café had multiple owners, the **statement of owner's equity** would need to include separate entries for each owner's share, making it a bit more complex, but the basic principles would still apply. Each owner's withdrawals, contributions, and share of the profits would be tracked individually.

Balance Sheet

The **balance sheet** illustrates one of the core principles of accounting:

ASSETS = LIABILITIES + EQUITY

This equation is the foundation of how a business's financial position is assessed. In simple terms, it shows that everything a company owns (**assets**) is financed either by borrowing (**liabilities**) or through the owner's investment and existing profits (**equity**).

Let's take the example of a small **café**. At the end of December, the café's **balance sheet** might show **$28,700** in **assets**.

Category	Amount ($)
Assets	
Cash	$8,500
Accounts receivable	$1,200
Inventory	$5,500
Equipment	$12,000
Other assets	$1,500
Total Assets	**$28,700**

Liabilities	
Accounts payable	$6,000
Unearned revenue	$1,800
Salaries and wages payable	$2,000
Interest payable	$100
Total Liabilities	**$9,900**

Equity	
Owner's capital balance	$18,800
Total Equity	**$18,800**
Total Liabilities + Equity	**$28,700**

This **$28,700** is the total value of everything the café owns. However, to understand where this number comes from, we need to break it down further. This total is composed of two key elements: **liabilities** and **equity**.

Liabilities represent what the café owes to others, including suppliers and employees. The **total liabilities** for the café amount to **$9,900**.

Liabilities & Equity	Amount ($)
Liabilities	
Accounts payable	$6,000
Unearned revenue	$1,800
Salaries and wages payable	$2,000
Interest payable	$100
Total Liabilities	**$9,900**

Equity represents the owner's claim on the business after all liabilities have been settled. In this case, the café's equity is the owner's **capital balance**, which is the owner's stake in the business. After accounting for all liabilities, the café owner retains **$18,800** in equity.

Equity	Amount ($)
Owner's capital balance	$18,800
Total Equity	**$18,800**

The **total equity** equals **$18,800**, which represents the owner's portion of the business after all debts have been paid.

$$\text{Total Assets} = \text{Total Liabilities} + \text{Total Equity}$$
$$\$28{,}700 = \$9{,}900 + \$18{,}800$$

The balance sheet differs from other financial statements like the income statement or cash flow statement because it doesn't cover a period of time. Instead, it provides a **snapshot** of the business's financial position at a specific moment. For example, while an income statement might show your revenues and expenses for the entire month of December, your balance sheet shows the value of your assets, liabilities, and equity as of **December 31st**.

Balance sheets are typically prepared at the end of significant periods, such as a quarter or a fiscal year. Businesses sometimes choose to operate on a **fiscal year** instead of a calendar year for accounting and tax purposes. Let's say you own a small clothing store, and the busiest months are during the holiday season. You might choose to end your fiscal year in February rather than December to capture the post-holiday sales in your yearly reports.

While **fiscal years** are more common for larger corporations, smaller businesses, like sole proprietorships or partnerships, can still apply to use a fiscal year. This is typically done by filing **IRS Form 1128** in the U.S., which is an application to change or adopt a different tax year.

Balance Sheet Structure and Formats

The basic structure of a **balance sheet** remains consistent whether a business uses a **calendar year** (January to December) or a **fiscal year** (any twelve-month period that ends on a different date). It will always list the company's **assets**, **liabilities**, and **equity**. What may vary is the **format** used to present the information.

The format used in the **café's balance sheet** we discussed earlier is known as the **"report form"**. This layout lists all of the **assets** at the top, with the **liabilities** and **equity** below. There's another common format called the **"account form"**, where **assets** are listed on the left side, and **liabilities** and **equity** are displayed on the right.

This **left-right structure** is frequently used in accounting because it aligns with the concept of **debits** and **credits** (which we'll explore in more depth in Chapter 3). It helps visualize the balance between what a business owns (assets) and how those assets are financed (through either debt or equity).

For example, if the café's balance sheet were presented in **account form**, you would see **$28,700** in **assets** listed on the left, and the combined **liabilities** of **$9,900** and **equity** of **$18,800** on the right.

Assets		Liabilities & Equity	
Cash	$2,500	Accounts payable	$6,000
Accounts receivable	$1,200	Unearned revenue	$1,800
Inventory	$1,000	Salaries & wages payable	$2,000

Equipment	$3,000	Interest payable	$100
Other assets	$21,000	**Total Liabilities**	**$9,900**
Total Assets	**$28,700**	Owner's capital balance	$18,800
		Total Equity	$18,800
		Total Liabilities + Equity	**$28,700**

Understanding Equity and the Equation

Let's focus for a moment on **equity**, which is an essential part of the balance sheet. In the café's balance sheet, we can see the **owner's capital balance** listed under equity. This amount reflects how much of the business the owner actually "owns" after all debts (liabilities) have been paid off.

Another way to look at it is by rearranging the equation:

Assets − Liabilities = Equity

This version highlights that equity is what remains for the owner after settling all debts. When I first learned accounting, I remember asking why we don't use this version more often. The reason is practical: accounting uses a system of **debits** and **credits**, which we'll dive into later, and the original formula is more convenient in that structure. But both expressions are valid and mathematically correct.

Why the Balance Sheet Matters

Unlike other financial statements, like the **income statement** (which shows profit) or the **statement of owner's equity** (which shows changes in equity), the **balance sheet** doesn't focus on a single output number like net income. Instead, it offers a **snapshot** of the business's overall assets and debts at a specific moment in time. This is often used to compare to prior periods for a picture of how the businesses financial health and liquidity is changing over time.

Let's use an example. Imagine your café has total **assets** of **$28,700** and total **liabilities** of **$9,900**. This looks pretty good on paper because you have more than enough assets to cover your debts. But, if you dig deeper, you might realize something important: only **$8,500** of those assets are in **cash**.

If suddenly all of your debts (liabilities) were due at the same time, you wouldn't have enough cash on hand to pay them immediately. You'd likely need to sell off other assets, such as inventory or equipment, to raise the necessary funds. This is where the concept of **liquidity** becomes important—how easily can your assets be converted into cash to cover immediate expenses?

The **balance sheet** helps you (and your accountant) understand key financial issues, like:

> **Debt structure** – How much debt does your business owe, and is it manageable?
>
> **Liquidity** – Do you have enough cash or easily convertible assets to cover immediate obligations?
>
> **Sustainability** – Can your business keep running smoothly with its current cash flow?

For example, even though your café seems healthy overall, a closer look at the **liquidity** (cash on hand) might reveal potential problems if all debts were due at once. By analyzing the balance sheet, you can spot these risks early and make adjustments to ensure long-term financial stability.

Statement of Cash Flows

The **statement of cash flows** is a financial report that shows the movement of cash into and out of a business over a specific period. Its main purpose is to ensure the business has enough cash available to pay off its debts while avoiding having too much cash on hand, which could increase the risk of theft or fraud. This is also an important tool to ensure there is enough cash on hand to maintain day-to-day operating expenses and may help spot potential cash shortfalls before they happen.

This statement is divided into three sections, corresponding to the **three main business activities**:

> **Operating activities** (day-to-day running of the business)
>
> **Investing activities** (purchasing equipment or long-term assets)
>
> **Financing activities** (raising funds or paying off debts)

Operating Activities:

This section captures cash transactions related to the core operations of the business, essentially, how the company earns revenue and incurs expenses in its primary activities. For example, cash received from customers for sales and cash paid to suppliers for inventory are included here. Consider a local bakery: the cash it collects from daily bread sales and the payments it makes for flour and utilities fall under operating activities. A positive cash flow in this section indicates that the company's regular operations are generating sufficient cash to maintain and grow the business.

Investing Activities:

Investing activities reflect cash flows associated with the acquisition and disposal of long-term assets and investments. This includes purchasing equipment, buying or selling property, or investing in other businesses. For instance, if our bakery decides to buy a new oven to increase production, the cash spent would be recorded as an outflow in this section. Similarly, selling an old delivery van would be an inflow. Negative cash flow in investing activities isn't necessarily a bad sign; it often means the company is investing in its future capabilities and growth.

Financing Activities:

This section deals with cash flows related to changes in the company's capital structure. It includes transactions like borrowing or repaying loans, issuing or buying back shares, and paying dividends. For example, if the bakery takes out a loan to renovate its storefront, the loan proceeds are a cash inflow in financing activities. Conversely, repaying that loan or distributing profits to owners as dividends would be cash outflows. Analyzing this section helps understand how the company finances its operations and growth, and how it returns value to its shareholders.

It's worth noting at this stage that the **cash flow statement** related to the **income statement**, but they won't necessarily align.

Cafe statement of Cash Flows

For the Month Ending on 12/31/2023

Category	Amount ($)
Cash Flows from Operating Activities	
Cash flows from sales	+$7,200
Outgoing cash from operating activities	-$5,900
Net Cash Flow from Operations	**+$1,300**
Cash Flows from Investing Activities	
Equipment purchase	-$4,500
Net Cash Flow from Investing	**-$4,500**
Cash Flows from Financing Activities	
Owner's withdrawal	-$2,000
Net Cash Flow from Financing	**-$2,000**
Net Cash Flow	**-$5,200**
Cash position at the beginning of the period	+$13,700
Current cash position	**+$8,500**

When preparing a statement of cash flows, there are two primary methods businesses can use: the **Direct Method** and the **Indirect Method**. Both methods ultimately produce the same total net cash flow amount, but they differ significantly in the way they calculate and present cash flow from operating activities.

The Direct Method

The **Direct Method** clearly and explicitly shows the sources and uses of cash. It lists specific cash inflows (such as cash collected from customers) and cash outflows (such as cash payments to suppliers or employees). This approach provides an easy-to-follow summary of cash transactions, making it straightforward to see exactly where cash is coming from and going.

Example:

Let's continue with our bakery example. For a given month, the direct method would report cash flow from operations like this:

Operating Activities (Direct Method)	Amount ($)
Cash received from customers	12,000
Cash paid for inventory (ingredients)	(4,500)
Cash paid for salaries	(3,000)
Cash paid for rent	(1,000)
Net cash flow from operating activities	**3,500**

This method clearly outlines each main cash transaction. You know exactly how much cash customers brought in, how much cash you paid to suppliers, how much went out in salaries, rent, and so forth.

The Indirect Method

The **Indirect Method**, in contrast, is less direct, it starts with the net income figure from your income statement and adjusts it to arrive at the actual cash generated or spent in operating activities. This involves adjusting for items that impact net income but don't affect cash immediately, such as depreciation, or changes in working capital like accounts receivable and inventory.

Example:

Returning to our bakery, imagine your income statement shows a net income of $4,000. You then adjust it as follows:

Operating Activities (Indirect Method)	Amount ($)
Net Income	4,000

Adjustments:	
Depreciation Expense (non-cash expense)	+500
Decrease in Inventory (sold more than purchase	+1,000
Increase in Accounts Payable (bills unpaid yet)	+500
Increase in Accounts Receivable (sales on credit, ash not yet collected)	-2,500
Net cash flow from operating activities	**3,500**

The indirect method starts with net income and then adjusts it for all non-cash items and working capital changes to reflect the true cash position.

While both the Direct and Indirect methods ultimately arrive at the same net cash flow figure, they differ significantly in their approach, clarity, and ease of preparation. The Direct Method offers a transparent view of a business's cash transactions, explicitly listing cash inflows (such as money received from customers) and outflows (such as money spent on inventory or rent). This makes it particularly valuable for business owners or stakeholders who prefer seeing a straightforward, detailed snapshot of exactly how cash moves in and out. However, despite this transparency, many businesses find the Indirect Method simpler and quicker to prepare, especially when already using accrual accounting systems. This is because the indirect method conveniently starts with net income from the income statement and then adjusts for non-cash items like depreciation and changes in working capital accounts such as accounts receivable or inventory.

This simplicity explains why most small and medium-sized businesses prefer using the Indirect Method; it requires less detailed tracking of individual cash transactions. On the other hand, larger businesses, or those prioritizing greater financial transparency, may choose the Direct Method or even present both methods to provide stakeholders with comprehensive insights into their cash management. Ultimately, the choice depends on balancing the business's size, the audience's needs for detailed information, and the complexity involved in preparing the cash flow statement.

Why Cash Flow and Income Don't Always Match

Let's say your café made **$8,200** in total sales in December, but the **cash received** was only **$6,760**. Why the difference? This happens because of the method of accounting used: **accrual basis accounting** versus **cash basis accounting**.

In **accrual basis accounting**, transactions are recorded when they occur, even if no cash has changed hands yet. For instance, if a customer buys $1,500 worth of products on credit in December, you would still record that amount as **revenue** for December, even though you haven't received the cash yet. Similarly, if you buy supplies worth $200 on your company credit card, those will count as **expenses** in December, even though you won't pay the bill until January.

In contrast, **cash basis accounting** only records transactions when cash actually moves. If you were using cash accounting, the $1,500 sale wouldn't be recorded until the customer pays, and the $200 expense wouldn't count until you pay your credit card bill. This is why **accrual accounting** often shows a more accurate picture of a business's financial performance, while **cash accounting** reflects the actual cash position. The use of cash accounting can also create difficulties in keeping track of who still owes you money and which suppliers you still owe. Because of this, some small businesses keep their official books for tax purposes on a cash basis while maintaining a set of accrual based books as well to keep track of these payment agreements.

Most small businesses prefer **cash basis accounting** because it's simpler. However, larger businesses like corporations making $30M over three years (as 2024, could be different in future years) are required by the IRS to use **accrual basis accounting**.

Best Practices: Accrual Accounting and Cash Flow

A smart approach is to use **accrual basis accounting** while also maintaining a **statement of cash flows**. This way, you get the best of both worlds: accurate financial data from accrual accounting and real-time awareness of how much cash you actually have on hand.

For example, if your café uses accrual accounting, you might record $200 in supply expenses for December, even if you won't pay that bill until January. The **cash flow statement** will reflect when the cash actually leaves your bank account, helping you avoid liquidity problems.

Cash Flows from Investing and Financing Activities

The second part of the cash flow statement tracks **cash flows from investing activities**. These include purchases of long-term assets like equipment or property. For example, if your café buys a new espresso machine, the cash spent on that equipment will be recorded as a **negative cash flow** from investing activities.

The third section covers **cash flows from financing activities**, which includes raising or repaying funds. If your business issues stock or takes out a loan, the cash received is reported here. For smaller businesses, this section also tracks **owner contributions** and **owner withdrawals**. If you, as the owner, invest $5,000 into your café, it will show up as an **owner contribution**. If you withdraw money for personal use, it will be recorded as an **owner's withdrawal**.

How Financial Statements Work Together

An experienced accountant, given the necessary data, can create reliable and insightful financial statements. While the types of accounts used might differ depending on the business's size or industry, the **structure** of each statement is consistent across companies. For example:

> - An **income statement** reports a business's **revenues** and **expenses** over a period, with the result being **net income**.
> - A **statement of cash flows** is divided into **operating**, **investing**, and **financing** activities, showing cash movements in each category.
> - A **balance sheet** always includes sections for **assets**, **liabilities**, and **equity**—where assets must equal the sum of liabilities and equity.

These statements aren't isolated from each other; they're interconnected. Certain figures flow from one statement to another, creating a complete financial picture for a given period. For instance:

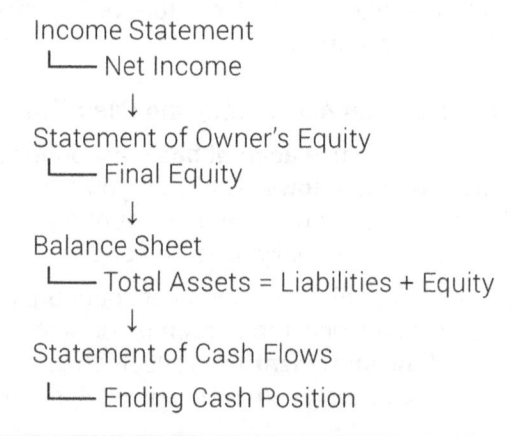

```
Income Statement
    └── Net Income
            ↓
Statement of Owner's Equity
    └── Final Equity
            ↓
Balance Sheet
    └── Total Assets = Liabilities + Equity
            ↓
Statement of Cash Flows
    └── Ending Cash Position
```

> - The **net income** from the **income statement** feeds into the **statement of owner's equity**, impacting the owner's capital balance.
> - The **final equity balance** from the statement of owner's equity then appears on the **balance sheet**.
> - The **statement of cash flows** shows where cash has come in and gone out, giving a real-time view of liquidity based on all operating, investing, and financing activities.

This interconnected nature of financial statements helps to provide a comprehensive view of a business's financial health. If these connections seem complex now, don't worry! We'll continue exploring each statement's construction and use throughout in chapter 5, so you can see exactly how they work together in real-world scenarios.

Cash Basis vs Accrual Basis

Earlier we mentioned the two types of accounting that can be used practically, Cash Basis and Accrual Accounting, now we will look at them in more detail as these methods differ primarily in *when* income and expenses are recorded.

Cash Basis Accounting (also referred to as Cost-Based Accounting in some contexts)

Cash Basis Accounting recognizes income only when the payment is received and similarly, expenses are only recognized when cash is paid out. It's a simpler method often adopted by smaller businesses, or freelancers whose transactions typically involve immediate payments.

For example, if a freelance graphic designer completes a project worth $2,000 in December but only receives the money in January, Cash Basis Accounting records that $2,000 in January when the cash arrives, not in December when the work was done. The same applies to expenses. If the designer buys a new computer in December but pays for it in installments, the expense gets recorded only when the actual payment is made each month, rather than when the computer is first acquired.

The main advantage of Cash Basis Accounting is its simplicity and clear focus on actual cash flow. Looking at the books will tell you how much money the business has on-hand. However, one drawback is that it doesn't match revenues and expenses to the period in which they are truly earned or incurred. This can create a distorted view of profitability: big payments received at the start of a month might make that month seem more profitable than it actually is, while a large expenditure delayed to the following month can inflate profits in the current month.

It's also worth noting that a big advantage in being cash-basis comes in the form of tax savings. A business can plan when to receive cash or structure payments made and received in a way that might be advantageous for their tax situation.

Cash Basis Accounting is ideal for small-scale operations with straightforward transactions, where tracking immediate cash flow is enough to gauge overall financial health. It's also typically easier to manage because you don't track accounts receivable (money owed by customers) or accounts payable (money your business owes to suppliers) until the cash actually moves.

Accrual Basis Accounting

Accrual Basis Accounting recognizes income and expenses in the period in which they are earned or incurred, *regardless* of when the money changes hands. It provides a more accurate snapshot of a business's financial performance by matching related revenues and expenses in the same reporting period. This method is preferred (and often required by law or regulatory bodies) for larger corporations because it allows for a more realistic assessment of profitability and financial health.

Imagine a construction company that completes a $50,000 job in December but will only be paid by the client in February. Under Accrual Basis Accounting, the $50,000 revenue is recorded in December, reflecting the fact that the company *earned* that amount in December. Similarly, if the company receives construction materials in December with payment due 60 days later, those expenses are recorded in December. Although the cash might not physically move until January or February, the economic event, earning revenue or incurring an expense, happened in December.

The advantage is clear: your financial statements reflect the business's true performance and profitability for each period, regardless of cash flow timing. Investors, stakeholders, and management get a better understanding of how the company is really doing from month to month or quarter to quarter, without fluctuations caused by late customer payments or delayed supplier invoices. However, Accrual Accounting is more complex because you must track accounts receivable, accounts payable, prepaid expenses, and accrued liabilities.

Choosing the Right Method

> - **Cash Basis** is generally suitable for very small businesses or freelancers with uncomplicated operations. It's easy to implement and helps you see how much cash is available at any given time.
>
> - **Accrual Basis** is the standard for mid-size and large companies, or any organization that wants (or needs) a detailed understanding of its economic performance. It ensures you recognize income when it's earned and expenses when they're incurred, offering a more accurate portrayal of profitability over time.

In practice, many small businesses start with Cash Basis Accounting due to its simplicity but eventually switch to Accrual Basis Accounting as they grow and need better financial insights. As your operation expands, you'll likely enter into more complex transactions, long-term projects, credit sales, payment plans, and so on, which require the clarity that only Accrual Accounting can provide. That's why it's widely used (and often mandated by following GAAP) in larger corporations, where reliable, standardized financial reporting is essential for stakeholders, lenders, investors, and regulatory compliance.

Chapter 2 Assessment Test

1. **What is the main purpose of financial accounting?**

    a. To help managers make internal business decisions.

    b. To prepare financial reports for external stakeholders.

    c. To record only cash transactions.

2. **Which of the following is NOT one of the four key financial statements?**

    a. Statement of Cash Flows

    b. Statement of Investments

    c. Income Statement

3. **What does the Income Statement primarily show?**

    a. The company's net profit or loss over a specific period.

    b. The total assets and liabilities of the company.

    c. The owner's personal financial status.

4. **What is the purpose of the Statement of Owner's Equity?**

    a. To track changes in the owner's stake in the business over time.

    b. To list all of the company's cash inflows and outflows.

    c. To calculate the company's net profit.

5. **Which of the following is a core component of a balance sheet?**

    a. Revenue

    b. Owner withdrawals

    c. Liabilities

6. **How does the accounting equation ensure financial accuracy?**

    a. It balances total revenue with total expenses.

    b. It shows that assets are always equal to liabilities plus equity.

    c. It calculates cash flow from operations.

7. **Why don't net income and cash flow always match?**

   a. Because accrual accounting records transactions when they occur, not when cash is exchanged.
   b. Because net income includes only cash transactions.
   c. Because businesses pay taxes on a different schedule.

8. **Which section of the Statement of Cash Flows includes purchases of long-term assets like equipment?**

   a. Operating activities
   b. Investing activities
   c. Financing activities

9. **What is the main difference between cash basis and accrual basis accounting?**

   a. Cash basis records transactions only when cash is exchanged, while accrual basis records them when they are earned or incurred.
   b. Cash basis is used only by large corporations, while accrual basis is for small businesses.
   c. Cash basis requires double-entry bookkeeping, while accrual basis does not.

10. **How are the financial statements interconnected?**

    a. The net income from the income statement flows into the statement of owner's equity.
    b. The balance sheet and income statement are completely independent of each other.
    c. The statement of cash flows is created first, and then the income statement is prepared.

Answers

1. What is the main purpose of financial accounting?

Correct Answer: (b) To prepare financial reports for external stakeholders.
Financial accounting focuses on providing accurate financial statements to investors, lenders, and other external parties.

2. Which of the following is NOT one of the four key financial statements?

Correct Answer: (b) Statement of Investments
The four main financial statements are Income Statement, Statement of Owner's Equity, Balance Sheet, and Statement of Cash Flows. There is no "Statement of Investments."

3. What does the Income Statement primarily show?

Correct Answer: (a) The company's net profit or loss over a specific period.
The Income Statement details revenues and expenses, helping determine whether the business made a profit or incurred a loss.

4. What is the purpose of the Statement of Owner's Equity?

Correct Answer: (a) To track changes in the owner's stake in the business over time.
This statement shows how owner's equity is affected by net income, contributions, and withdrawals.

5. Which of the following is a core component of a balance sheet?

Correct Answer: (c) Liabilities
The Balance Sheet consists of three sections: Assets, Liabilities, and Equity.

6. How does the accounting equation ensure financial accuracy?

Correct Answer: (b) It shows that assets are always equal to liabilities plus equity.
The accounting equation (Assets = Liabilities + Equity) is the foundation of double-entry bookkeeping, ensuring that every transaction keeps the books balanced.

7. Why don't net income and cash flow always match?

Correct Answer: (a) Because accrual accounting records transactions when they occur, not when cash is exchanged.
In accrual accounting, revenue and expenses are recorded when they are earned or incurred, regardless of when cash is received or paid.

8. Which section of the Statement of Cash Flows includes purchases of long-term assets like equipment?

Correct Answer: (b) Investing activities
Investing activities track cash flows related to purchasing or selling long-term assets such as property, equipment, or investments.

9. What is the main difference between cash basis and accrual basis accounting?

Correct Answer: (a) Cash basis records transactions only when cash is exchanged, while accrual basis records them when they are earned or incurred.
Cash basis accounting recognizes transactions when cash is received or paid, while accrual basis accounting records them when they occur, providing a more accurate picture of financial performance.

10. How are the financial statements interconnected?

Correct Answer: (a) The net income from the income statement flows into the statement of owner's equity.
Net income from the Income Statement affects Owner's Equity, which is then reflected in the Balance Sheet.

CHAPTER 3

The Accounting Equation

> *The numbers tell the story, and if you learn the lessons the numbers are teaching, you will be able to see the future.*
>
> —Robert Kiyosaki,
> author of Rich Dad Poor Dad

So far, we've taken a broad look at accounting, focusing primarily on financial statements as the final product. Think of these statements as the polished version of all the financial activity within a business. However, to create this polished outcome, we need to start with the "raw materials" of accounting. This includes all the data, source documents (like invoices and receipts), organized filing systems, precise data-entry rules, journal entries, and other bookkeeping essentials. These tools are fundamental to producing financial statements that are accurate and valuable for business insights.

In this chapter, we're diving deep into the "behind-the-scenes" work that makes those polished financial statements possible. Here, we'll look at how each transaction is recorded, tracked, and ultimately compiled into usable financial data. For small business owners especially, understanding this foundational process can be a game-changer in using accounting to make informed decisions and streamline operations.

Double-Entry Accounting

The core principle of accounting revolves around a simple equation: **Assets = Liabilities + Equity**. This formula, known as the *fundamental accounting* *equation*, first introduced in Chapter 1, forms the basis of all financial records and is what keeps everything in balance on the balance sheet. Achieving this balance relies on a key method known as *double-entry accounting*.

Double-entry accounting ensures that any change to one account is offset by a corresponding change in another. This approach guarantees that assets will always equal liabilities plus equity, no matter how many transactions take place.

A quick tip before we move on: One of our contributors has created a helpful and free website filled with visuals and illustrations that can really make the accounting equation (and the financial statements that follow) easier to understand.

Feel free to check it out as you continue through the next chapters, follow the link or scan the QR code:

https://www.accountingequation.io/

How Double-Entry Works in Practice

Let's say I run a small café and decide to buy a coffee grinder for $2,500. Here's how double-entry accounting would handle this:

1. I **subtract $2,500** from my **cash account** (an asset).
2. I **add $2,500** to my **equipment account** (also an asset).

In this scenario, the cash account is *credited* by $2,500, while the equipment account is *debited* by $2,500. The important thing to note is that while both accounts are on the asset side of the equation, double-entry ensures they balance out without affecting the liabilities or equity.

In accounting, **debits and credits** are like two sides of a scale. When you credit an account, you decrease it if it's an asset but increase it if it's a liability or equity. When you debit an account, you increase it if it's an asset and decrease it if it's a liability or equity. Though it may feel counterintuitive at first, understanding this flow is critical.

On payday, suppose I pay my employees a total of $5,000. In this case, the transaction affects both my cash and liability accounts:

> - I subtract $5,000 from **cash** (asset), reducing my cash balance.
> - I subtract $5,000 from **wages payable** (liability), reducing my outstanding liabilities.

Here, instead of adjusting two asset accounts, I'm adjusting both an asset and a liability. This transaction, like all in double-entry accounting, keeps the equation in perfect balance.

Assets

Assets are anything a business owns that holds financial value, whether immediately accessible or expected to bring value in the future. These range from tangible items like cash and property to more intangible items, such as *accounts receivable (AR)*, which represent future cash flows owed to the business.

For example, if a bakery buys an industrial oven, this oven becomes a new asset. Similarly, cash in the bank, office furniture, and even customer invoices awaiting payment are considered assets, although they offer value in different ways.

Accounts Receivable (AR): The Promise of Future Cash

Let's say Sarah runs a catering company, and she has an agreement to cater a corporate event for $5,000. The event goes off without a hitch, but the client has arranged to pay in 30 days. Sarah can record this $5,000 as an increase to her AR (asset) account, as well as an increase to her sales (revenue) account, because it represents incoming cash, even if the funds haven't hit her bank yet. When the payment is finally received, Sarah would:

> - **Debit (add to)** her cash account by $5,000.
> - **Credit (reduce)** her AR account by $5,000.

By recording this future income in AR, Sarah's records give a complete picture of her business's financial position, even if she hasn't yet been paid.

Asset accounts provide a forward-looking view of a business's strength. *Accrual basis accounting*, which records income and expenses when they are earned or incurred, relies on these forward-leaning assets and liabilities to give a snapshot of business health. This way, businesses can track not just their cash but their commitments, expected inflows, and financial obligations in a comprehensive way.

Intangible Assets

Intangible assets, such as *patents*, *trademarks*, *copyrights*, and *brand names*, bring unique long-term value to a business, even if they lack immediate cash value. This does not mean they are any less critical; quite the opposite—they often drive brand loyalty and competitive edge in the market. For example, *Starbucks* holds valuable intangible assets in its brand identity, proprietary coffee blends, and customer loyalty programs. These assets aren't physical, yet they create immense value by attracting and retaining customers worldwide.

In 2022, Starbucks reported intangible assets valued in the billions, underscoring the brand's influence and customer base. In tech, *Microsoft* is another example with extensive intangible assets, including software patents and copyrights, as well as the brand's reputation itself, which collectively boost the company's valuation and market position.

The Role of Franchising in Intangible Assets

Consider a real-world example of franchise value. When an individual becomes a *Subway* franchisee, they gain access to Subway's brand recognition, operational guidance, and customer loyalty. In exchange, they typically pay a fee, which Subway records as income derived from an intangible asset: its brand and franchise systems. Suppose a Subway franchisee pays a $30,000 initial franchise fee with a ten-year agreement. Rather than treat the entire $30,000 as a one-time expense, this cost is recorded as an *intangible asset* and amortized (gradually expensed) over the ten years.

In this case:

- **Annual Amortization Expense**: Each year, the franchisee records $3,000 ($30,000 ÷ 10 years) as an *amortization expense*.
- **Balance in Asset Account**: This expense is deducted from the intangible asset account, ensuring the balance sheet accurately reflects the asset's decreasing value over time.

Although both **amortization** and **depreciation** involve allocating the cost of an asset over its useful life, they apply to different types of assets:

- **Depreciation** relates to tangible assets like buildings, machinery, and vehicles.
- **Amortization** applies to intangible assets, such as a franchise license or a patent.

By amortizing intangible assets, businesses distribute the cost over time, presenting a balanced financial outlook that matches the asset's gradual impact on the business. This distribution fulfills the Matching Principle we discussed in Chapter 1.

Consider Chris, a local entrepreneur who recently invested in a franchise for a popular coffee brand, "CaféPro." After two years, Chris's balance sheet begins to reflect the accumulated amortization of his franchise license, which he purchased for $50,000 over a ten-year period. In the asset section of his balance sheet, the original licensing value is gradually reduced by annual amortization. Each time amortization is adjusted (or recognized) an entry is also made to an amortization expense account to show the impact on net income. Accumulated amortization is what is known as a contra account, which is an account with an abnormal balance. This means that it is listed as an asset on the balance sheets with a negative balance. Normal account balances will be discussed in more detail later.

After two years, Chris would have recorded $10,000 in accumulated amortization, decreasing the book value of his franchise asset by $5,000 annually. Just like depreciation on physical assets such as equipment, the accumulated amortization account serves to adjust the recorded value of intangible assets over time, providing a realistic view of their remaining worth.

Chris's CaféPro Franchise Balance Sheet (Partial)

For the Year Ending on 12/31/26

Assets		
Cash		$6,246
Accounts Receivable		$395
Inventory		$2,100
Total Current Assets		**$8,741**
Property, Plant, Equipment		
Equipment		$2,570
Less: Accumulated Depreciation - Equipment	$1,028	$1,542
Total Property, Plant, Equipment		**$1,542**
Intangible Assets		
Franchise License		$50,000
Less: Accumulated Amortization - Franchise License	$10,000	$40,000
Total Intangible Assets		**$40,000**
Total Assets		**$50,283**

When it comes to typical business expenses, like spending $800 on coffee supplies, the accounting is straightforward: Chris's Supplies Expense account would increase, and his Cash would also decrease by the same amount. In double-entry accounting, assets will always balance with the sum of liabilities and equity, making it clear where funds are used and how they impact the financial position.

Now, back to the franchise license. When Chris first acquired the $50,000 license from CaféPro, he paid cash up front, which means his Cash (asset) decreased by $50,000, while his Franchise License (also an asset) increased by the same amount. If he decides to amortize this license evenly over ten years, he will reduce the franchise license's value by $5,000 each year while recording a $5,000 amortization expense on the equity side. This ensures that assets, liabilities, and equity remain balanced as always.

Using a Loan to Fund Intangible Asset Purchases

But what if Chris didn't have $50,000 available? Suppose he secured a small business loan to cover the cost. In this scenario, his accountant would increase Notes Payable (a liability) by $50,000 and increase Cash (an asset) by the same amount. Once he uses the loan funds to pay for the franchise, the transaction would shift $50,000 from his Cash account to his Franchise License account. As Chris repays the loan, Cash will decrease accordingly, while Notes Payable will reflect his reduced loan balance over time.

Another example: suppose Chris, before launching his CaféPro franchise, already had $20,000 in cash he was willing to put toward the $50,000 franchise licensing fee, and he decided to borrow the remaining $30,000 from a lender. How would an accountant record this transaction?

In this case, the franchise license (an asset account) would increase by $50,000, representing the full cost of the franchise license. Chris's cash account would decrease by $20,000, which is the amount he personally contributed. Meanwhile, the loans payable account (a liability account) would increase by $30,000, reflecting the amount he borrowed. This transaction would result in a net increase of $30,000 on the assets side of the balance sheet and a corresponding increase of $30,000 on the liabilities side, keeping the accounting equation balanced.

The franchise license would then be amortized over its useful life, just as if Chris had paid for it entirely with his own cash. Each year, he would increase the expense account (reducing equity) by $5,000 and simultaneously decrease the franchise license (asset account) through accumulated amortization by $5,000.

Patents

Another common type of intangible asset you'll encounter in accounting is the *patent*. Patents represent valuable rights granted by the government, giving a company the exclusive ability to manufacture or sell a unique invention for a set period of time. However, because patents have a limited useful life, their cost is gradually amortized, similar to other intangible assets.

In many industries, patents expire or lose their practical usefulness over time. For instance, **pharmaceutical companies** often rely on patents to protect new drugs, but these patents have strict expiration dates. Once expired, generic versions can be produced, drastically reducing the patent's value. In technology, a patent might become outdated well before its legal expiration, as the rapid pace of innovation can make certain inventions obsolete quickly. Therefore, businesses should choose amortization periods that reflect the asset's expected usefulness, not just its legal duration.

Let's walk through a hypothetical example of accounting for a patent, using a tech company that's developed an innovative *antivirus software program*.

> **Step 1: Patent Acquisition:** *The company files for and acquires the patent for its antivirus software, incurring a total cost of $35,000, paid in cash*. This transaction would decrease the **cash** (asset) account by $35,000 and increase the **patent** (asset) account by $35,000.

> **Step 2: Determine Useful Life:** *After careful consideration, the company decides that the patent is likely to be useful for seven years*. This timeframe will guide the amortization process.

> **Step 3: First Year Amortization:** At the end of the first year, the company records $5,000 in amortization expense ($35,000 divided by seven years). This is done by increasing the **amortization expense** (reducing equity) by $5,000 and reducing the **patent** (asset) account by $5,000.

> **Step 4: Patent Defense Costs:** *In the second year, a competitor challenges the patent in court*. The company successfully defends its patent but incurs $12,000 in legal fees. To record this, the accountant adds $12,000 to the **patent** account and deducts $12,000 from **cash**.

> **Step 5: Adjust Amortization for Additional Costs:** After adding the $12,000 in defense costs, the patent's adjusted value is $42,000. However, only six and a half years of useful life remain. The company now calculates a new annual amortization: **$7,000 per year** ($42,000 divided by approximately 6 years).

> **Final Amortization Process:** Each year, for the next six years, the company will record **$7,000 in amortization expense**. This means the **patent** (asset) account is reduced by $7,000 each year, and the **equity**

account reflects this annual expense. This way, the company's balance sheet stays aligned, always reflecting *Assets = Liabilities + Equity*.

When it comes to intangible assets like patents, trademarks, or copyrighted works, *initial value* on the balance sheet is based on **direct production costs**. For a patent, this might include attorney fees and filing expenses. For a logo or cartoon character, the value would reflect costs such as legal fees for trademarking and payments to designers or artists.

But what happens when one intangible asset becomes far more valuable than another, even if both were created with similar initial costs?

Q: Suppose a studio pays an artist $500 to design two characters—one becomes a worldwide sensation while the other fades into obscurity. How can these two assets be valued the same on the balance sheet?

A: *Intangible assets are typically recorded at production cost* until sold. So, both characters would be valued at $500 initially, regardless of one character's rising popularity.

However, when a company *sells* an intangible asset, it's then recorded at the sale price. If, for example, a studio sold the rights to the popular character for $50 million, the buyer would record that intangible asset at $50 million, reflecting its *market value*. But companies can't just increase the value of their intangible assets on their own balance sheets based on assumed or perceived market worth. Conversely, the selling company would remove any remaining amount for that character from their books and record the difference between its remaining value on the book and the amount it sold for as income. This example follows a key accounting principle called the *"Historical Cost Principle."*

Goodwill: The Value Beyond Tangibles

"Goodwill" is an intangible asset that represents the *extra value* a company brings to the table beyond its physical assets and financial performance. Think of goodwill as the *brand reputation* and *customer loyalty* a business has built over time. This value might derive from producing high-quality products, having exceptional customer service, a loyal client base, or a well-trained and dedicated team.

For example, a well-loved local coffee shop with a loyal customer base and a reputation for great service has goodwill. This goodwill might make it more valuable than another café with the same physical assets but without that reputation.

Companies don't assign a dollar amount to their own goodwill—it would be highly subjective and could easily mislead investors. Instead, *goodwill is only recorded during a business acquisition.*

Here's how it works:

When Company A buys Company B, it often pays more than the fair market value of Company B's assets. This difference in purchase price reflects the goodwill associated with Company B's brand, reputation, and customer relationships.

Let's say a large coffee chain buys out our well-loved local coffee shop for $1 million. If the coffee shop's physical assets and inventory are valued at $700,000, the additional $300,000 paid would be recorded as goodwill on the acquiring company's balance sheet.

Understanding Goodwill: Real-World Example

Imagine *TechCorp*, a large technology firm, which already has $4 billion worth of **goodwill** recorded on its balance sheet. Now, TechCorp decides to acquire a smaller, innovative company called *InnovaTech*. At the time of purchase, InnovaTech has $3 million in assets and $2 million in liabilities, resulting in a *net asset value* of $1 million. However, TechCorp sees strategic value in acquiring InnovaTech, particularly its technology patents and skilled workforce, so it agrees to pay $5 million in cash to acquire the company.

Here's how this impacts TechCorp's balance sheet:

1. **Initial Acquisition and Goodwill Calculation:** When TechCorp acquires InnovaTech, it adds InnovaTech's $3 million in assets and $2 million in liabilities to its own books, giving TechCorp a $1 million increase in net assets. But since TechCorp paid $5 million, it ends up with a net reduction of $4 million in net assets on its balance sheet. This creates a discrepancy because now the *assets side is not balanced* with liabilities and equity.

Account	Change	Explanation
Cash	- $5,000,000	Cash paid to acquire InnovaTech
Assets acquired	+ 3,000,000	Innova Tech's total assets added to TechCorp
Liabilities acquired	+ $2,000,000	InnovaTech's liabilities added to TechCorp
Net change in assets	- $2,000,000	$3M – $5M cash = net reduction before goodwill
Change in liabilities + equity	+ $2,000,000 (liabilities only)	No change in equity yet
Result:	**Unbalanced**	The accounting equation is off by $4M

2. **Recording Goodwill:** To balance the books, TechCorp records **goodwill**, an intangible asset that accounts for the extra value paid beyond InnovaTech's net assets. The difference between the purchase price ($5 million) and the net asset value ($1 million) is $4 million, which is added to the *goodwill* account. Now, TechCorp's *assets are equal to liabilities plus equity*, and the goodwill accurately reflects the additional value TechCorp sees in InnovaTech, such as its unique technology and brand reputation.

Account	Change	Explanation
Goodwill	+ $4,000.000	Added as an intangible asset to reflect value paid above net assets
		(Purchase price $5M − Net assets $1M)
Total change in assets	+ $4,000.000	This offsets the earlier $4M imbalance caused by paying more than the net assets acquired
Change in liabilities + equity	No change	Goodwill only affects the asset side
Result:	Balanced	Assets now equal liabilities + equity

3. **Why Pay Extra? The Strategic Value of Goodwill:** TechCorp didn't overpay out of goodwill alone, it saw potential in InnovaTech's technology that could drive future growth and expand its market share. By recording this premium as goodwill, TechCorp acknowledges the value InnovaTech brings beyond its physical assets, like its patents, team expertise, and industry relationships.

4. **Goodwill Impairment – When Things Go Wrong:** Unlike other assets, goodwill is not amortized because it's considered to have an indefinite lifespan. However, if something impacts TechCorp's brand or InnovaTech's value, such as a product scandal or legal issue, the goodwill might lose value. For instance, if TechCorp's new InnovaTech-based product fails and leads to negative press, TechCorp may choose to **write down** (reduce) the goodwill on its balance sheet. This is known as a *goodwill impairment*, and it's recorded as an expense on the income statement, reducing both the goodwill asset and the equity account to keep the accounting equation balanced.

Key Takeaway: Goodwill allows companies to reflect the intangible but valuable assets acquired in a purchase. It captures the "extra" value paid for benefits like a strong brand, loyal customers, or proprietary technology—assets that don't show up in a company's physical inventory but are essential to its competitive advantage.

Liabilities

In accounting, **liabilities** are obligations that a business has to settle in the future. These are values expected to leave the business, such as amounts owed to suppliers, lenders, or customers who paid in advance for services yet to be provided.

One type is **Accounts Payable (AP)**, which represents money owed to other businesses for supplies or services received but not yet paid for. When a company orders office supplies or raw materials on credit, it records this under accounts payable, showing a short-term commitment to pay the vendor.

For example, think of a well-known coffee chain like Starbucks. When Starbucks buys coffee beans from suppliers but doesn't pay immediately, it incurs a liability in the form of **Accounts Payable (AP)**. This AP represents the amount Starbucks owes to suppliers until the payment is completed.

Another form is **Notes Payable**, which typically refers to loans taken from banks or other lenders. Unlike AP, notes payable often involve formal agreements and may carry interest. These can be short- or long-term, depending on the loan's repayment terms. For example, a business might take out a three-year loan to purchase equipment, creating a longer-term liability on its books.

Lastly, we have **Unearned Revenue**, which applies when a business receives payment upfront for services or goods it has not yet delivered.

Imagine a famous personal trainer, "FitFlow," who charges clients a $10,000 fee for a year of personal coaching, payable upfront. FitFlow collects the $10,000 in January but delivers services monthly throughout the year. When FitFlow receives the money, it records $10,000 in **Unearned Revenue** (a liability) because it owes future services to the client. As each month passes and services are provided, a portion of this unearned revenue shifts from a liability to a revenue account, reflecting the income earned month by month.

We'll show two transactions:

1. The initial payment received (recorded as unearned revenue).
2. The revenue recognized after one month (when part of the service is delivered).

Step 1: Recording the Initial Payment

TRANSACTION RECORD	NOTE	DATE	ACCOUNT	ASSETS
1	Client pays FitFlow	1/1/2023	Cash	$10,000

ACCOUNT	LIABILITIES	+	ACCOUNT	EQUITY
Unearned Revenue	$10,000		Revenue	-

FitFlow receives $10,000 in cash, which increases the Cash account (asset). At the same time, this payment creates a $10,000 liability (Unearned Revenue), as FitFlow owes the service over the next 12 months.

Step 2: Recognizing Revenue After One Month of Service

TRANSACTION RECORD	NOTE	DATE	ACCOUNT	ASSETS
2	Monthly service completed	2/1/2023	Cash	-

ACCOUNT	LIABILITIES	+	ACCOUNT	EQUITY
Unearned Revenue	- $833,33		Revenue	$833,33

After delivering one month of service, FitFlow reduces the Unearned Revenue account by $833.33 (1/12 of the initial payment) and recognizes this as earned Revenue. This amount is now part of FitFlow's equity because it reflects income earned.

Each month, FitFlow would continue to record a similar entry, gradually transferring $833.33 from Unearned Revenue (liability) to Revenue (equity) until the full $10,000 is earned by the end of the 12-month period.

Unearned revenue, as demonstrated in the FitFlow example, works similarly to **notes payable** but with an important difference. With unearned revenue, the liability decreases as the business delivers the agreed-upon service or product. For **notes payable**, however, the liability decreases through actual cash payments toward the debt.

Consider a small tech startup, **ByteBoost**, that takes out a $20,000 loan to purchase equipment. This loan is recorded as a **note payable** on ByteBoost's balance sheet, representing an obligation to pay back the bank. Here, the note payable shows the principal amount the business owes, while an **interest payable** account would track the interest ByteBoost has to pay on top of the principal.

"Notes" are essentially promises to repay, and they can be issued to any party willing to extend credit, banks, suppliers, or even investors. The term note is often used interchangeably with loan. Since most lenders charge interest, **notes payable** are often paired with **interest payable** accounts. This interest is an additional cost of borrowing and must be tracked as part of the company's expenses.

Before diving further into the specifics of handling notes and interest payable, it's essential to understand two foundational terms in accounting: **debits** and **credits**. These concepts are the basis of **double-entry accounting** and are crucial for recording every transaction accurately.

Debits & Credits

We've held off on introducing **debits** and **credits** until now to avoid overwhelming you with accounting jargon. By now, you should have a basic idea of how **double-entry accounting** works. If you've followed along, you know that each accounting transaction impacts at least two accounts, and that **assets** must always equal the total of **liabilities** plus **equity**.

Let's break down some basic principles to make things clearer:

> 1. Every transaction requires at least two accounts to be adjusted.
> 2. The total amount debited must equal the total amount credited.

Up until now, we've been using "increase" and "decrease" to describe changes in accounts. For example, if a business pays a bill in cash, we might say that cash (an asset) decreases, and accounts payable (a liability) also decreases by the same amount. This way of thinking is perfectly fine, but using **debits** and **credits** provides a more standardized and accurate way to track transactions.

So, What Are Debits and Credits?

In accounting, **debits** and **credits** are tools used to increase or decrease accounts. They might seem confusing at first, especially since their meanings can differ from how these words are used in everyday language.

Imagine this scenario: when I return an item to a store, they might give me a "store credit" that I can use to buy something else. But in accounting, "credit" doesn't always mean "money you receive." Instead, **debits and credits have specific effects depending on the type of account** they're applied to.

Here's a basic rule to remember:

> ▸ **Asset Accounts**: When we add to an asset account (like cash), we **debit** it. When we reduce an asset, we **credit** it.
> ▸ **Liability and Equity Accounts**: When we increase a liability or equity account, we **credit** it. When we decrease a liability or equity account, we **debit** it.

An Example to Illustrate

Imagine a small café, **Coffee Craze**, that buys $200 worth of coffee beans on credit. Here's how this transaction would look in debits and credits:

> - **Inventory** (an asset) increases because Coffee Craze now has more beans to sell. So, we **debit** the Inventory account for $200.
> - **Accounts Payable** (a liability) also increases since the café owes $200 to its supplier. We **credit** Accounts Payable for $200.

This is what the entry would look like:

Date	Account	Debit	Credit
01/05/2023	Inventory	$200	
	Accounts Payable		$200

Every transaction works in this dual way: one account is debited, and another is credited, keeping everything balanced according to the accounting equation.

The "Opposite" Logic

One of the trickiest things about debits and credits is that they work in a way that may feel counterintuitive. For example:

> - When you **withdraw money from a bank account**, in accounting terms, you're **crediting** your cash account, even though you're actually taking money out.
> - Likewise, when you **add money to an account**, you're **debiting** it.

This can feel odd at first because it's not how these words are used in banking, which is most people's experience with these words. But once you get the hang of it, using **debits and credits** becomes second nature and becomes quite simple.

Think of it Like Balancing Scales

The concept of debits and credits is like a perfectly balanced scale. Every debit must have an equal credit, keeping the books balanced. So if you add a $200 debit on one side, you need a $200 credit on the other. This balance is the heart of **double-entry accounting** and ensures accuracy in financial records.

As you practice with debits and credits, these terms will become more intuitive. Just remember, every transaction involves at least two accounts: one debit and one credit.

Here's a clear table to illustrate the basic concept of **debits** and **credits** for different types of accounts. This shows common actions and whether each action results in a debit or credit, with explanations to reinforce the rules.

Account Type	Action	Debit or Credit	Explanation / Example
Asset (e.g., Cash)	Increase	Debit	If we receive $500 in cash, we debit the Cash account by $500.
Asset (e.g., Cash)	Decrease	Credit	If we pay a $100 bill, we credit the Cash account by $100.
Liability (e.g., Accounts Payable)	Increase	Credit	When we buy goods on credit for $300, we credit Accounts Payable by $300.
Liability (e.g., Accounts Payable)	Decrease	Debit	When we pay an outstanding invoice Of $200, we debit Accounts Payable by $200.
Equity (e.g., Owner's Capital)	Increase	Credit	If the owner invests S 1,000 in the business, we credit Owner's Capital by $1,000.
Equity (e.g., Owner's Capital)	Decrease	Debit	If the owner withdraws $500, we debit Owner's Capital by $500.
Revenue (e.g., Sales Revenue)	Increase	Credit	When we sell a product for $200, we credit Sales Revenue by $200.
Expense (e.g., Rent Expense)	Increase	Debit	If we pay $600 in rent we debit Rent Expense by $600.

Quick Reference Notes

- *Asset Accounts: **Debit** to increase, **credit** to decrease.*
- *Liability Accounts: **Credit** to increase, **debit** to decrease.*
- *Equity Accounts: **Credit** to increase, **debit** to decrease.*
- *Revenue Accounts: **Credit** when recording sales or income.*
- *Expense Accounts: **Debit** when recording expenses.*

	ASSETS	LIABILITIES	EQUITY
CREDITS	Decrease Assets	Increase Liabilities	Increase Equity
ASSETS	Increase Assets	Decrease Liabilities	Decrease Equity

One more Example

Let's consider a **law firm** that receives a payment from a client's insurance company. The insurance company pays $150,000 to cover legal fees for a client involved in a case. Here's how the entries would look:

> ▷ For the **law firm**: The accountant **debits** the Cash account by $150,000, increasing it, because cash was received. At the same time, they **credit** Accounts Receivable (another asset) by $150,000 to reduce it, as the amount owed is now paid.
>
> ▷ For the **insurance company**: The accountant **credits** the Cash account by $150,000 to show a decrease in cash, and **debits** Accounts Payable (a liability) by $150,000 to reduce the amount they owed to the law firm.

Equity accounts operate similarly to liability accounts when it comes to debits and credits, with a few unique characteristics that we'll cover in the next section. Essentially, equity increases with credits and decreases with debits, just like liabilities.

ADE LOR

There's a popular and very useful trick to help you remember **how debits and credits affect different types of accounts**—it's the acronym **ADE LOR**.

> ▷ **ADE** stands for **Assets, Drawings, and Expenses**. These accounts are on the **left side** of the accounting equation, meaning they **increase with debits** and **decrease with credits**.
>
> ▷ **LOR** stands for **Liabilities, Owner's Equity, and Revenue**. These are on the **right side**, meaning they **increase with credits** and **decrease with debits**.

This simple memory aid can be a lifesaver when you're learning how to record journal entries properly.

Account Type	Group	Normal Balance	Debit Effect	Credit Effect
Assets	A (ADE)	Debit	Increases	Decreases
Drawings	D (ADE)	Debit	Increases	Decreases
Expenses	E (ADE)	Debit	Increases	Decreases
Liabilities	L (LOR)	Credit	Decreases	Increases
Owner's Equity	O (LOR)	Credit	Decreases	Increases
Revenue	R (LOR)	Credit	Decreases	Increases

The Left and Right Sides on a transaction

Debits go on the left, and credits go on the right – This is a key rule in accounting, remember this!

The fundamental accounting equation: **Assets = Liabilities + Equity**, naturally aligns with this left-right logic. **Assets** are typically on the left side of this equation, while **liabilities** and **equity** are on the right.

> ▹ **Assets**: Most of the time, your asset accounts will have **debit balances** (since assets generally represent things the business owns or has). For example, your checking account, equipment, and property balances are typically positive, reflecting the resources available to your business.
>
> ▹ **Liabilities**: On the other side, **liabilities** are expected to have **credit balances**. It's normal for a business to owe money for things like accounts payable, taxes due, or customer deposits on orders. These liabilities grow as the business operates and incurs more obligations.

Understanding Normal vs. Abnormal Balances

Generally:

> ▹ **Asset accounts** should have debit balances. If an asset account shows a credit balance, this often signals an error. However, there are rare cases when a credit balance in an asset account is possible—like when a bank account is overdrawn.
>
> ▹ **Liability accounts** should have credit balances. If a liability account ends up with a debit balance, it's often due to a mistake in recording, unless there's an unusual situation (e.g., a refund to a customer).

In accounting, **debits and credits** are frequently abbreviated as **"Dr."** for debit and **"Cr."** for credit. You'll likely see these abbreviations in journal, ledgers, and other places where the shorthand is more convenient.

Now that we have a basic understanding of **debits and credits**, let's see how they apply in the context of **notes payable**, a common type of liability for businesses that take out loans.

A Detailed Example: GreenWave's New Solar Project Loan

Imagine **GreenWave Energy**, a company specializing in renewable energy solutions, wanting to expand by building a large solar farm. To cover the initial costs, they take out $2 million from a bank on March 15, 2023, using part of their existing facilities as collateral.

Step 1: Recording the Loan

Once the financing is finalized, GreenWave records the loan as follows:

- **Debit**: Cash accounts for $2 million (increasing their assets).
- **Credit**: Notes Payable account for $2 million (increasing their liabilities).

#	Note	Date	Assets (Account / Amount)	Liabilities (Account / Amount)	Equity
1	Financing	3/15/2023	Cash / $2,000,000	Notes Payable / $2,000,000	-

This entry means GreenWave now has $2 million in cash for the project, but they also owe $2 million to the bank.

Step 2: Monthly Interest Accrual

The loan has an interest rate of **4 percent per year**, which accrues monthly. Although GreenWave's first payment isn't due until three months later, they need to recognize the interest expense as it builds up each month.

Monthly Interest Calculation:

$$2,000,000 \times 0.04 \div 12 = \$6,666.67$$

GreenWave accrues $6,666.67 in interest each month.

Monthly Accounting Entry:

- **Credit**: Interest Payable (a liability account) by $6,666.67, increasing the liability.
- **Debit**: Interest Expense (an expense account) by $6,666.67, recording the expense incurred.

#	Note	Date	Liabilities (Account / Amount)	Equity (Account / Amount)
2	Accrued Interest	4/1/2023	Interest Payable / $6,666.67	Expense / ($6,666.67)
3	Accrued Interest	5/1/2023	Interest Payable / $6,666.67	Expense / ($6,666.67)
4	Accrued Interest	6/1/2023	Interest Payable / $6,666.67	Expense / ($6,666.67)

Even though GreenWave hasn't made a cash payment yet, this entry shows that the company has an additional $6,666.67 in liability each month due to accruing interest. Following **accrual accounting** principles, they record the expense as it happens rather than waiting until payment.

> - **Expense Accounts** are **debited** as costs like interest build up.
> - **Liability Accounts** like **Interest Payable** are **credited** as obligations increase.

Recording accrued interest each month keeps GreenWave's financial records accurate, showing the full extent of their obligations in real time. This transparency helps the company plan its cash flow and avoid unexpected expenses when it's time to pay.

On **June 15**, they make their first payment of **$45,000**. Based on their **amortization schedule**, this payment is split as follows:

> - **$20,000 toward accrued interest (3 months at $6,666.67 per month).**
> - **$25,500 toward reducing the loan principal.**

Here's how the entries look in GreenWave's accounting records:

#	Note	Date	Assets (Account / Amount)	Liabilities (Account / Amount)	Equity
5	Loan Payment	6/15/2023	Cash / ($45,000)	Interest Payable / ($20,000) Notes Payable / ($25,000)	-

> - Cash is credited by $45,000, reflecting the payment leaving GreenWave's bank account.
> - Interest Payable is debited by $20,000 to clear the accrued interest liability for the last three months.
> - Notes Payable is debited by $25,000, reducing the loan principal balance.

After this payment, the **loan principal** is reduced from **$2,000,000** to **$1,975,000**. Interest continues to accrue monthly based on this new balance at the 4% annual rate.

Monthly Interest Calculation on New Principal:

$1,975,000 \times 0.04 \div 12 = \$6,583.33$

Each month, GreenWave accrues $6,583.33 in interest on the updated loan principal.

Monthly Interest Accrual Entry (for July, August, etc., until the next payment):

#	Note	Date	Liabilities (Account / Amount)	Equity (Account / Amount)
6	Accrued Interest	7/1/2023	Interest Payable / $6,583.33	Expense / ($6,583.33)

With each loan payment, a portion goes toward interest, and the remaining amount reduces the principal, much like a home mortgage. As the principal decreases over time, the amount of interest accrued each month also decreases. This results in a gradual shift where more of each payment goes toward paying down the principal rather than interest.

This process is known as **amortization** and is detailed in an **amortization schedule** provided by the lender. The schedule helps the accountant track how much of each payment applies to interest versus principal, ensuring accurate entries.

Equity

In accounting, **equity** represents what's left over after all a company's liabilities are paid off. We can see this in the **fundamental accounting equation**:

Assets − Liabilities = Equity

This form of the equation highlights the essence of equity: the **net assets** that belong to the owners of the business after settling debts. However, equity can be a bit more nuanced than simply subtracting liabilities from assets.

On the **balance sheet**, equity is divided into accounts like **owner's equity** (for sole proprietorships or partnerships) and **stockholder equity** (for corporations). These accounts show who holds claims on the business's net assets. In addition, equity is affected by **revenue** and **expense** accounts, which capture the regular inflows and outflows of money as part of the company's operations.

Expenses: The Cost of Keeping the Lights On

Imagine you own a small **coffee shop**. Running your shop involves a range of ongoing expenses. You need to pay for rent, utilities, employee salaries, and the interest on your business loan. These **expenses** represent the routine costs of keeping the business going and serving customers.

What's important to understand here is that **expenses reduce equity**. When you pay your monthly rent, that money is going out of the business, never to return. Unlike spending on equipment or inventory, which brings in assets you can potentially resell, paying rent or utilities provides no lasting asset. These costs are just part of doing business.

So, every time you pay these operating expenses, they're recorded in expense accounts, which then decrease my equity.

Revenue: The Lifeblood of the Business

Now let's look at **revenue**, the opposite of expenses. Revenue is the money flowing **into** the business from regular operational activities. When customers buy a cup of coffee, a bag of beans, or a muffin, that's revenue.

Revenue is recorded in revenue accounts and represents an **increase in equity**. Every sale brings in cash (or another form of payment), adding value to the business and boosting the owners' stake in it. Unlike an owner's personal investment in the business, revenue is generated by the business itself through its daily activities.

Understanding Equity in a Small Business

Small business's equity works technically different than a large corporation, although the foundational concepts are the same. Small businesses don't have stockholders or issue dividends. Instead, the owner's personal investment in the business and the business's retained earnings represent the equity. Let's break down the main types of equity accounts for small businesses.

Key Equity Accounts in a Small Business

1. **Owner's Capital Balance / Owner's Equity**: This account shows the owner's claim on the assets of the business. It's essentially the business's total equity balance and appears on the **balance sheet** as the main equity account.

2. **Owner's Contributions**: When an owner injects their own funds into the business, this account records that contribution. Think of it as increasing the owner's "stake" in the business. This account is usually found on **ledgers** and the **statement of owner's equity**.

3. **Owner's Withdrawals**: When an owner takes money out of the business for personal use, it's recorded here. Withdrawals reduce the owner's capital balance and are similar to dividends, though they don't follow the same rules as corporate dividends.

4. **Revenues**: This account records money flowing **into** the business from its regular operations, such as sales. Revenues increase the owner's equity because they add to the business's net assets.

5. **Expenses**: This account captures the costs the business incurs to keep running, like rent, payroll, and utilities. Expenses reduce the owner's equity, as they represent outflows of assets that don't bring in anything resellable in return.

With these equity accounts in mind, we can expand the accounting equation:

Assets = Liabilities + (Owner's Contributions − Owner's Withdrawals + Revenues − Expenses)

This expanded form emphasizes how each component affects **equity**. Essentially, **equity** is the net effect of the owner's investments and withdrawals, along with the business's profits (revenues minus expenses).

In small businesses, this total **equity** is often represented by the **owner's capital balance** on the balance sheet.

Can Equity Be Negative?

While it's uncommon to see a **negative asset** balance (a credit balance in an asset account) or a **negative liability** balance (a debit in a liability account), it is possible to have a **negative equity** balance. This happens when the business's liabilities exceed its assets, resulting in a **negative owner's capital balance**. This could mean the business is in financial trouble, but it might not be unexpected, especially if it's the early stages or during a difficult financial period.

Debits and Credits in Equity

Since **equity** is on the right side of the fundamental accounting equation, any increase in equity is recorded as a **credit**, and any decrease in equity is recorded as a **debit**. Here's a quick breakdown:

- **Owner's Contributions**: When the owner adds funds to the business, it's recorded as a **credit** to equity, increasing the capital balance.
- **Owner's Withdrawals**: When the owner takes money out of the business, it's recorded as a **debit**, reducing the capital balance.
- **Revenues**: An increase in revenue is recorded as a **credit**, which raises the owner's equity.
- **Expenses**: An increase in expenses is recorded as a **debit**, which lowers the owner's equity.

Example of Accounting for Leo's Pet Supplies

Leo, a passionate pet lover, decides to open **Leo's Pet Supplies**, a small store specializing in high-quality pet food and accessories. As a sole proprietor, Leo's equity in the business is directly affected by all income, expenses, and personal investments or withdrawals.

Leo has saved **$80,000** to start his business. He deposits this amount into a new business checking account specifically for **Leo's Pet Supplies**.

Transaction 1: Initial Investment

ASSETS	=	LIABILITIES	+	EQUITY
Cash	$80,000			Owner's Contributions
Previous Balance	Total Assets: $0	Total Liabilities: $0 Total Equity: $0		
Operation	+$80,000 (Cash)			+$80,000 (Owner's Contributions)

This amount is recorded as an *increase in Owner's Contributions* under **Equity**, since it's Leo's personal investment in the company. Because he isn't borrowing or using credit, there's no entry in **Liabilities**. The total **Assets** of the business are **$80,000**, which matches the amount in **Equity**.

Next, Leo pays **$2,500** as a refundable security deposit for his rental space and **$1,800** for his first month's rent.

Transaction 2: Rent and Security Deposit

ASSETS	=	LIABILITIES	+	EQUITY	
Cash	$75,700			Owner's Contributions	
Security Deposit	$2,500			Rent Expense	-$1,800
Previous Balance	Total Assets: $80,000	Total Liabilities: $0		Total Equity: $80,000	
Operation	+$2,500 (Security Deposit), -$1,800 (Rent Expense)				
New Balance	Total Assets: $78,200	Total Liabilities: $0		Total Equity: $78,200	

The **$2,500** is listed as an **asset** under *Security Deposit*, as he expects to get this back when his lease ends.

The **$1,800 rent** is recorded as an *expense* under **Equity**, which reduces the owner's stake in the business. Assets decrease by **$4,300** to reflect the cash outflow, balanced by the **Security Deposit** and the decrease in **Equity** due to the rent expense.

Leo purchases shelves, a cash register, and storage units for **$15,000**. This equipment is essential for his store operations.

Transaction 3: Equipment Purchase

ASSETS	=	LIABILITIES	+	EQUITY
Cash	$60,700			Owner's Contributions
Security Deposit	$2,500			Rent Expense
Equipment	$15,000			
Previous Balance	Total Assets: $78,200	Total Liabilities: $0		Total Equity: $78,200
Operation	-$15,000 (Cash), +$15,000 (Equipment)			
New Balance	Total Assets: $78,200	Total Liabilities: $0		Total Equity: $78,200

This purchase doesn't involve any **Liabilities** because he isn't using credit. Instead, the equipment is added as an **asset** under *Equipment*. There's no change in **Equity** because buying equipment is a long-term investment in the business, not an expense. **Total Assets** remain the same, as the **$15,000** reduction in *Cash* is offset by the **$15,000** addition in *Equipment*.

Next, Leo places an order for **$5,000** worth of pet supplies with a supplier, which he purchases on credit, meaning he'll pay at the end of the month.

Transaction 4: Inventory Purchase on Credit

	ASSETS	=	LIABILITIES	+	EQUITY	
	Cash	$60,700	Accounts Payable	$5,000	Owner's Contributions	
	Security Deposit	$2,500			Rent Expense	
	Equipment	$15,000			Inventory Expense	-$5,000
Previous Balance	Total Assets: $78,200		Total Liabilities: $0		Total Equity: $78,200	
Operation			+$5,000 (Accounts Payable)			
New Balance	Total Assets: $78,200		Total Liabilities: $5,000		Total Equity: $73,200	

This creates a new entry in **Liabilities**, as he owes **$5,000** to his supplier, which is recorded under *Accounts Payable*. The **$5,000** purchase is recorded as an **Inventory Expense**.

In his first week, Leo makes **$3,200** in sales from his pet supplies. He also hires an employee and accrues **$500** in payroll expense, although the payment will be made at the end of the next week.

Transaction 5: Sales and Payroll Expense

	ASSETS	=	LIABILITIES	+	EQUITY	
	Cash	$63,900	Accounts Payable	$5,000	Owner's Contributions	
	Security Deposit	$2,500	Accrued Payroll	$500	Revenue	+$3,200
	Equipment	$15,000			Rent Expense	
					Inventory Expense	-$500
					Payroll Expense	
Previous Balance	Total Assets: $78,200		Total Liabilities: $5,000		Total Equity: $73,200	
Operation	+$3,200 Cash (Sales Revenue)		+$500 (Accrued Payroll)			
New Balance	Total Assets: $81,400		Total Liabilities: $5,500		Total Equity: $75,900	

The **sales revenue** is recorded as a **credit** to increase equity, as revenue boosts the owner's stake in the business. The corresponding **debit** to cash reflects the increase in assets from sales. Meanwhile, **accrued payroll** is recorded as a liability because the expense is incurred but not yet paid. Payroll expense is **debited** (reducing equity), and **accrued payroll** (a liability) is **credited**.

Later, Leo receives a **$300 utility bill** and decides to withdraw **$2,000** from the business for personal use.

Transaction 6: Utility Bill and Owner's Withdrawal

ASSETS		=	LIABILITIES		+	EQUITY	
Cash	$61,600		Accounts Payable	$5,000		Owner's Contributions	
Security Deposit	$2,500		Accrued Payroll	$500		Revenue	
Equipment	$15,000					Rent Expense	
						Inventory Expense	
						Payroll Expense	
						Utility Expense	-$300
						Owner's Withdrawals	-$2,000
Previous Balance	Total Assets: $81,400		Total Liabilities: $5,500			Total Equity: $75,900	
Operation	-$2,300 (Cash outflow)						
New Balance	Total Assets: $79,100		Total Liabilities: $5,500			Total Equity: $73,600	

The **$300 utility payment** is recorded as an *expense* which flows into **Equity** since it's a normal business cost, which decreases the owner's stake in the business. The **$2,000 withdrawal** is recorded as an *Owner's Withdrawal* under **Equity** because it's money taken out of the business for personal purposes. Both payments are taken from **Cash** under **Assets**, so there's no impact on **Liabilities**. **Assets** decrease by **$2,300** to reflect the cash outflow, balanced by the corresponding decreases in **Equity** for utilities and the owner's withdrawal.

One day a water pipe bursts, causing **$1,500** in damage. However, after agreeing to cover a portion of the repair cost, the landlord promises to reimburse Leo **$1,000** for the repairs. Although Leo hasn't received this reimbursement yet, he has a right to collect it in the near future. In accounting, this type of expected payment from a third party is known as a **receivable**, which represents an asset. The business is effectively owed $1,000 by the landlord, and therefore it has future economic value.

Transaction 7: Repairs and Reimbursement

ASSETS		=	LIABILITIES		+	EQUITY	
Cash	$60,100		Accounts Payable	$5,000		Owner's Contributions	
Security Deposit	$2,500		Accrued Payroll	$500		Revenue	
Equipment	$15,000					Rent Expense	
Reimbursement Receivable	$1,000					Inventory Expense	
						Payroll Expense	
						Utility Expense	
						Repairs Expense	-$500
						Owner's Withdrawals	
Previous Balance	Total Assets: $79,100		Total Liabilities: $5,500			Total Equity: $73,600	
Operation	-$1,500 (Cash for Repair), +$1,000 (Reimbursement Receivable)					-$1,500 (Repairs Expense), +$1,000 (Reimbursement)	
New Balance	Total Assets: $78,600		Total Liabilities: $5,500			Total Equity: $73,100	

The **$1,500 repair payment** is recorded as a **Repairs Expense** under **Equity**, reducing the owner's stake in the business due to this unexpected cost. Meanwhile, the **$1,000 reimbursement** is recorded in **two places**:

1. **Under Assets** as **Reimbursement Receivable**, showing the amount Leo is due to receive from the landlord in the future.

2. **Under Equity** as **Reimbursement**, partially offsetting the Repairs Expense and reducing the net impact of the repair on the owner's equity.

With the end of the month approaching, Leo needs to take care of his monthly rent. He heads to the landlord's office and pays **$1,800** to cover his storefront for the upcoming month. This payment is recorded as a **Rent Expense** in the business's books, which reduces his **Equity** since it's an essential cost of keeping the business running. It also reduces his **Cash** by **$1,800**, reflecting the money that left his account for the rent.

Shortly after, Leo receives good news: the **$1,000 reimbursement** from his landlord for a recent repair has finally arrived. This reimbursement had previously been recorded as an **Accounts Receivable** under **Assets**, anticipating the money Leo was owed. Now that it's been received, his **Cash** goes up by **$1,000**, and the **Accounts Receivable** is decreased, and subsequently removed from his books since the landlord has settled his debt. This adjustment moves the receivable into cash but doesn't impact Equity or Liabilities.

Business has also been good this month. Leo's pet supply store has generated **$5,500** in revenue from sales. He records this as **Revenue** which impacts **Equity**, boosting his ownership equity in the business. The sales bring in an additional **$5,500** in **Cash** under **Assets**, representing the income flowing into the business.

Leo then remembers the outstanding balance he owes his supplier. He takes **$5,000** from his **Cash** and pays off the debt for inventory he purchased on credit earlier. This payment clears his **Accounts Payable** under **Liabilities** since he no longer owes the supplier anything. The inventory itself had already been accounted for in Equity when it was first acquired, so this payment affects only **Cash** and **Liabilities**.

Finally, Leo pays his employee's accrued payroll, a balance of **$500** that he had recorded as a liability. Handing over the payment reduces his **Cash** by **$500** and clears the **Accrued Payroll** liability since the amount has now been paid.

Transaction 8: End of the Month

	ASSETS		=	LIABILITIES		+	EQUITY	
	Cash	$59,300		Accounts Payable	$0		Owner's Contributions	
	Security Deposit	$2,500		Accrued Payroll	$0		Revenue	+$5,500
	Equipment	$15,000					Rent Expense	-$1,800
							Inventory Expense	
							Payroll Expense	
							Utility Expense	
							Repairs Expense	
							Owner's Withdrawals	
Previous Balance	Total Assets: $78,600			Total Liabilities: $5,500			Total Equity: $73,100	
Operation	-$1,800 (Rent), +$5,500 (Sales Revenue), +$1,000 (Reimbursement received), -$5,000 (Supplier payment), -$500 (Payroll payment)							
New Balance	Total Assets: $76,800			Total Liabilities: $0			Total Equity: $76,800	

Note: In our simplified example, we recorded the employee's payroll as a single **$500 Payroll Expense** impacting **Equity**. However, in a real business scenario, payroll costs typically include additional expenses related to taxes and employer contributions. Specifically:

> ▸ **Social Security and Medicare Taxes (FICA)**: Employers in the United States are required to match their employee's contributions to Social Security (6.2%) and Medicare (1.45%), which adds up to an extra **7.65%** of wages.
>
> ▸ **Federal and State Unemployment Taxes (FUTA and SUTA)**: Employers also contribute to unemployment insurance, which varies by state but is generally around **0.6% to 6%** for FUTA and additional rates for SUTA.

Including these taxes would mean that, in practice, the total payroll expense for a $500 wage could be **$538.25** (adding 7.65% for FICA), plus any applicable state and federal unemployment taxes. For simplicity, we've excluded these in our example to focus on the core accounting entries, but businesses should be aware of these additional obligations. Luckily there are payroll support options for companies of all sizes who will typically handle calculating, withholding and remitting payroll taxes, but for cash planning purposes it is important to understand the basics of what your responsibilities will be as the employer.

Creating the Income Statement, balance sheet, and a cash flow statement

As Leo prepares for the end of the month, he asks us to help him put together three key financial statements for his pet supply shop: an **income statement**, a **balance sheet**, and a **cash flow statement**. With the detailed records we've kept in his ledgers, creating these reports will be straightforward.

Our first step is to go over Leo's current account balances. This will give us a clear view of his business's financial standing and provide the foundation for each of the financial statements we'll create.

Assets

Account	Amount
Cash	$59,300
Security Deposit	$2,500
Equipment	$15,000
Total Assets	**$76,800**

Liabilities

Account	Amount
Accounts Payable	$0
Accrued Payroll	$0
Total Liabilities	**$0**

Equity

Account	Amount
Owner's Contributions	$80,000
Revenue	$8,700
Rent Expense	-$3,600
Inventory Expense	-$5,000
Payroll Expense	-$500
Utility Expense	-$300
Repairs Expense	-$500
Owner's Withdrawals	-$2,000
Total Equity	**$76,800**

To start with, we'll create an **income statement** for Leo's pet supply shop, which summarizes his **total revenue** and **total expenses** over a specific period.

Income Statement

For the Month Ending on 10/31/2024

Revenues	Amount
Sales Revenue	$8,700
Total Revenues	**$8,700**

Expenses	Amount
Rent Expense	($3,600)
Inventory Expense	($5,000)
Payroll Expense	($500)
Repairs Expense	($500)
Utility Expense	($300)
Total Expenses	**($9,900)**

Net Income ($1,200)

Net Loss ($1,200)

All of Leo's revenue this period comes from sales of pet supplies, while his expenses are divided across several categories. In accounting, expenses are grouped into different **expense accounts** to show where money is spent. Leo's expenses fall into four main categories:

1. **Rent** – covering the cost of his shop space.
2. **Materials** – representing the portion of supplies and goods used in sales.
3. **Payroll** – wages for his employee.
4. **Repairs and Maintenance** – any costs associated with maintaining his shop.

After reviewing Leo's records, we find that his **total expenses** add up to **$9,600**. This includes the **entire $5,000** spent on materials, which we're recording as an expense this period instead of tracking any remaining inventory as an asset.

With these expenses, Leo's income statement for the month shows a **net loss of $900**.

Next, we'll construct a **Statement of Owner's Equity** and a **Balance Sheet** for Leo's Pet Supplies.

Statement of Owner's Equity

For the Month Ending on 10/31/2024

Owner's Equity on 10/01/2024	Amount
Add: Revenue (Net Income)	$8,700
Less: Rent Expense	($3,600)
Less: Inventory Expense	($5,000)
Less: Payroll Expense	($500)
Less: Repairs Expense	($500)
Less: Utility Expense	($300)
Less: Owner's Withdrawals	($2000)
Total Owner's Equity on 10/31/2024	$76.800

Balance Sheet
Leo's Pet Supplies
As of 10/31/2024

Assets

Assets	Amount
Cash	$59,300
Security Deposit	$2,500
Equipment	$15,000
Total Assets	**$76.800**

Liabilities and Equity

Liabilities	Amount
Accounts Payable	$0
Accrued Payroll	$0
Total Liabilities	**$0**

Equity	Amount
Owner's Contributions	$80,000
Revenue	$8,700
Rent Expense	($3,600)

Inventory Expense	($5,000)
Payroll Expense	($500)
Utility Expense	($300)
Repairs Expense	($500)
Owner's Withdrawals	($2,000)
Total Equity	**$76,800**

Liabilities + Equity $76,800

One of the advantages of running a sole proprietorship like Leo's is that the **business's equity value reflects Leo's personal ownership stake**. From the balance sheet, we see that Leo maintains a significant claim on the company's assets, thanks to his initial contribution of $80,000 in seed money. Liabilities are zero.

Now, imagine if Leo had taken out a bank loan for the initial $80,000 instead of investing his personal savings. His balance sheet would look very different. In that case, the business's creditors (the bank) would have a larger claim on the company's assets, as the liability for the loan would reduce Leo's overall equity. Over time, Leo would need to consistently turn profits and make loan payments to build his stake in the business.

Let's pivot to the **Statement of Cash Flows**, which provides insights into how cash moves in and out of the business. Cash flow activities are typically categorized into three groups:

1. **Operating Activities**: The core day-to-day expenses and revenues, like sales, rent, or payroll.
2. **Investing Activities**: Long-term expenditures, such as buying equipment or making a refundable deposit.
3. **Financing Activities**: Funds raised through contributions or loans, or cash withdrawn by the owner.

Statement of Cash Flows

For the Month Ending on 10/31/2024

Operating Activities

Activity	Amount
Cash inflows from sales	$8,700
Cash outflows for rent	($3,600)

Cash outflows for payroll	($500)
Cash outflows for repairs	($500)
Cash outflows for utilities	($300)
Net Cash from Operating Activities	**$3,800**

Investing Activities

Activity	Amount
Cash inflows from sales	($2,500)
Cash outflows for rent	($15,000)
Net Cash from Investing Activities	**($17,500)**

Financing Activities

Activity	Amount
Cash inflows from sales	$80,000
Cash outflows for rent	($2,000)
Net Cash from Financing Activities	**$78,000**

Net Change in Cash $64,300
Beginning Cash Balance $0
Ending Cash Balance $59,300

Net Change in Cash $59,300

Let's revisit one of Leo's initial cash flows. After contributing $80,000 to the business, this amount was debited into the cash account, marking it as **cash from financing activities**. It represents money introduced into the business by the owner.

In another transaction, Leo paid $4,300 for his store's first month of rent ($1,800) and security deposit ($2,500). These cash flows are split between **operating activities** (the rent) and **investing activities** (the security deposit). The rent reflects an ongoing business cost, while the deposit is categorized as an investment since it's recoverable in the future.

At the end of the reporting period, Leo's cash flow statement helps us double-check the numbers. It summarizes and categorizes all cash inflows and outflows, ensuring the **cash balance in the statement aligns with the balance sheet**.

However, creating this report isn't always so straightforward. For example, payments for accrued expenses (like payroll or supplier balances) often occur later than the actual expense is incurred, so we have to carefully track when cash leaves the business. Another tricky situation involves **partial reimbursements**, like the $1,000 Leo's landlord promised for repair costs. The initial $1,500 repair cost was a cash outflow, but the reimbursement added back $1,000, requiring clear tracking to ensure the numbers reconcile.

This kind of complexity is one reason **some smaller businesses choose to use the cash accounting method,** which allows them to **record expenses only when cash is actually paid,** avoiding the need to track accruals and timing differences in day-to-day bookkeeping.

With these insights in hand, we can present Leo's **Statement of Owner's Equity** and **Balance Sheet**, followed by a **Statement of Cash Flows**, to provide a complete financial snapshot of his pet supply shop. Let's dive into the numbers!

Understanding Equity in a Corporation

If you've been following the financial journey of Leo's Pet Supplies, you already understand the basics of double-entry accounting, which apply just as well to a small neighborhood shop as they do to a multinational corporation. While the math is the same, corporations introduce a unique twist: **stockholders' equity**. Let's dive into the world of corporate accounting and unravel how equity operates at this level.

In corporations, ownership is spread across **stockholders**, who contribute capital in exchange for shares of stock. Unlike Leo's sole proprietorship—where equity reflects his personal investment—corporations issue **common stock** to represent stockholder ownership.

ASSETS = LIABILITIES + STOCKHOLDERS' EQUITY

STOCKHOLDERS' EQUITY = COMMON STOCK + RETAINED EARNINGS

RETAINED EARNINGS = REVENUES - EXPENSES - DIVIDENDS

Imagine the tech startup "TechFuture Inc." Issues 10,000 shares at $50 per share, raising $500,000 in capital. Here's how that transaction would be recorded:

- **Debit**: Cash (Asset) $500,000
- **Credit**: Common Stock (Equity) $500,000

The beauty of common stock is that it gives stockholders both **ownership rights** and a share in the company's success through dividends.

Some corporations also issue **preferred stock**, which operates differently from common stock. Preferred stockholders don't have voting rights, but they enjoy **priority dividends**, which makes their investment attractive to those seeking consistent returns.

For instance, if TechFuture Inc. issues $200,000 in preferred stock, it would be recorded in a **separate preferred stock equity account**. This segregation ensures clarity when analyzing the financial health of a corporation.

Retained earnings are the portion of a corporation's profits that it keeps rather than distributing as dividends. These funds might be used to open new offices, develop products, or handle day-to-day operations.

For example: TechFuture Inc. earns $300,000 in profit this year but chooses to pay $100,000 in dividends to its stockholders. The remaining $200,000 is added to retained earnings:

> - **Credit**: Retained Earnings (Equity) $200,000

The retained earnings account grows as the company succeeds, building a financial cushion for future projects or unexpected downturns.

When a corporation declares dividends, it's essentially sharing its profits with its stockholders. Let's say TechFuture Inc. pays $100,000 in dividends:

> - **Debit**: Dividends (Equity) $100,000
> - **Credit**: Cash (Asset) $100,000

This payout reduces the company's equity and cash but enhances investor trust and satisfaction. It's worth noting that dividends don't always come in cash; they can also take the form of additional shares or other assets.

Equity accounts in corporations operate under the same rules as in other types of businesses:

> - **Credits increase equity**: Think of common stock issues, retained earnings, or revenue.
> - **Debits decrease equity**: Examples include dividend payouts and expenses.

Here's a simple breakdown of normal account balances:

> - **Assets (like cash)**: Normally debit balances.
> - **Liabilities (like loans)**: Normally credit balances.
> - **Equity (like stock)**: Normally credit balances.
>   - **Exceptions**: Expense and Dividend accounts have **debit balances** since they reduce equity.

The structure of a corporation's equity offers a detailed snapshot of its financial health and strategy. For instance:

> - A company with **a large retained earnings account** and low liabilities likely has resources for expansion or innovation.
> - A company heavily reliant on loans might have less financial stability, but it can still grow through careful planning and profit reinvestment.

Retained Earnings

Retained earnings serve as a crucial component of a corporation's equity, reflecting the profits it has chosen to reinvest in the business rather than distribute to its shareholders.

Calculated as **revenues – expenses – dividends**, are a direct driver of stockholder equity. Let's break it down with a practical example:

Imagine a corporation generates **$120M in revenue**, incurs **$100M in expenses**, and issues **$10M in dividends**. This leaves **$10M in retained earnings**, which boosts the equity of its stockholders. It's a similar process to how small businesses see an increase in owner equity when profits exceed expenses—it's just scaled up.

It's important to distinguish between cash inflows:

> - **Financing Activities**: Loans or stock sales usually belong to creditors, who hold a legal claim on repayment.
> - **Operating Activities**: Profits from business operations are the property of the business or its stockholders.

Even when some profits are used to cover liabilities, retained earnings always result in a **net increase in stockholder equity**.

Example: AquaClear Industries

Let's examine **AquaClear Industries**, a fictional company specializing in sustainable water filtration systems. The company is funded by **$5M in stock issuance** and **$3M in business loans**. Over its first quarter of operations, here's what happens:

1. $5,000,000 in Common Stock Issued

AquaClear raises money from investors by issuing common stock.

> - **Debit**: Cash (increases as money is received).
> - **Credit**: Common Stock (stockholder equity increases).

2. $3,000,000 in Business Loans Secured

The company takes out loans to cover early-stage operational costs.

- **Debit**: Cash (increases).
- **Credit**: Notes Payable (liabilities increase).

3. $250,000 Loan Payment Made

After the first quarter, AquaClear begins paying down its loan balance.

- **Debit**: Notes Payable (liability decreases).
- **Credit**: Cash (asset decreases).

4. $2,000,000 Spent on Equipment and Supplies

The company purchases manufacturing equipment and materials for its filtration systems.

- **Debit**: Other Assets (equipment and supplies increase).
- **Credit**: Cash (asset decreases).

5. $6,500,000 in Revenue Earned

AquaClear sells its systems, earning **$4,000,000 in cash** and **$2,500,000 on credit** (accounts receivable).

- **Debit**: Cash and Accounts Receivable (assets increase).
- **Credit**: Revenue (stockholder equity increases).

6. $4,000,000 in Expenses Incurred

The company faces operational costs, including production and salaries.

- **$3,000,000** paid in cash.
- **$1,000,000** remains unpaid (accounts payable).
- **Debit**: Expenses (stockholder equity decreases).
- **Credit**: Cash and Accounts Payable (assets and liabilities adjust).

7. $500,000 Dividends Issued to Stockholders

At the end of the quarter, AquaClear rewards its stockholders with dividend payments.

- **Debit**: Dividends (equity decreases).
- **Credit**: Cash (asset decreases).

Simplified Ledger for AquaClear Industries

Transaction	Debit	Credit
Common Stock Issued	Cash ($5,000,000)	Common Stock ($5,000,000)
Business Loan Secured	Cash ($3,000,000)	Notes Payable ($3,000,000)
Loan Payment	Notes Payable ($250,000)	Cash ($250,000)
Equipment Purchased	Other Assets ($2,000,000)	Cash ($2,000,000)
Revenue Earned	Cash ($4,000,000), Accounts Receivable ($2,500,000)	Revenue ($6,500,000)
Expenses Incurred	Expenses ($4,000,000)	Cash ($3,000,000), Accounts Payable ($1,000,000)
Dividends Issued	Dividends ($500,000)	Cash ($500,000)

By the end of its first quarter, AquaClear Industries is poised for growth. Its retained earnings reflect the company's profitability, while proper tracking of equity, assets, and liabilities ensures financial clarity. Compare this with our earlier small-business example of Leo's Pet Supplies, and you'll see the same fundamental principles in action—only with larger numbers and different complexities!

Retained Earnings Statement
End of Quarter (all dollar amounts in thousands)

Item	Amount ($)
Retained Earnings at the beginning of the period	$ -
Plus: Net income	$ 2,000
Subtotal	$ 2,000
Less: Dividends issued	$ 500
Retained Earnings at the end of the period	$ 1,500

Retained earnings are tracked using a **retained earnings statement**, which is updated for each accounting period. This statement reflects AquaClear Industries' retained earnings after one quarter, showing how profits contribute to stockholder equity even after accounting for dividends.

AquaClear Industries
Balance Sheet
As of the End of QI 2024

Assets	
Cash	$7,500,000
Accounts Receivable	$2,000,000
Equipment	$5,000,000
Inventory	$1,500,000
Prepaid Expenses	$500,000
Total Assets	**$16,500,000**

Liabilities	
Accounts Payable	$2,500,000
Notes Payable	$1,000,000
Accrued Expenses	$500,000
Total Liabilities	**$4,000,000**

Stockholder's Equity	
Common Stock	$8,000,000
Retained Earnings	$4,500,000
Total Equity	**$12,500,000**

Total Liabilities and Equity $16,500,000

Retained earnings are listed alongside common stock in the **equity section** of the company's balance sheet. However, it's essential to understand the distinction between these two components:

- **Common Stock**: Represents the initial and ongoing investments made by shareholders.
- **Retained Earnings**: Represents the portion of net income the company has retained for reinvestment rather than distributing to stockholders as dividends.

Chapter 3 Assessment Test

1. **What is the fundamental accounting equation?**

   a. Assets = Revenue + Expenses

   b. Assets = Liabilities + Equity

   c. Liabilities = Assets - Expenses

2. **What does double-entry accounting ensure?**

   a. Every transaction impacts only one account.

   b. Total debits equal total credits.

   c. Assets are always greater than liabilities.

3. **How does purchasing equipment with cash affect the accounting equation?**

   a. Assets increase, and liabilities increase.

   b. Assets decrease, and equity decreases.

   c. One asset increases, and another asset decreases.

4. **Which of the following is an example of an intangible asset?**

   a. Equipment

   b. Patents

   c. Inventory

5. **What happens when a company receives $5,000 in accounts receivable through the sale of services?**

   a. Cash increases, and accounts payable increases.

   b. Accounts receivable increases, and revenue increases.

   c. Accounts receivable decreases, and cash increases.

6. **How is amortization different from depreciation?**

   a. Amortization applies to tangible assets, and depreciation applies to intangible assets.

b. Amortization applies to intangible assets, and depreciation applies to tangible assets.

   c. Both terms are used interchangeably.

7. **What is goodwill in accounting?**

   a. Physical assets like machinery and land.

   b. A liability that represents future obligations.

   c. An intangible asset representing extra value paid during an acquisition.

8. **Which type of account increases with a credit?**

   a. Asset accounts

   b. Liability accounts

   c. Expense accounts

9. **If a company pays off a $5,000 liability, how is the accounting equation affected?**

   a. Assets decrease, and liabilities decrease.

   b. Assets increase, and equity decreases.

   c. Liabilities increase, and equity increases.

10. **What is the purpose of recording debits and credits?**

    a. To ensure assets always exceed liabilities.

    b. To accurately track increases and decreases in accounts.

    c. To simplify the income statement preparation.

Answers

1. What is the fundamental accounting equation?

Correct Answer: b) Assets = Liabilities + Equity
This equation is the foundation of accounting and ensures all financial records stay balanced.

2. What does double-entry accounting ensure?

Correct Answer: b) Total debits equal total credits.
Double-entry accounting maintains balance by recording every transaction in at least two accounts.

3. How does purchasing equipment with cash affect the accounting equation?

Correct Answer: c) One asset increases, and another asset decreases.
Cash decreases, and equipment increases, keeping the total assets unchanged.

4. Which of the following is an example of an intangible asset?

Correct Answer: b) Patents
Intangible assets include non-physical items like patents, trademarks, and goodwill.

5. What happens when a company receives $5,000 in accounts receivable through the sale of services?

Correct Answer: b) Accounts receivable increases, and revenue increases.
Accounts receivable records the promise of future cash, while revenue reflects income earned.

6. How is amortization different from depreciation?

Correct Answer: b) Amortization applies to intangible assets, and depreciation applies to tangible assets.
Amortization gradually reduces the value of intangible assets, while depreciation applies to physical assets.

7. What is goodwill in accounting?

Correct Answer: c) An intangible asset representing extra value paid during an acquisition.
Goodwill reflects the premium paid for a business beyond its tangible and identifiable intangible assets.

8. Which type of account increases with a credit?

Correct Answer: b) Liability accounts
Liability and equity accounts increase with credits, while asset accounts increase with debits.

9. If a company pays off a $5,000 liability, how is the accounting equation affected?

Correct Answer: a) Assets decrease, and liabilities decrease.
Cash (an asset) decreases, and the liability is reduced, keeping the equation balanced.

10. What is the purpose of recording debits and credits?

Correct Answer: b) To accurately track increases and decreases in accounts. Debits and credits ensure that every transaction is properly recorded and the accounting equation stays balanced.

CHAPTER 4

Recording Transactions

> *Numbers have an important story to tell. They rely on you to give them a clear and convincing voice.*
>
> – Stephen Few,
> Data Visualization Expert

Up to this point, we have examined accounting from a broad perspective. While financial statements represent the end result, creating them requires careful preparation and organization. Behind every financial report lies a foundation of essential elements: raw data, source documents, systematic filing methods, precise data-entry procedures, journal entries, and fundamental bookkeeping tools. All these components must be properly managed to generate accurate and useful financial information for any business. In this chapter, we will explore the detailed mechanics of accounting and its day-to-day practices.

Every transaction a business makes is like a piece of a puzzle that, when put together, reveals the full picture of its financial story. Recording these transactions properly ensures that the image is clear, complete, and useful for making informed decisions.

Now that you have a firm grasp of the **fundamental accounting equation** and the principles of **double-entry accounting**, you've overcome some of the most conceptually challenging parts of accounting. Lucky for us, accounting mathematics is primarily rooted in basic addition and subtraction.

The real complexity of accounting lies not in its calculations but in its **organization and analysis**. One of the most common things I see when small business owners are setting up their books is understanding when an account belongs on the income statement (revenue or expense) and when it belongs on the balance sheet (assets, liabilities, and equity). Gaining an understanding of how to organize your data is the first step in ensuring clear financial data.

In this chapter, we'll dive into the tools and methods accountants and bookkeepers rely on to:

> - Identify relevant financial data.
> - Organize this data effectively.
> - Ensure accuracy and reliability in reporting.

For business owners, understanding these processes demystifies essential concepts like "**journal entries**" and "**trial balances**." If you're a business owner who prefers to take control of your own bookkeeping, the guidance in this chapter will equip you with the knowledge to manage your financial records with confidence.

Every transaction starts with a **source document**—a record that proves a transaction has occurred and provides the details needed to record it accurately. Think of it as the first link in the chain of accounting.

For example, imagine Leo, from our earlier pet supply store example. If Leo buys a shipment of dog food, the **invoice from the supplier** serves as the source document. If he writes a check to cover advertising expenses, that check is another source document. These records are essential for verifying the changes to various accounts in the business's books.

Here are examples of source documents you'll encounter in everyday transactions:

> - **Invoices**: Received for purchases or issued to customers for sales.
> - **Receipts**: Proof of payment or funds received.
> - **Bank Statements**: To track deposits, withdrawals, and fees.
> - **Checks**: Evidence of payments made by the business.
> - **Bills**: Detailing amounts owed for services or products.
> - **Credit Card Statements**: Showing business expenses charged to the account.
> - **Time Cards**: For payroll calculations.
> - **Packing Slips**: Received with delivered goods.

> **Deposit Slips**: Proof of funds deposited into a business account.

A good source document should clearly outline the following:

> **Description of the transaction**: What was bought or sold.
>
> **Amount**: The total cost or revenue.
>
> **Authorization**: Signatures, stamps, or logos that validate the transaction.

What is an Invoice?

At its core, an **invoice** is a vital document used in business transactions between two parties: the buyer and the seller. The seller provides goods or services, and the buyer owes money in return. But how much does the buyer owe? What exactly are they paying for? When is the payment due? An invoice answers all these questions.

It's essentially a formal request for payment sent by the seller to the buyer. The invoice includes an itemized list of goods or services provided, the total amount owed, and the payment terms. Once the buyer receives the invoice, they send the payment, completing the transaction.

A typical invoice includes several important elements:

> **Names and Addresses:** The seller's and buyer's names and contact details.
>
> **Invoice Number:** A unique identifier for the invoice, often sequential (e.g., Invoice #1038).
>
> **Invoice Date:** The date the invoice was issued, which starts the clock for when payment is due.
>
> **Payment Terms:** Details like "Net 30 Days," indicating payment is due within 30 days of the invoice date.
>
> **Description of Goods/Services:** An itemized list of what the buyer is paying for. Being specific helps avoid confusion or delays.
>
> **Subtotal and Tax:** The breakdown of the total cost, including applicable sales tax.
>
> **Total Amount Due:** The final amount the buyer must pay, inclusive of taxes.

For example, an invoice for custom design services might include a description of the work, a quantity of 1, a rate of $350, and an 8% sales tax, resulting in a total amount of $378.

Are Invoices and Sales Receipts the Same?

No, there's a key difference:

> - An **invoice** is a request for payment, issued before payment is made.
> - A **receipt** serves as proof of payment, issued after the payment has been received.

What's the Difference Between a Sales Invoice and a Purchase Invoice?

The difference lies in perspective:

> - A **sales invoice** is what the seller calls it.
> - A **purchase invoice** is what the buyer calls it. You may also hear the buyer refer to a purchase invoice as a bill. They're the same document, just viewed from opposite sides of the transaction.

What is a T-Account?

A **T-Account** is a simple visual tool used in accounting to represent the activity of an account. It gets its name because it's shaped like a capital letter "T," which helps clearly distinguish between **debits** and **credits** recorded in the account.

Imagine splitting the "T" into two sides:

> - The **left side** is where **debits** are recorded.
> - The **right side** is where **credits** are recorded.

This structure makes it easy to track the impact of transactions on an account over time, ensuring that every debit and credit is accounted for and balanced.

While **T-Accounts** and the **general ledger** serve similar purposes in accounting—tracking and recording transactions, there are key differences in how they are used and presented. Both tools help accountants organize financial data, but they are suited to different stages of the accounting process and offer distinct advantages depending on the situation.

T-Accounts are best for **learning** and for breaking down individual transactions to understand how debits and credits work. They are a conceptual tool used to explain the mechanics of double-entry accounting. For beginners, as well as seasoned accountants, they offer clarity when analyzing the flow of transactions. However, sometimes even experienced accountants will refer back to T accounts when facing a particularly complex entry that will effect many accounts, to ensure all debits and credits are balanced and recorded properly.

The **general ledger** is a more formal and organized record of all transactions in a business. It is the central accounting system where **every account**—assets, liabilities, equity, revenue, and expenses—has its own detailed record. The ledger consolidates **all T-Account activity** in one place, providing an ongoing summary of account balances.

GL	Description	Debit	Credit	Reference		GL NUMBER		100		200	
100	CASH	50,00	80,00			GL DESCRIPTION		CASH		INVENTORY	
200	INVENTORY	200,00	100,00					50,00	80,00	200,00	100,00
									30,00	100,00	

In a T-Account, whether the **Closing Balance** appears on the **debit side** or the **credit side** depends on whether the balance is **positive** or **negative**.

For **asset accounts** (like Cash), debits increase the balance, and credits decrease it. If the total debits exceed the total credits, the balance is positive, and it will appear on the **debit (left)** side of the T-Account.

However, if the total credits exceed the debits for an asset account, the balance becomes **negative**. In this case, the closing balance will appear on the **credit (right)** side instead. This negative balance often indicates an **overdraft** or a shortfall in the account. Here you will find an excel file where you can practice with T Accounts. Scan the QR code or go to the link:

https://docs.google.com/spreadsheets/d/1H7HnTPy6Xta32yAsM-83fKAshAxg8zun2/edit?usp=drive_link&ouid=115451442075974404873&rtpof=true&sd=true

Journal Entries and General Ledgers

Before transactions make their way into formal **ledgers**, they must first be recorded as **journal entries**. Think of journal entries as the first draft of your financial story. Each entry documents the specifics of a transaction, showing how it affects your accounts with a **debit** (on the left) and a **credit** (on the right). To avoid confusion, credits are typically placed one line below and indented slightly to separate them visually from the debits.

Why is this step so important? A **journal entry** serves as a chronological record of every business transaction. Whether you're running a local bakery or managing a large corporation, this timeline is crucial for tracking financial activity and identifying patterns over time.

Example of a Journal Entry

Date	Account	Debit ($)	Credit ($)	Explanation
2024-10-15	Cash	1,000		Received payment from customer
2024-10-15	Accounts Receivable		1,000	Cleared outstanding invoice
2024-10-16	Office Supplies Expense	200		Purchased office supplies
2024-10-16	Cash		200	Paid in cash
2024-10-18	Rent Expense	1,800		Paid monthly rent
2024-10-18	Cash		1,800	Deducted cash for rent payment

Here's why journalizing is essential: it creates a **chronological record** of all business activities, allowing transactions to be traced over time. For a small business, the journal might start simply, but as the business grows, the number of accounts and the complexity of the transactions multiply.

For example, imagine a boutique pet supply store, like Leo's Pet Supplies. Each week, transactions such as inventory purchases, sales revenue, rent payments, and payroll need to be recorded. Over time, tracking all these accounts accurately using basic ledgers becomes challenging because of the volume of transactions that need to be managed. That's where journal entries come in—they serve as the foundation for the **general ledger**, a comprehensive repository of all account balances and transaction histories.

The General Ledger

The **general ledger** is the organized collection of all account information. Whether it's **assets**, **liabilities**, or **equity**, every account in the ledger has:

1. **A current balance**: Reflecting the account's present value.
2. **A transaction history**: Detailing every change to the account based on journal entries.

For example:

> - **Asset accounts** (like cash or inventory) typically have **debit balances**.
> - **Liability and equity accounts** (such as accounts payable or revenue) usually carry **credit balances**, except for expenses and owner withdrawals, which reduce equity.

GENERAL LEDGER FOR LEO'S PET SUPPLIES

Date	Description	Debit	Credit	Balance
Oct 1	Owner's contribution	$80,000		$80,000
Oct 3	Security deposit		$2,500	$77,500
Oct 5	Rent payment		$1,800	$75,700
Oct 10	Equipment purchase		$15,000	$60,700
Oct 15	Sales revenue	$3.200		$63,900
Oct 20	Utility payment		$300	$63,600
Oct 25	Payroll payment		$500	$63,100
Oct 28	Repairs payment		$1,500	$61,600
Oct 30	Reimbursement received	$1.000		$62,600
Oct 31	Rent payment (2nd month)		$1,800	$60,800
Oct 31	Supplier payment		$5,000	$55,800

ACCOUNTS PAYABLE

Date	Description	Debit	Credit	Balance
Oct 10	Inventory purchase		$5,000	$5,000
Oct 31	Payment to supplier	$5,000		$0

OWNER'S CONTRIBUTIONS

Date	Description	Debit	Credit	Balance
Oct 1	Initial investment		$80,000	$80,000

REVENUE

Date	Description	Debit	Credit	Balance
Oct 15	Sales revenue		$3,200	$3,200
Oct 31	Sales revenue		$5,500	$8,700

EXPENSES

Date	Description	Debit	Credit	Balance
Oct 3	Security deposit	$2,500		$2,500
Oct 5	Rent (1st month)	$1,800		$4,300
Oct 20	Utility bill	$300		$4,600
Oct 25	Payroll expense	$500		$5,100
Oct 28	Repairs expense	$1,500		$6,600
Oct 31	Rent (2nd month)	$1,800		$8,400

REIMBURSEMENT RECEIVABLE

Date	Description	Debit	Credit	Balance
Oct 28	Repairs reimbursement due	$1,000		$1,000
Oct 30	Reimbursement received		$1,000	$0

In today's world, much of this process is automated using **accounting software**, which updates ledgers automatically as transactions are entered. Programs like QuickBooks, Xero, or Wave simplify bookkeeping for small businesses, saving time and reducing the chance of human error.

However, even with automation, it's essential to keep **physical records** like receipts, invoices, and contracts for auditing purposes and tax compliance.

Even small businesses benefit from having a straightforward filing system for organizing source documents. For example:

- **Assets**: Include receipts for purchases, property documents, and bank statements.
- **Liabilities**: Store bills, loan agreements, and contracts with suppliers.
- **Equity**: Divide this into sections:
- **Expenses**: Payroll, rent, utilities, and other operating costs.
- **Revenue**: Sales invoices, payment receipts, and deposit slips.

Investing in labeled folders or a small filing cabinet can prevent headaches during tax season and streamline audits. Today there are also a variety of options for scanning and retaining paper documents in organized digital folders or cloud-based databases, eliminating the need to keep physical records. Many business owners find it helpful to create a folder structure by year, with subfolders for categories like receipts, invoices, and bank statements.

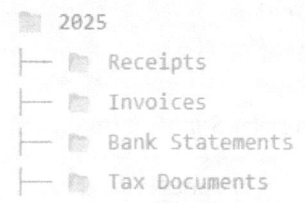

```
📁 2025
├── 📁 Receipts
├── 📁 Invoices
├── 📁 Bank Statements
├── 📁 Tax Documents
```

Remember: well-organized records are a business owner's best friend.

Chart of Accounts

The **chart of accounts (COA)** is like the backbone of your business's financial records. It's essentially a list that organizes all the different accounts you'll use to track your money—where it's coming from, where it's going, and what it's doing in between. You can think of the chart of accounts as a sort of table of contents to your General Ledger. Often it will provide summary data such as account number, account name and sometimes account balance and account type (revenue, expense, asset, liability, equity).

Think of it as a **filing system** for your business finances. Just as you wouldn't want to toss all your paperwork into one messy drawer, the COA helps you categorize transactions into neat and manageable groups. With a well-designed COA, you can find what you're looking for quickly—whether it's last month's rent payment or how much revenue you made on a specific product.

Even a small business, like *Leo's Pet Supplies*, may have 10–20 accounts to track things like **cash, sales, and rent expenses**. For larger companies, the number of accounts can balloon into the thousands, with entire teams of accountants managing them. Regardless of size, every business depends on its COA to stay organized.

How Accounts are Categorized

Accounts are typically grouped by type, with each type represented by a number range. For instance:

- **101–199**: Asset accounts
- **201–299**: Liability accounts
- **301–399**: Equity accounts
- **401–499**: Revenue accounts
- **501–599**: Expense accounts
- **601-699:** Other income accounts
- **701-799:** Other expense accounts

- **801-899**: Tax adjustments (rare)
- **901-999**: Uncategorized

Here's a simple example of how *Leo's Pet Supplies* might set up its COA:

Account Number	Account Number
101	Cash
102	Security Deposit
201	Accounts Payable
301	Owner's Contributions
401	Sales Revenue
501	Rent Expense

The beauty of the COA is that it's **flexible**. As your business grows, your COA can expand to accommodate new accounts. For example:

- If Leo decides to open a second store, he might create:
    - **101.1**: Cash – Main Store
    - **101.2**: Cash – Second Store
- If he starts selling pet grooming services, he could add:
    - **402**: Grooming Revenue

And if he takes on a business partner, he might create separate equity accounts:

- **301.1**: Owner's Contributions – Leo
- **301.2**: Owner's Contributions – Partner

Clear and specific account names are **crucial**. Imagine naming an account simply "Cash." Does it refer to your checking account? Physical cash in a register? By using precise names like "Cash – Bank of America – Main Store," you eliminate confusion. If you have multiple accounts at the same bank another common practice would be to include the last four digits of the account number in the name as well.

The same rule applies to other accounts. For example, instead of naming an expense account "Utilities," you could create subcategories like:

- Utilities – Electricity
- Utilities – Internet

This level of detail makes it easier to track exactly where your money is going. It is always better to be more detailed. That is the ability to roll all of the individual utility accounts up to a total utilities number if you don't need the detail is much easier than trying to go back later and figure out which portion of the utilities went to a specific category like electricity.

Sub-Ledgers: Specialized Tools

In addition to the **general ledger**, which tracks all accounts, businesses often create **sub-ledgers** to focus on specific areas. For example:

> - **Sales Ledger**: Tracks income from different products or services.
> - **Purchase Ledger**: Details all expenses, such as vendor payments.
> - **Accounts Receivable Ledger**: Keeps tabs on customers who owe you money.

While the general ledger provides an overview, these sub-ledgers allow businesses to **zoom in** on specific areas for better management.

Practical Tips for Building Your Chart of Accounts

> 1. **Think Ahead**: Spend time designing your COA before recording transactions. Planning saves headaches later. Ensure that your structure leaves plenty of room for growth in each category. As your business grows it is likely your chart of accounts will as well.
> 2. **Stick to Consistency**: Once an account name or number is set, use it across all systems.
> 3. **Regular Maintenance**: Periodically review your accounts to ensure they still align with your business operations.

As Leo discovered, a well-thought-out chart of accounts makes life easier, whether you're a sole proprietor or a Fortune 500 CFO.

Subsidiary Ledger (Subledger)

As we said, your general ledger serves as the main financial record, containing summarized information about all your accounts, assets, liabilities, equity, revenues, and expenses.

For example, your general ledger might show a total of $5,000 under the account "Accounts Receivable," which indicates that customers owe your business a total of $5,000, but it doesn't show exactly which customers owe money or how much each owes individually.

Here's where the subsidiary ledger comes in. Subsidiary ledgers provide detailed, specific information supporting certain general ledger accounts, typically for accounts receivable, accounts payable, or inventory.

Continuing with Leo's Pet Supplies example, your general ledger might show a total of $5,000 in accounts receivable. However, the subsidiary ledger breaks this total down into individual customer accounts, providing precise details like:

Customer Name	Amount Owed ($)	Due Date
Emily's Cat Haven	$1,500	April 15
PetWorld Supplies	$1,500	April 20
Friendly Paws Vet	$1,000	May 5
Downtown Pet Grooming	$1,500	May 10
Total	**$5,000**	

Utilizing both ledgers in tandem provides a structured, layered approach to accounting, significantly reducing errors and discrepancies. Subsidiary ledgers, which detail specific individual transactions, serve as foundational building blocks, ensuring that summarized totals reflected in the General Ledger are precise and dependable.

Additionally, distinguishing clearly between the General Ledger and Subsidiary Ledgers enhances **auditing efficiency**. Auditors depend on the detailed breakdown found in subledgers to verify and trace individual transactions, confirming their accuracy and validity.

Moreover, maintaining and regularly reconciling both types of ledgers helps businesses quickly identify inconsistencies or unusual patterns, thereby aiding in fraud detection and prevention.

Trial Balance

Once you've set up your **general ledger** and started recording transactions, the next step in maintaining accurate books is creating a **trial balance**.

The **trial balance** is essentially a summary of all the balances in your general ledger accounts. Its main purpose is to verify that the total **debit balances** equal the total **credit balances**. If the two sides don't match, it's a red flag that something may have gone wrong in your accounting records. An important reason that many companies opt to use accounting software is that it will not allow you to go out of balance due to built in controls ensuring each transaction has a matching transaction of the opposite type. Of course, this still does not guarantee accuracy if an amount was mistyped or the wrong account was selected.

Here's how it works:

1. **Debits** represent increases in asset accounts or decreases in liability and equity accounts.
2. **Credits** represent increases in liability and equity accounts or decreases in asset accounts.
3. Every transaction is recorded using **double-entry accounting**, meaning every debit has a corresponding credit.

Let's revisit *Leo's Pet Supplies* and calculate its trial balance.

Trial Balance as of December 31, 2024

Account Name	Debit	Credit
Assets		
Cash	$20,000	
Accounts Receivable	$15,000	
Inventory	$10,000	
Equipment	$50,000	
Liabilities		
Accounts Payable		$12,000
Loans Payable		$25,000
Equity		
Owners Capital		$50,000
Revenue and Expenses		
Revenue		$40,000
Operating Expenses	$32,000	
Totals	**$127,000**	**$127,000**

Since the **debit and credit totals are equal**, Leo's trial balance checks out!

While balancing the debits and credits is a good sign, it's not a guarantee that your books are error-free. For example:

- If you accidentally post a transaction to the wrong account but use the correct debit and credit amounts, the trial balance will still match.
- If you record an equal debit and credit with the wrong figures, the balance will also appear correct.

That's why the trial balance is just one step in maintaining accurate records. It can highlight potential errors but doesn't catch every mistake. Another key to maintaining accurate records is account reconciliation. That is, for any account whose balance can be verified from an outside source, such as a bank statement, the account balance in the books is compared to that on the statement, and if they do not match you can further investigate each individual transaction to find the variance.

What to Do If Your Trial Balance Doesn't Match

If the **debits don't equal the credits,** here's a systematic process to track down the error:

- **Check Your Math:** Start with the basics. Recalculate the totals in your debit and credit columns, simple addition errors are often the culprit. As mentioned earlier, most businesses don't rely on manual records, and accounting software will usually calculate totals automatically. However, if you do have to do math manually, a good rule of thumb to always do your addition twice. Pro tip: If the error in your Trial Balance is divisible by 9, it's probably a transposition error. For example, you entered $3500 as $5300- the difference is $1800, which is perfectly divisible by 9.)

- **Review Account Balances:** Double-check the balances in your general ledger. If one of the account balances is off, it will throw off the entire trial balance.

- **Identify Misclassified Entries:** Look for debits that were mistakenly listed as credits (or vice versa). These errors cause the **difference in balances to equal twice the incorrect entry**. For example, if you accidentally recorded $500 as a credit instead of a debit, your totals would be off by $1,000.

- **Recompute Ledger Balances:** If the error still isn't clear, you'll need to go through each ledger account and recompute its balance from the beginning.

- **Verify Journal Entries:** Make sure every journal entry was correctly posted to its corresponding ledger account.

- **Double-Check Journal Entries:** Finally, review the original journal entries to confirm that every debit has an equal and corresponding credit.

Let's say Leo discovers a mismatch in his trial balance. His total debits are $127,500, while his total credits are $127,000, a difference of $500. Here's how he might troubleshoot:

- First, he checks his math and confirms the totals.

▶ Next, he reviews each account balance and discovers that his **pet food revenue of $250** was accidentally recorded as a debit instead of a credit. Fixing this error resolves the discrepancy. This is an example of when doing a bank reconciliation ahead of time would have already identified and corrected this error.

Prepaid Expenses & Unearned Revenues

Accounting is all about timing and precision, especially in **accrual-based accounting**. Unlike cash accounting, which only tracks when money physically moves, accrual accounting keeps tabs on the actual flow of business activity. This brings us to **prepaid expenses** and **unearned revenues**, two essential concepts that require special handling in financial records.

Prepaid Expenses: Paying Before You Use

Let's say Leo, from *Leo's Pet Supplies*, decides to launch an online advertising campaign for his shop. He prepays $12,000 for a six-month ad plan on a popular pet blog. While Leo hands over the full $12,000 upfront, his business hasn't yet received the full benefit of the advertising service. In accounting terms, this $12,000 is considered a **prepaid expense**, recorded as an **asset** since the service is yet to be consumed.

Here's what happens when the payment is made:

ENTRY DATE	ACCOUNT	DEBIT	CREDIT
2025 Jan 31	Prepaid Advertising (Asset)	12,000	
2025 Jan 31	Cash (Asset)		12,000

Now, as each month passes, Leo's accountant will **adjust the books** to reflect the portion of the advertising service that has been used. For instance, after one month, $2,000 worth of ads has been "consumed." The accountant will make an **adjusting journal entry** like this:

ENTRY DATE	ACCOUNT	DEBIT	CREDIT
2025 Feb 28	Advertising Expense (*Equity*)	2,000	
2025 Feb 28	Prepaid Advertising (*Asset*)		2,000

On the flip side, let's imagine Leo's friend Claire runs a pet grooming business. A customer pays Claire $1,200 upfront for a "12-month grooming package," even though the services haven't been delivered yet. This payment doesn't count as revenue, at least not yet. Instead, it's recorded as **unearned revenue**, a **liability**, since Claire owes services to her customer.

Here's how it looks at the time of payment:

ENTRY DATE	ACCOUNT	DEBIT	CREDIT
2025 Jan 1	Cash (Asset)	$1,200	
2025 Jan 1	Unearned Revenue (Liability)		$1,200

Every month, as Claire provides the grooming service, she recognizes part of the revenue:

ENTRY DATE	ACCOUNT	DEBIT	CREDIT
2025 Jan 31	Unearned Revenue (Liability)	$100	
2025 Jan 31	Revenue (Equity)		$100

By the end of the year, Claire's liability will have reduced to zero, and the $1,200 will be fully recognized as revenue. This information will also be important for future cashflow planning. The company needs to essentially save a portion of this cash that was received up front to pay for the labor and supplies as they are accrued at the time of delivering the service.

Accounting Periods: Snippets of Time

Adjustments are made at the end of an **accounting period**—whether that's monthly, quarterly, or yearly. This practice is based on the **periodicity assumption**, which states that a business's life can be divided into meaningful chunks of time.

Imagine a painting business that buys $18,000 worth of paint supplies, expecting it to last for the next 12 months. However, in the first month, they take on a large project and use $6,000 worth of supplies. Instead of dividing the total evenly over 12 months, they adjust the books to match actual usage:

- Debit: Supplies Expense (Equity) $6,000
- Credit: Prepaid Supplies (Asset) $6,000

If the following month is quieter, and they only use $500 worth of supplies, the adjusting entry reflects that change:

- Debit: Supplies Expense (Equity) $500
- Credit: Prepaid Supplies (Asset) $500

This level of precision ensures that the company's financial records are accurate, timely, and relevant.

A Word on Practicality

Not every adjustment needs to be made daily or even weekly, referencing back to materiality and significance for your business size. Small businesses, like Leo's, usually align their adjustments with their **monthly financial statements**. Larger corporations, however, may have more frequent adjustments or automated systems to track asset usage in real-time. There are also a variety of methods for accounting for the cost of the product, as this often needs to include raw materials, labor, and a portion of overhead costs. In fact, this can become such a complex process that cost accounting is its own subfield.

The Bigger Picture

Prepaid expenses and unearned revenues are just two examples of how accrual accounting reflects the true financial activity of a business. Adjusting entries are the bridge between day-to-day transactions and meaningful financial statements, ensuring that your records tell the whole story—whether you're running a local shop or a multinational corporation.

Cehapter 4 Assessment Test

1. **What is the purpose of a source document in accounting?**

   a. To balance the general ledger.
   b. To verify and provide details of a financial transaction.
   c. To prepare trial balances.

2. **Which of the following is an example of a source document?**

   a. A T-account
   b. An invoice
   c. A trial balance

3. **What is the key difference between an invoice and a receipt?**

   a. An invoice is proof of payment, and a receipt is a request for payment.
   b. An invoice is a request for payment, and a receipt is proof of payment.
   c. Both are identical documents.

4. **What is the primary function of a T-Account?**

   a. To visually represent debits and credits for an account.
   b. To summarize account balances for the month.
   c. To calculate net income.

5. **Where are transactions first recorded before being posted to the general ledger?**

   a. Trial balance
   b. Journal entries
   c. Sub-ledgers

6. **What does a Chart of Accounts (COA) represent?**

   a. A categorized list of all the accounts used in a business.
   b. A list of financial statements.
   c. A summary of total assets.

7. **If a business prepays $12,000 for advertising services over six months, how is it initially recorded?**

   a. Debit Prepaid Advertising (Asset), Credit Cash (Asset).
   b. Debit Advertising Expense, Credit Cash.
   c. Debit Unearned Revenue, Credit Cash.

8. **What happens when a portion of unearned revenue is earned?**

   a. A liability increases, and an asset decreases.
   b. A liability decreases, and revenue increases.
   c. An asset decreases, and an expense increases.

9. **What does the trial balance verify?**

   a. That total revenues exceed expenses.
   b. That total debits equal total credits.
   c. That financial statements are ready for reporting.

10. **Why might a business use subsidiary ledgers in addition to a general ledger?**

    a. To track detailed financial information about specific accounts, such as customer balances.
    b. To replace the general ledger entirely.
    c. To create financial statements.

Answers

1. What is the purpose of a source document in accounting?

Correct Answer: (b) To verify and provide details of a financial transaction.
Source documents, such as invoices and receipts, serve as proof of transactions and provide the necessary details to record them accurately.

2. Which of the following is an example of a source document?

Correct Answer: (b) An invoice
An invoice is a source document because it verifies a financial transaction and provides payment details.

3. What is the key difference between an invoice and a receipt?

Correct Answer: (b) An invoice is a request for payment, and a receipt is proof of payment.
An invoice is sent before payment as a request for funds, while a receipt is issued after payment as proof that it has been received.

4. What is the primary function of a T-Account?

Correct Answer: (a) To visually represent debits and credits for an account.
T-Accounts help accountants track how transactions affect an account by organizing debits (left side) and credits (right side).

5. Where are transactions first recorded before being posted to the general ledger?

Correct Answer: (b) Journal entries
Journal entries serve as the initial record of transactions before they are categorized and summarized in the general ledger.

6. What does a Chart of Accounts (COA) represent?

Correct Answer: (a) A categorized list of all the accounts used in a business.
The COA organizes all accounts into categories such as assets, liabilities, revenue, and expenses to facilitate financial tracking.

7. If a business prepays $12,000 for advertising services over six months, how is it initially recorded?

Correct Answer: (a) Debit Prepaid Advertising (Asset), Credit Cash (Asset).
Since the service hasn't been received yet, it is recorded as a prepaid expense (an asset). Each month, a portion of this will be expensed.

8. What happens when a portion of unearned revenue is earned?

Correct Answer: (b) A liability decreases, and revenue increases.
Unearned revenue is a liability because the business owes services or goods. As the business delivers on its obligation, liabilities decrease and revenue increases.

9. What does the trial balance verify?

Correct Answer: (b) That total debits equal total credits.
The trial balance ensures that double-entry accounting has been applied correctly and that all transactions are balanced.

10. Why might a business use subsidiary ledgers in addition to a general ledger?

Correct Answer: (a) To track detailed financial information about specific accounts, such as customer balances.
Subsidiary ledgers provide more detailed tracking of specific transactions, such as amounts owed by individual customers, while the general ledger contains summarized totals.

CHAPTER 5

FINANCIAL STATEMENTS

> *If you can't describe what you are doing as a process, you don't know what you're doing.*
>
> – W. Edwards Deming,
> composer and economist

We provided a cursory review of Financial Statements in Chapter 2 and also created Financial Statements for Leo's Pet Supplies in Chapter 3. Now, we'll break down the **income statement**, **balance sheet**, and **statement of cash flows** to further understand how each provides unique insights into a business's financial health. Each of these statements is critical in both **financial** and **managerial accounting**, but each has its own limitations. While an income statement shows profits, it may not fully capture cash flow; the balance sheet reflects assets and liabilities but doesn't convey how cash moves over time. Using these statements together allows for a clearer, more comprehensive view of a business's performance.

To ensure accurate and comparable results, accountants typically generate these statements at specific, **consistent intervals**. This consistency enables us to make **like-for-like comparisons**, helping businesses track trends and respond strategically.

In the previous chapters, we explored examples from small businesses. Now, let's consider a larger company: **TechGear**, a mid-sized electronics distributor. For a business of this size, a single income statement might reveal an impressive net income, but without examining its cash flow statement, TechGear's cash reserves may tell a different story. Imagine TechGear has generated high sales revenue on paper, yet because much of that revenue is tied up in unpaid invoices, the company struggles to meet immediate cash obligations. This example highlights the importance of analyzing each statement collectively to get an accurate picture of a business's ability to grow, invest, and stay competitive.

While many of the principles we'll discuss are valuable for companies of all sizes, some sections, such as those covering **Depreciation Methods**, are especially relevant. Whether you're looking to strengthen your knowledge for academic purposes or practical application, these tools are essential in refining your financial perspective and making informed decisions.

Breaking Down the Income Statement

An income statement is an essential report that every business owner, from a small shopkeeper to a corporate executive, wants to understand. At its core, it answers a straightforward question: did **revenues** exceed **expenses**? This information reveals whether the business is operating at a **profit** or a **loss**.

Consider our café, where revenue streams come from coffee, pastries, and other food sales. Each month, the owner reviews an income statement that deducts expenses like ingredients, rent, and staff wages. This statement helps the owner determine if specific costs, like seasonal promotions or new suppliers, are paying off.

When businesses grow, the income statement becomes even more critical and detailed. For instance, a regional retail company, let's call it **TechWorld**, might operate multiple locations, each contributing unique revenue streams with varying profit margins. For TechWorld, the income statement reveals overall profits while breaking down performance by **product line** and **location**, helping to identify which areas are thriving and which may need adjustments.

Corporate Income Statements

A corporate income statement provides additional detail by categorizing **sales revenue**, **cost of goods sold**, and **operating expenses**. For example, a tech retailer like TechWorld might experience high sales from new product launches. Still, the income statement could reveal that expenses in areas like shipping or customer support are impacting profit margins. This insight helps the company make strategic decisions on whether to adjust prices, reduce costs, or focus on high-performing products.

TechWorld

Income Statement

For the Year Ending on 12/31/2024 (all dollar amounts in millions)

Category	Amount ($)
Revenues	
Sales revenue	$12,450,000
TOTAL REVENUES	**$12,450,000**
Expenses	
Cost of goods sold	$5,100,000
Selling/General/Admin expense	$4,000,000
Depreciation/Amortization	$150,000
Income tax expense	$750,000
TOTAL EXPENSES	**$10,000,000**
Net income	**$2,450,000**

Let's say **TechWorld** ended the year with a net income of **$2.45 million**. As a corporation, TechWorld can choose to distribute part of this profit to its shareholders in the form of dividends. This distribution is recorded in the company's **retained earnings statement**, which tracks profits kept in the company for reinvestment.

For instance, if TechWorld anticipates a net income of **$2.45 million** and decides to issue **$500,000** in dividend payments, its retained earnings statement might look like this:

TechWorld

Retained Earnings Statement

For the Year Ending on 12/31/2024

Category	Amount ($)
Beginning retained earnings	$10,000,000
Add: Net income	+$2,450,000
Less: Dividends	-$500,000
Ending retained earnings	**$11,950,000**

Retained earnings represent the portion of **net income** that a business keeps to reinvest in its operations, rather than distributing it as dividends. In accounting terms, retained earnings function similarly to **owner's equity** and are shown on the **balance sheet**.

In this example, **TechWorld** starts with **$10 million** in retained earnings. After adding the net income of **$2.45 million** and subtracting the **$500,000** in dividends, TechWorld ends the year with **$11.95 million** in retained earnings.

Retained earnings statements are valuable tools for both existing and potential shareholders. They provide insight into a company's approach to **dividend distribution**. Some investors prefer companies that pay regular and generous dividends, as this offers immediate returns. Others may be drawn to companies that choose to **reinvest** most of their earnings into the business for growth opportunities, expecting that this will increase the value of their investment over time. The retained earnings statement is a good combination of the income statement and balance sheet, showing both profitability and how those profits are used, allowing a quick way to determine if the business strategies and growth align with an individual's investment strategy.

In previous examples, we saw how an **income statement** can be used by small business owners, like our café owner, to make internal management decisions (an example of **managerial accounting**). When combined with a retained earnings statement, as in the case of a larger corporation like **TechWorld**, income statements become valuable for shareholders to evaluate a company's financial health and dividend policies. Because shareholders are **external parties**, this application is considered **financial accounting** rather than managerial.

Income Statements for Other Purposes

Income statements also have applications beyond just internal management and shareholder analysis:

1. **Tax Preparation**: The income statement provides a clear record of **taxable revenues** and **deductible expenses**. This information is crucial for preparing tax filings and ensuring the business accurately reports its financial activity (we'll cover tax-specific details in Chapter 7).

2. **Comparing Yearly Performance**: Another common use of income statements is to analyze **year-over-year data**. By comparing income statements from previous years, a business can identify trends, spot growth opportunities, or recognize areas that may require cost control.

TechWorld

Income Statement

2021 - 2024 (all dollar amounts in millions)

Category	2024	2023	2022	2021
Revenues				
Sales revenue	$12,450,000	$11,800,000	$10,300,000	$9,700,000
TOTAL REVENUES	$12,450,000	$11,800,000	$10,300,000	$9,700,000
Expenses				
Cost of goods sold	$5,150,000	$4,950,000	$4,500,000	$4,200,000
Selling/General/Admin expense	$4,000,000	$3,800,000	$3,500,000	$3,200,000
Depreciation/Amortization	$150,000	$140,000	$130,000	$120,000
Income tax expense	$750,000	$720,000	$680,000	$650,000
TOTAL EXPENSES	$10,000,000	$9,160,000	$8,810,000	$8,170,000
Net income/loss	$2,450,000	$2,190,000	$1,490,000	$1,530,000

Comparing **year-by-year data** on an income statement provides essential insights for both **internal management** and **external investors**. Let's take our example of **TechWorld**, the tech retailer we've been discussing. Suppose that TechWorld's sales revenue in 2023 was notably higher than in 2024. Management would want to investigate this shift to understand whether the drop was due to changes in consumer demand, increased competition, or a decrease in marketing efforts.

For **managers**, this kind of analysis helps pinpoint what they've done well or needs improvement. For instance, if TechWorld notices a spike in costs for 2024, they might look into whether these were essential expenses (like investments in new technology) or if there were inefficiencies that need addressing. **Income statements** across multiple years can reveal patterns, allowing managers to make informed decisions about budgeting, product development, or scaling back operations. This is another area where using various classifications when entering data allows data to be easily viewed from many perspectives such as sales by customer to see who your largest customers are, or profit by product.

External investors and **creditors** are also keenly interested in year-over-year data. A steady increase in net income over the years might attract new investors, signaling that TechWorld is stable and growing. Likewise, a lender considering a loan to TechWorld will appreciate that the company has consistently generated profits and covered its liabilities.

Earnings Per Share (EPS)

One useful metric for stockholders is **Earnings Per Share (EPS)**. EPS is calculated by dividing the **net income** by the total number of **shares outstanding**. This metric shows how much profit is made per share of stock, offering a clear picture of the company's profitability on a per-share basis.

For example, if TechWorld has **1 million shares** outstanding and earns a net income of **$2.45 million** in 2024, its EPS would be **$2.45 per share**. If in 2023, TechWorld had a net income of **$2.19 million**, the EPS for that year would be slightly lower. This comparison helps shareholders see how the company's profitability per share has changed over time, giving them insights into its financial health and growth. This can be especially useful in investing because market value is driven strongly by intangible assets such as demand and customer loyalty. This can be misleading because it doesn't always align with the actual monetary value of the company or its ability to pay its liabilities.

EPS is particularly useful for comparing a company's performance over different periods (intracompany comparisons). However, it's less effective for comparing between companies (intercompany comparisons) because companies issue different amounts of shares. For example, a small company with few shares may have a higher EPS than a large corporation, but that doesn't necessarily mean it's more profitable in absolute terms.

Calculating Earnings Per Share (EPS) in More Detail

In our previous example, we calculated **Earnings Per Share (EPS)** by dividing the **net income** by the **total number of shares outstanding**. For instance, if a company with 10 shareholders earned $100 in profit, its EPS would simply be **$10 per share** ($100 net income divided by 10 shares). This straightforward formula works well for basic calculations and gives investors a quick insight into profitability.

However, when it comes to **formal financial reporting** that complies with accounting standards like **GAAP** (Generally Accepted Accounting Principles), the calculation becomes a bit more nuanced. The formal EPS formula typically looks like this:

$$\text{EPS} = \frac{\text{Net Income} - \text{Preferred Dividends}}{\text{Total Common Shares Outstanding}}$$

This formula introduces a new element: **preferred dividends**. Preferred dividends are payments made to **preferred shareholders**—a category of stockholders who receive a fixed dividend before any profits are distributed to common shareholders. Since **EPS** primarily reflects earnings for **com-**

mon stock, any dividends paid to preferred stockholders are subtracted from **net income** before calculating EPS.

To keep it simple, the idea is that **EPS focuses on the portion of profits available to common shareholders**, which means that preferred dividends are not part of the calculation.

Why EPS Matters

EPS offers a standardized method to measure a company's profitability on a **per-share basis**. It helps investors compare how much profit a company generates per share across different time periods. So, if TechWorld had 1 million common shares and made a net income of $2.45 million, but it also paid out $450,000 in preferred dividends, the EPS for common shareholders would be:

$$\text{EPS} = \frac{2,450,000 - 450,000}{1,000,000} = 2.00$$

This means each share earned $2.00 in profit for the year, after accounting for preferred dividends.

Why Preferred Dividends Are Subtracted

In calculating **Earnings Per Share (EPS)**, preferred stock dividends are subtracted from **net income** because preferred stockholders have priority when it comes to **dividends** and other payouts. In other words, the amount left over after paying preferred dividends is what's available for common shareholders, so we focus on this adjusted figure. This ensures that **EPS** accurately reflects the income available specifically for **common stockholders**.

Understanding Weighted Average Shares

Another detail in the EPS calculation is the **weighted average** of common shares outstanding over the reporting period. Unlike a simple count of shares at the end of the year, the weighted average accounts for fluctuations in the number of outstanding shares throughout the period. Shares can change due to events like issuing new shares or share buybacks, and this weighted method gives a more precise average overtime.

Example Calculation

Let's return to our TechWorld example for simplicity. Imagine TechWorld had **5 million shares** on January 1, 2024, but later issued another **1 million shares** on July 1, 2024. The weighted average calculation would consider the extra shares only for the portion of the year they were in circulation, rather than assuming all shares existed for the full year. The weighted average shares calculation would be 5M (full year) + 1M X ½ year (July 1-Dec 31) = 5.5M shares.

If we approximate the weighted average to be **5.5 million** shares (5M during the whole year, plus 1M for a half year calculates to 5.5M over the whole year) over the year, and assume TechWorld's net income is **$2.45 million**, the EPS would be calculated as:

$$\text{EPS} = \frac{2,450,000}{5,500,000} = 0.45$$

Thus, each share earned approximately **45 cents** over the year. For investors and shareholders, this number provides insight into the profitability of each share in relation to the total shares issued and available.

EPS in Financial vs. Managerial Accounting

EPS is primarily used in **financial accounting** for comparing profitability over time within the same company (known as **intracompany comparison**). For TechWorld's investors, tracking EPS over several years reveals whether the company is effectively generating returns per share.

From a **managerial accounting** standpoint, however, managers within TechWorld might focus more on **net income** itself as a simpler way to gauge overall profitability without delving into per-share metrics. Net income gives a direct view of total profits, which is crucial for making decisions on spending, budgeting, and internal investment.

Stock Transactions and Financial Statements

It's important to note that issuing new shares or paying dividends doesn't impact the **income statement** directly. When a company issues stock, it's raising capital, but this isn't considered **revenue**—it's recorded in **equity accounts** and appears on the **balance sheet**. Similarly, when dividends are paid to shareholders, these aren't recognized as an **expense** on the income statement. Instead, dividend payments reduce retained earnings, which is reflected in the **statement of retained earnings** and the balance sheet.

Understanding the Balance Sheet

To see how **assets, liabilities, and equity** interact on a balance sheet, let's take a closer look at **TechWorld's balance sheet**. While TechWorld is not a multibillion-dollar corporation, the same **accounting principles** apply, whether the company is large or small: **total assets** must equal the combined total of **liabilities and equity**. This is the foundation of the **fundamental accounting equation**, as we learned in earlier chapters.

Let's say TechWorld has **$3 million** in assets. Of this, about **$1.5 million** might come from liabilities (debts owed to creditors), and the remaining **$1.5 million** represents the owner's equity or what shareholders own outright. This balance sheet alignment shows how assets are "financed" through either debt or owner equity, a crucial perspective for both **managers** and **investors**.

Current vs. Long-Term Assets and Liabilities

When assessing **current** and **long-term assets** and **liabilities**, a **one-year threshold** typically helps classify these categories on the **balance sheet**:

> - **Current assets** are those expected to be **converted into cash within a year**. For example, **cash, accounts receivable**, and **inventory** generally fall under this category because they support the day-to-day operational needs of the business.
> - **Long-term assets** include things like **property, equipment**, and **investments** that the business intends to hold onto for more than a year. These assets are essential to the company's long-term growth and stability but aren't as easily converted into cash.

Let's say TechWorld owns a warehouse valued at **$800,000**. While this is a significant asset, selling it to meet immediate financial needs is not practical because it would disrupt the business's operations. By categorizing it as a **long-term asset**, TechWorld clarifies to investors that this asset is intended to support the business over the long term, rather than meeting short-term obligations.

On the **liability side** of the balance sheet, the same one-year rule applies:

> - **Current liabilities** are debts expected to be **paid within the next year**. Examples include **accounts payable**, short-term loans, and upcoming tax payments.
> - **Long-term liabilities** include obligations like **mortgages**, bonds payable, or other loans that the company expects to pay off over a longer period.

Tech World

Balance Sheet

For the Year Ending on 12/31/2024 (all dollar amounts in millions)

Assets	
Current Assets	
Cash and cash equivalents	$2,500
Accounts receivable	$1,200
Inventory	$750

Other current assets	$150
TOTAL CURRENT ASSETS	$4,600
Long-Term Assets	
Property	$1,000
Equipment	$900
Long-term investments	$500
Other assets	$200
TOTAL LONG-TERM ASSETS	$2,600
TOTAL ASSETS	**$7,200**

Liabilities	
Current Liabilities	
Accounts payable	$1,100
Notes payable	$800
Other current liabilities	$300
TOTAL CURRENT LIABILITIES	$2,200
Long-Term Liabilities	
Long-term debt	$700
Other long-term liabilities	$150
TOTAL LONG-TERM LIABILITIES	$850
TOTAL LIABILITIES	**$3,050**

Equity	
Stockholder equity	$2,500
Retained earnings	$1,650
TOTAL EQUITY	**$4,150**
TOTAL LIABILITIES PLUS EQUITY	**$7,200**

Exceptions to the One-Year Rule

Some businesses, depending on their industry, use a **longer threshold than one year** to classify current assets, especially if their **operating cycle** extends beyond a year.

Take, for instance, a **vineyard**. The entire process—from planting and harvesting grapes to aging the wine—might take **18 months or more**. Even though it takes longer than a year for the vineyard to turn a barrel of wine into cash, that barrel of wine is still considered a **current asset** because it's part of the vineyard's normal operating cycle. In this case, the operating cycle, not the calendar year, defines what is current.

Understanding Liquidity Through the Liquidity Ratios

One of the main reasons executives, investors, and lenders scrutinize **balance sheet components** is to assess a company's **liquidity**, or its ability to meet **short-term financial obligations**. A key measure of this is the **current ratio**.

The **current ratio** is calculated as:

$$\text{Current Ratio} = \frac{\text{Current Assets}}{\text{Current Liabilities}}$$

For instance, using TechWorld as an example, let's say that as of December 31, 2024, **TechWorld's current assets** are **$4.6 million**, and its **current liabilities** total **$2.2 million**. Plugging these values in:

$$\text{Current Ratio} = \frac{4,600,000}{2,200,000} = 2.09$$

With a current ratio of **2.09**, TechWorld has more than twice the amount of **liquid assets** needed to cover its short-term debts, which signals a healthy level of liquidity. Generally, a **current ratio over 1** indicates that the company is liquid enough to cover its immediate obligations, while a ratio of **2 or above** is seen as ideal, showing a strong financial buffer.

The **current ratio** is just one of several **liquidity ratios** used to assess a company's ability to meet short-term obligations. Others are discussed below:

> - **Quick Ratio**: Excludes inventory from current assets, focusing on assets that can be quickly converted to cash.
> - **Cash Ratio**: Measures the company's cash and cash equivalents against its current liabilities, giving an even more immediate sense of liquidity.

Quick Ratio	How to Evaluate
Formula: $\text{Quick Ratio} = \dfrac{\text{Cash + Accounts Receivable + Marketable Securities}}{\text{Current Liabilities}}$	**Interpretation**: The quick ratio is a tighter measure than the current ratio because it focuses only on the most liquid assets—those that can quickly be turned into cash. A quick ratio of **1 or higher** is typically reassuring, as it suggests the company can cover its immediate debts without selling inventory.
Cash Ratio	**How to Evaluate**
Formula: $\text{Cash Ratio} = \dfrac{\text{Cash}}{\text{Current Liabilities}}$	**Interpretation**: The cash ratio provides the most immediate view of liquidity since it only considers cash on hand. A cash ratio of 1 means the company has enough cash alone to cover its current liabilities, which is a very secure position to be in financially.

Explanation of Terms:

> - **Accounts Receivable (AR)**: *Money owed to the company by its customers.*
> - **Marketable Securities**: *Short-term investments that can be quickly sold for cash, such as stocks or bonds.*
> - **Current Liabilities**: *Debts the company expects to pay off within the next year.*

In addition to ratios, **working capital** is another critical indicator. Defined as:

Working Capital = Current Assets − Current Liabilities

For **TechWorld**, with **$4.6 million** in current assets and **$2.2 million** in current liabilities, the working capital would be:

Working Capital = 4,600,000 - 2,200,000 = 2,400,000

A **positive working capital** balance of **$2.4 million** means TechWorld has sufficient resources to handle its short-term liabilities comfortably. A **negative working capital** balance, however, would signal potential financial trouble, as it suggests that the company might struggle to cover its immediate debts without seeking external funding or tapping into long-term assets.

While **working capital** is a useful measure of a company's liquidity, an exceptionally high working capital balance isn't necessarily a positive sign. High working capital might indicate that too much money is tied up in **inventory** (a current asset that may not generate immediate cash flow) or that the business is **inefficiently collecting accounts receivables** (also a current asset), which can weaken cash flow.

For instance, if **TechWorld** consistently increases its working capital but has a large portion tied up in unsold products or delayed customer payments, this could signal inefficiencies. Just as too little working capital can lead to cash flow issues, an excessive amount suggests that funds aren't being used optimally for growth or investment.

Solvency Ratios

To assess the *long-term financial stability* of a business, we use **solvency ratios**. While liquidity ratios focus on short-term obligations, solvency ratios give a sense of whether a business can meet its debts over the long haul. One of the most commonly used solvency ratios is the **debt-to-asset ratio**:

$$\text{Debt-to-Asset Ratio} = \frac{\text{Total Liabilities}}{\text{Total Assets}}$$

This ratio helps us understand what percentage of the company's assets is financed through debt. For example, if **TechWorld** has a debt-to-asset ratio of 45%, this means that 45% of the company's assets are funded by loans or other liabilities. Higher ratios can indicate a higher reliance on borrowed funds, which in turn increases the financial risk for **equity holders** (or investors).

Let's imagine TechWorld is expanding and takes on more debt to open additional locations. While this can accelerate growth, it also raises the debt-to-asset ratio. In difficult times, equity holders (who are last in line to get paid in a bankruptcy situation) bear a higher risk if the company faces financial hardship.

Equity Differences: Corporations vs. Small Business

The **equity section** of a balance sheet varies depending on the business structure. For a sole proprietor, like our café example earlier, **owner's equity** reflects the owner's total claim on the business's assets. In a corporation, however, equity is split into **stockholder equity** and **retained earnings**.

For instance, **TechWorld**, if it were a corporation, might show **$2.5 billion in stockholder equity** on its balance sheet. This amount represents funds raised from shareholders when the company initially issued shares. It's important to note that this **stockholder equity** figure does not fluctuate with the daily market price of the stock. It's a fixed record of the capital raised by issuing stock, not the current trading value or market of those shares. This is where the concept of goodwill comes in. People are willing to pay more than the initial value of a share because of perceived and realized increases in the companies value.

Key Takeaways on Stockholder Equity:

> ▸ **Stockholder Equity** is the accumulated capital from shareholders and doesn't change with stock market fluctuations.

> Capital from **debt** (like loans or bonds) is recorded under **liabilities**, while capital from **stock issuance** remains within **equity**.

The distinction between **equity accounts** in a corporation and a sole proprietorship (or similar business structure) can be understood by examining the *fundamental accounting equation*. Here's how it differs for each:

> - Corporation:
>   Assets = Liabilities + (Common Stock + Retained Earnings)
> - Sole Proprietorship:
>   Assets = Liabilities + Owner's Equity

In a **corporation**, equity is divided into **common stock** and **retained earnings**. *Common stock* represents the capital raised from stockholders when shares are issued. This is recorded as an equity account, signifying the contributions of shareholders toward the company's assets. *Retained earnings*, on the other hand, refer to the accumulated net income that remains in the company after dividends are paid out. Although retained earnings belong to the stockholders, they're reinvested into the business, often for growth and expansion.

Let's say *TechWorld*, issues stock to fund new product lines. When stock is sold, **cash** (an asset) increases, and so does **common stock** (an equity account). In the case of a profitable year, **retained earnings** also increase, reflecting the portion of profits kept in the business rather than distributed to shareholders as dividends.

In contrast, a **sole proprietorship** (or a partnership or LLC) does not have **common stock** or **retained earnings** accounts because these businesses do not issue stock or pay dividends. Instead, they operate with a single **owner's equity** account, which fluctuates with owner contributions and withdrawals. Any profits or losses for the period are added or subtracted from this account, reflecting the owner's personal claim on the business.

For instance, consider a **small café** owned by a single individual. If the owner makes a personal investment (often referred to as a contribution) into the café, it's recorded as an increase in *owner's equity*. Similarly, if the owner withdraws cash (often called a distribution), it decreases *owner's equity*. There's no need to track retained earnings or dividends, as the entire equity belongs to the single owner.

Depreciation and Asset Valuation

When businesses purchase **long-term assets** like equipment or property, they often don't immediately report the entire purchase cost as an expense. Instead, they **depreciate** these assets over time. Depreciation spreads the asset's cost over its useful life, which allows the business to match expenses with the revenue generated from the asset. (Remember the Matching Principle from Chapter 1).

Imagine a **professional content creator** who invests $4,000 in high-end video equipment to improve production quality. Instead of recording the $4,000 as an expense immediately, the creator might choose to depreciate it over four years, recording an annual expense of $1,000. This approach aligns the expense with the asset's productive use over time.

On the **balance sheet**, this would be reflected in two parts:

1. The **original cost** of the asset (e.g., $4,000 for equipment).
2. An **accumulated depreciation** account that shows the cumulative depreciation recorded over the years.

Example: TechWorld's Equipment Depreciation

In the case of **TechWorld**, let's say the balance sheet originally lists equipment valued at **$800,000**. Over several years, **$300,000** of this value has been depreciated, leaving an **adjusted equipment value** of **$500,000**. This accumulated depreciation provides a more accurate picture of the asset's current worth, which is particularly useful for stakeholders evaluating TechWorld's financial health.

Assets	Amount
Current Assets	
Cash and cash equivalents	$1,500,000
Accounts receivable	$1,200,000
Inventory	$300,000
Total Current Assets	**$3,000,000**
Long-Term Assets	
Property	$600,000
Equipment	$800,000
Less: Accumulated depreciation – equipment	$(300,000)
Adjusted Equipment Value	**$500,000**
Long-term investments	$400,000
Total Long-Term Assets	**$1,500,000**
Total Assets	**$4,500,000**

By using depreciation, **TechWorld** can reflect not only the original cost of its assets but also their *remaining value* as they age. This method helps business owners, investors, and potential lenders to understand how much life remains in TechWorld's equipment, which can influence decisions about whether it's time for replacements, upgrades, or further investments.

In this way, **depreciation** isn't just about spreading out costs for tax purposes, it's about keeping the financial statements honest and relevant, showing both historical costs and realistic asset values over time.

Methods of Depreciation

When deciding how to depreciate assets, there are several factors and judgment calls to consider. Some assets lose value more quickly than others, which means they may need to be depreciated over a shorter timeframe. For instance, a computer used in a tech company might have a high depreciation rate, as technology becomes outdated rapidly. Meanwhile, a delivery truck might retain some resale value even after years of use.

Certain assets, like land, are unique in that they generally don't lose value over time and therefore aren't depreciated. Similarly, investments in stocks or bonds are not depreciated because their value is based on market fluctuations rather than wear and tear.

In the United States, the IRS provides some basic guidelines for depreciation in *Publication 946*. These guidelines outline different types of assets and suggest reasonable depreciation schedules. For example, office furniture might be depreciated over a seven-year period, while vehicles typically follow a five-year depreciation schedule.

Example: Depreciating a Delivery Van for TechWorld

Imagine TechWorld purchases a delivery van for $50,000. Even though the van is expected to wear down over time, it's also likely to have some resale value—maybe it can be sold for parts after many years of use. The remaining value at the end of its useful life is called the **residual value** or **salvage value**. If TechWorld estimates the van's salvage value at $5,000, then only $45,000 of the purchase price will be depreciated over time.

The IRS especially doesn't want assets over-depreciated, because this would reduce a business's taxable income, and doing so would also complicate tax reporting in the event the business sold their depreciated asset.

This concept of residual value is crucial because it helps companies avoid depreciating assets to a point where their book value drops to zero, despite the asset still holding some market value. In other words, salvage value is the amount you could expect to sell the asset for after it has reached its useful life.

Straight Line Depreciation

Straight line depreciation is the simplest and most straightforward method for spreading the cost of an asset over its useful life. Let's say TechWorld buys a $6,000 3D printer. Based on its projected wear and technological changes, TechWorld estimates it'll be useful for five years and have no resale value at the end. Using straight line depreciation, TechWorld would write off $1,200 each year as a **depreciation expense** ($6,000 divided by five years). This approach keeps things simple by charging the same depreciation amount every year.

But what if TechWorld expects to sell that printer for $500 after five years? In that case, the **depreciable cost** would be $5,500 ($6,000 purchase price minus $500 salvage value). Dividing this $5,500 over five years results in a yearly depreciation of $1,100, keeping the asset's eventual resale value in mind.

Declining Balance Depreciation

The declining balance method is useful for assets that lose a lot of value early on, like cars or tech equipment. Instead of the same amount of depreciation year over year, this method allows for a **higher depreciation** in the asset's first years. For example, if TechWorld decides to depreciate the 3D printer using a declining balance method at a 200% rate, it would write off 20% of the printer's original cost (excluding salvage value) in the first year, which would be $1,200 ($6,000 × 20%). The second year, 20% would be taken off the remaining $4,800 book value, and so forth. This method makes sense when an asset is expected to contribute most of its productivity or value early in its life.

Full Depreciation on Purchase

For items that lose their value almost immediately, some businesses opt to **fully depreciate** them as soon as they're purchased. Small items like low-cost office furniture or accessories, which won't hold value for long, can be written off at once. This is sometimes allowed for tax purposes, especially if the asset's cost is below a certain threshold. It is important for your company to have a policy that identifies a threshold to take full depreciation in the year of purchase. The de minimus safe harbor allows business to deduct certain long-term assets at a maximum dollar amount of $2,500.

This method makes things simple by handling depreciation all at once, but it's not suitable for assets expected to last multiple years, or businesses with minimal revenue and expenses, as it doesn't reflect their value or usage over time and may portray your business as less-profitable for that year.

In addition to the straight-line and declining balance methods, two other approaches are Sum-of-the-Years-Digits and Units of Production Method.

Sum-of-the-Years-Digits (SYD) Method

The SYD method is an accelerated depreciation technique that allocates higher depreciation expenses in the earlier years of an asset's useful life, gradually decreasing over time. This approach aligns with the assumption that assets are more productive or lose value more rapidly in their initial years.

How it is calculated:

1. **Determine the Asset's Useful Life:** Identify the total number of years the asset is expected to be in service.
2. **Compute the Sum of the Years' Digits:** Add together the digits for each year of the asset's useful life. For example, for an asset with a 5-year lifespan: 5 + 4 + 3 + 2 + 1 = 15. Alternatively, use the formula:

$$\text{Sum of Years' Digits} = \frac{n(n+1)}{2}$$

where n is the useful life in years.

1. **Calculate the Depreciation Fraction for Each Year:** For each year, divide the remaining lifespan by the sum of the years' digits.
2. **Determine the Depreciable Base:** Subtract the asset's salvage value (residual value) from its initial cost.
3. **Compute Annual Depreciation Expense:** Multiply the depreciable base by the depreciation fraction for each respective year.

Practical Example:

Assume a company purchases machinery for $100,000, with an estimated useful life of 5 years and a salvage value of $10,000.

1. **Depreciable Base:** $100,000 (cost) - $10,000 (salvage value) = $90,000.
2. **Sum of the Years' Digits:** 5 + 4 + 3 + 2 + 1 = 15.
3. **Annual Depreciation Calculations:**
    - **Year 1:** (5 / 15) × $90,000 = $30,000.
    - **Year 2:** (4 / 15) × $90,000 = $24,000.
    - **Year 3:** (3 / 15) × $90,000 = $18,000.
    - **Year 4:** (2 / 15) × $90,000 = $12,000.
    - **Year 5:** (1 / 15) × $90,000 = $6,000.

This method results in a decreasing depreciation expense over the asset's life, reflecting its diminishing utility.

The significant advantage of using this method, is that it allows businesses to recognize higher depreciation expenses during the early years of an asset's life, precisely when the asset is typically at its most productive. This aligns the expense more closely with actual usage, reflecting a realistic portrayal of the asset's declining productivity over time. Additionally, higher depreciation expenses in the initial years can also provide notable tax advantages by reducing taxable income early on, offering businesses immediate financial relief. By lowering taxable income early, businesses can reinvest saved tax dollars back into their operations or growth strategies.

However, it's crucial for companies to remember that while accelerated depreciation provides these immediate financial and tax benefits, it also leads to lower net income figures in early reporting periods, potentially influencing stakeholder perceptions, investment evaluations, and key financial ratios. There is often a delicate balancing act business owners must play. If the company is more concerned with its tax liability than it is with attracting potential investors, they often utilize different strategies, such as depreciation method, to decrease their net income as low as possible in a given year to reduce the tax liability. On the other hand, if your company is seeking new investors so they can focus on growth, showing a higher profit is more likely to attract investors looking for residual income.

Units of Production Method

The Units of Production method is an effective way to calculate depreciation for assets whose usage is closely tied to their physical output or production level. Unlike other methods, this approach directly links depreciation expense to actual asset use, ensuring a precise match between the expense recorded and the benefits derived from the asset.

Calculation Steps:

1. **Estimate Total Production Capacity:** Determine the total number of units the asset is expected to produce throughout its useful life.

2. **Determine Depreciable Base:** Subtract the salvage value from the asset's initial cost:

Depreciable Base Cost of Asset — Salvage Value

3. **Calculate Depreciation Rate per Unit:** Divide the depreciable base by the total production capacity:

$$\text{Depreciation Rate per Unit} = \frac{\text{Depreciable Base}}{\text{Total Production Capacity}}$$

> 4. **Compute the annual depreciation expense** by multiplying the depreciation rate per unit by the actual number of units produced in the given year:

Annual Depreciation Expense = Units Produced in the Year * Depreciation Rate per Unit

Example: Imagine your business purchases a machine for $50,000, expecting it to have a salvage value of $5,000 after producing 100,000 units. Your depreciable base is:

$$\$50,000 - \$5,000 = \$45,000$$

Your depreciation rate per unit would then be:

$$\frac{\$45,000}{100,000 \text{ units}} = \$0.45 \text{ per unit}$$

If the machine produces 20,000 units in one year, your annual depreciation expense would be:

$$20,000 \text{ units} * \$0.45 = \$9,000$$

This method offers significant advantages by closely aligning depreciation with actual asset usage. It accurately matches expenses with revenue generated by the asset, reflecting its true economic benefit to the business. However, because depreciation varies according to production levels, this can lead to fluctuations in expenses from period to period, potentially complicating financial forecasting. Additionally, tracking asset usage accurately requires diligent record-keeping, adding administrative complexity compared to simpler methods like straight-line depreciation.

Modified Accelerated Cost Recovery System (MACRS)

The **Modified Accelerated Cost Recovery System (MACRS)** is the primary depreciation method required by the Internal Revenue Service (IRS) in the United States for tax reporting purposes. Unlike the straight-line or units of production methods, MACRS is specifically designed to help businesses recover the cost of assets more quickly, allowing for higher depreciation deductions in the early years of an asset's life. This accelerates cost recovery and reduces taxable income sooner, providing an immediate cash-flow benefit through lower tax bills in the early periods of asset use.

With MACRS, the IRS provides clearly defined depreciation schedules that categorize assets into different classes, based primarily on their expected useful life. Each class has a specific depreciation timeline. Common asset classes under MACRS include:

- **5-year property:** Vehicles, computers, and office equipment.
- **7-year property:** Office furniture, fixtures, and certain manufacturing equipment.
- **27.5-year property:** Residential rental property.
- **39-year property:** Commercial real estate like offices, warehouses, or retail stores.

Once you've identified the correct property classification, the IRS provides standardized depreciation percentages (tables) to use for each year of the asset's recovery period. The depreciation tables used for calculating MACRS (Modified Accelerated Cost Recovery System) depreciation can be found directly in **IRS Publication 946**. You can easily access these tables online through the IRS website (www.irs.gov), searching specifically for **Publication 946 (How to Depreciate Property).** This document is regularly updated, ensuring you always have the correct depreciation rates and schedules according to current tax regulations.

MACRS Calculation Example:

Imagine TechWorld invests in new computers for a total cost of $20,000. According to MACRS, computers are classified as 5-year property. The IRS provides the following approximate depreciation percentages for 5-year property under MACRS (half-year convention):

Year	MACRS Depreciation %	Depreciation Expense Calculation	Depreciation Expense
1	20%	$20,000 * 20%	$4,000
2	32%	$20,000 * 32%	$6,400
3	19.2%	$20,000 * 19.2%	$3,840
4	11.52%	$20,000 * 11.52%	$2,304
5	11.52%	$20,000 * 11.52%	$2,304
6	5.76%	$20,000 * 5.76%	$1,152

Notice how depreciation expenses under MACRS start out high in early years and decline gradually. By front-loading depreciation expenses, TechWorld is able to significantly reduce its taxable income and thus its tax bill during the initial years of asset ownership.

The MACRS method provides significant benefits by offering higher tax deductions early on, effectively freeing up cash flow for reinvestment or other operational expenses. Businesses often appreciate MACRS because of these immediate tax savings, especially when investing heavily in equipment and machinery. Moreover, since MACRS is standardized by the IRS, it simplifies the tax reporting process by clearly defining depreciation amounts for each asset category, eliminating guesswork.

However, while MACRS is beneficial from a tax perspective, it has some drawbacks when it comes to financial reporting. Using MACRS often results in discrepancies between tax reporting and financial accounting under U.S. GAAP, since GAAP usually prefers methods like straight-line depreciation for consistent and smooth expense reporting. These differences can result in complexity, requiring businesses to maintain separate depreciation schedules, one for financial reporting and another strictly for tax purposes.

Additionally, because MACRS front-loads depreciation expenses, assets appear to lose value quickly in the beginning. This accelerated approach can negatively affect short-term net income and other financial metrics, potentially impacting stakeholders' perceptions of financial performance.

U.S. GAAP vs. IRS Depreciation Methods: Understanding the Differences

When selecting depreciation methods, it's essential to understand that U.S. GAAP and IRS standards serve different purposes, leading to distinct preferences. U.S. GAAP emphasizes transparency, accuracy, and consistency in financial reporting, which is why businesses commonly adopt methods like Straight-Line, Units of Production, or Sum-of-the-Years-Digits (SYD). These methods clearly reflect the asset's usage, aligning expenses directly with revenues to offer stakeholders a realistic view of financial performance. On the other hand, the IRS favors the Modified Accelerated Cost Recovery System (MACRS), specifically designed to accelerate depreciation and quickly reduce taxable income. MACRS provides businesses with immediate tax benefits by front-loading depreciation expenses, thus lowering taxes owed in the asset's early years. However, once a company selects a depreciation method under GAAP, consistency is critical, and any changes must be clearly disclosed to maintain trust and clarity for investors and other stakeholders. Conversely, IRS regulations are more rigid, mandating adherence to the predefined MACRS schedules without deviation, prioritizing tax compliance over financial statement presentation.

Analyzing Cash Flow Statements

Just like other financial statements, the cash flow statement serves different purposes depending on who's reading it. Investors might check it for signs of regular dividend payments, while managers may focus on cash availability for future investments and day to day operations.

Let's use **TechWorld** as an example. The **final cash balance** shown on TechWorld's cash flow statement for **December 31, 2024**, is **$2,5 million**.

This figure aligns with the **cash account on TechWorld's balance sheet** for the same date, ensuring consistency across financial statements.

TechWorld Statement of Cash Flows

For the Year Ending on 12/31/24

Cash Flow Activities	Amount
Cash Flows from Operating Activities	
Cash actually received from sales	$900,000
Outgoing cash for operating expenses	$200,000
Net Cash Flow from Operations	**$700,000**
Cash Flows from Investing Activities	
Acquisition of smaller tech company (net of cash acquired)	($200,000)
Sale of unused assets	$50,000
Net Cash Flow from Investing	**($150,000)**
Cash Flows from Financing Activities	
Issuance of stock	$600,000
Repurchase of stock	($50,000)
Dividend payments	($150,000)
Net Cash Flow from Financing	**$400,000**
Net Cash Flow for the Period	**$950,000**
Cash Position at the Beginning of the Period	$1,550,000
Cash Position at the End of the Period	**$2,500,000**

Operating Cash Flow vs. Income Statement

Examining the **cash flows from operating activities** on TechWorld's statement, you'll notice a discrepancy between cash flows and the revenue and expenses reported on the income statement. Why does this happen? It's because, unlike the income statement, the cash flow statement only records actual cash receipts and payments. Essentially, the operating cash flow section is a summarized version of what the income statement would look like for a company reporting on a cash basis.

For instance, suppose **TechWorld** made **sales in December totaling $1,000,000**, but only received **$900,000** in cash. On the income statement (under accrual accounting), the full **$1,000,000** would be recorded as revenue. However, on the cash flow statement, only the **$900,000** actually received shows up as cash inflow. This distinction gives a clearer picture of the immediate cash available to meet obligations, which is essential for effective cash flow planning and management.

Impact of Non-Cash Expenses

Another difference between the income statement and cash flow statement lies in **non-cash expenses** like depreciation. While depreciation appears as an expense on the income statement, it doesn't impact cash flow directly. For example, TechWorld's **$800,000 warehouse** is depreciated over time, affecting **net income** on the income statement, but it doesn't reduce the company's cash on hand. Cash flow statements provide a "cleaner" view of available cash by excluding these "phantom expenses."

Cash Flow Analysis for Decision-Making

Cash flow statements are especially valuable for assessing the company's **liquidity** and **funding sources**. They reveal whether the company has sufficient cash from its core operations to sustain itself or if it's relying heavily on financing activities (like loans or stock issuance) or investment sales to maintain cash flow.

For instance, let's say **TechWorld** shows a substantial cash inflow from financing activities due to issuing a new round of stock. While this boosts cash flow temporarily, both investors and managers would be more interested in whether **core operations** consistently generate enough cash to keep the business financially healthy in the long term.

Examining TechWorld's Cash Flow Activities

The **cash flows from investing activities** provide a snapshot of TechWorld's strategic moves throughout the year. For example, let's say TechWorld spent around $200,000 acquiring a smaller tech company to expand its reach in a new market. The phrase *"net of cash acquired"* indicates that any cash assets from this acquisition were deducted from the purchase cost, effectively reducing TechWorld's total investment expense to $200,000.

In the **cash flows from financing activities**, we might see an entry where TechWorld decides to repurchase $50,000 worth of its own stock. Companies often buy back shares to signal confidence in their market value, potentially boosting share prices by reducing supply. If the strategy works, TechWorld can later issue new shares at higher prices, generating additional capital.

These activities—acquiring new businesses and repurchasing stocks, suggest a company in a **strong cash position**. With healthy cash reserves, TechWorld can afford to make speculative investments and pursue growth opportunities without immediately impacting its operational stability.

The **vitality of a company's cash position** is often evaluated by its *free cash flow* (FCF), which represents the cash available after covering necessary capital expenditures and dividend obligations. Free cash flow can be expressed as:

Free Cash Flow = Net Cash Flow from Operations - Capital Expenditures - Dividends Paid

Suppose TechWorld's **net cash flow from operations** is $700,000. We group its capital expenses—such as property and equipment purchases, and find a total of $150,000 (-200,000 + 50000). After subtracting dividends of $150,000, we calculate TechWorld's free cash flow as follows:

$700,000 - $150,000 − $150,000 = $400,000

With $400,000 in free cash flow, TechWorld has the flexibility to **reduce long-term debt, increase dividends, repurchase stock, or invest in new ventures**. High free cash flow is often seen as a marker of financial health, offering a company leeway for future growth and stability. Companies that can operate with little to no debt are especially attractive to investors because it means they are more likely to get their investment back if the business were to cease operations, as there are no creditors in line to be paid before the investors.

Using the Cash Flow Statement for Strategic Analysis

For **investors**, the cash flow statement offers insight into TechWorld's **long-term vision**. If a company is directing significant cash towards investments and acquisitions, it's clearly focused on growth. On the other hand, a higher proportion of cash flowing toward dividend payments may indicate a priority on shareholder returns. Investors might weigh these trends when assessing TechWorld's financial strategy.

From a **managerial accounting perspective**, the cash flow statement provides a clear view of TechWorld's actual cash position. Many business owners face situations where, despite a healthy income statement, cash seems to run dry. By tracking investment and financing activities separately, the cash flow statement helps TechWorld's managers make informed, sustainable decisions about cash usage, ensuring liquidity isn't compromised by less visible expenses.

Capital Expenditure vs. Revenue Expenditure

When running a business, you'll inevitably spend money, but not all expenses are treated the same way in accounting. Expenses generally fall into two main categories: **Capital Expenditures** and **Revenue Expenditures**. But what are the differences?

Capital Expenditure (CapEx)

Capital expenditure refers to the money your business spends on purchasing or improving long-term assets, items that provide benefits to your company over several years, not just within a single year. These are typically large, one-time investments intended to enhance the business's future earning potential.

Common examples include:

- Buying buildings, offices, or land
- Purchasing machinery and equipment
- Acquiring vehicles for business use
- Major upgrades or renovations to existing facilities

Imagine you own a small pizza restaurant. If you buy a high-quality pizza oven for $10,000, it's a substantial investment intended to serve your business for many years. This purchase is a **Capital Expenditure** because it provides long-term value beyond the current accounting year.

Revenue Expenditure

Revenue expenditures, on the other hand, are regular, short-term expenses necessary for your daily business operations. These costs are typically consumed within the same accounting year in which they're incurred. They're immediately recorded as **expenses** on your income statement, directly reducing your profits in the period in which they occur.

Common examples include:

- Monthly rent payments
- Salaries and wages
- Utility bills (electricity, water, internet)
- Regular repairs and maintenance
- Costs of goods sold (materials or inventory purchases)

Returning to the earlier example, the flour, tomatoes, and cheese you buy each week to make pizzas represent everyday operating costs, expenses directly related to your immediate, ongoing business operations. These ingredients are examples of **Revenue Expenditure** because they're consumed quickly, and their costs directly impact your profits within the same accounting period.

Clearly distinguishing between these two types of expenditures ensures your financial statements genuinely reflect your restaurant's profitability and true value. Mixing these up could either falsely inflate your profits or inaccurately portray your financial position, making informed business decisions challenging.

Example of Financial Statements

To help you clearly visualize how accounting records come together, I've included a practical Excel demonstration showing how real transaction data flows through the accounting process. In this file, you'll see examples of a structured ledger, a trial balance, an income statement, a balance sheet, and a cash flow statement. By examining this sample, you can get a clearer understanding of how financial information is organized, maintained, and analyzed in a real-world setting. Working with this illustrative example will reinforce your learning and provide a valuable reference as you build your accounting skills.

You will find it here:

https://docs.google.com/spreadsheets/d/1a_bT67OKjRepkHSTow4d66ts-jR4y2675/edit?usp=sharing&ouid=115451442075974404873&rtpof=true&sd=true

or scan the QR code:

Chapter 5 Assessment Test

1. **What is the main purpose of the income statement?**

    a. To display a company's cash flow.

    b. To summarize revenues and expenses, showing profit or loss.

    c. To list all assets and liabilities.

2. **Which of the following components appears on the balance sheet?**

    a. Total Revenue

    b. Liabilities and Owner's Equity

    c. Depreciation Expense

3. **What does the cash flow statement primarily track?**

    a. A company's income over time.

    b. Cash inflows and outflows from operations, investing, and financing.

    c. Changes in retained earnings.

4. **How is Earnings Per Share (EPS) calculated?**

    a. Net Income ÷ Total Liabilities

    b. (Net Income - Preferred Dividends) ÷ Weighted Average Shares Outstanding

    c. Net Income ÷ Total Assets

5. **What does the current ratio measure?**

    a. A company's short-term liquidity.

    b. The value of retained earnings.

    c. The total revenue compared to net income.

6. **What is the relationship between depreciation and the balance sheet?**

    a. Depreciation is listed as an asset.

    b. Depreciation reduces the value of long-term assets over time.

    c. Depreciation has no impact on the balance sheet.

7. **What does "Retained Earnings" represent on a balance sheet?**

   a. Dividends paid to stockholders.//
   b. Profits reinvested into the company after paying dividends.//
   c. Cash inflows from financing activities.

8. **Which of the following is an example of a capital expenditure?**

   a. Paying employee salaries.//
   b. Purchasing a new production facility.//
   c. Buying office supplies.

9. **What happens when a company repurchases its stock?**

   a. Total assets increase.//
   b. Cash decreases, and treasury stock is recorded.//
   c. Retained earnings increase.

10. **Why is free cash flow (FCF) important?**

    a. It shows a company's profitability based on accrual accounting.//
    b. It represents the cash available after necessary expenditures, helping with investment and financial decisions.//
    c. It measures how efficiently a company collects payments from customers.

Answers

1. What is the main purpose of the income statement?

Correct Answer: b) To summarize revenues and expenses, showing profit or loss.
The income statement reveals a company's financial performance by subtracting expenses from revenues to determine net income.

2. Which of the following components appears on the balance sheet?

Correct Answer: b) Liabilities and Owner's Equity
The balance sheet presents a snapshot of a company's assets, liabilities, and owner's equity at a specific moment.

3. What does the cash flow statement primarily track?

Correct Answer: b) Cash inflows and outflows from operations, investing, and financing.
The cash flow statement details how cash enters and exits a business through its core, investing, and financing activities.

4. How is Earnings Per Share (EPS) calculated?

Correct Answer: b) (Net Income - Preferred Dividends) ÷ Weighted Average Shares Outstanding
EPS focuses on profitability per share for common shareholders by excluding preferred dividends.

5. What does the current ratio measure?

Correct Answer: a) A company's short-term liquidity.
The current ratio evaluates a business's ability to meet short-term obligations using its current assets.

6. What is the relationship between depreciation and the balance sheet?

Correct Answer: b) Depreciation reduces the value of long-term assets over time.
Depreciation decreases the book value of long-term assets like machinery and buildings while spreading their cost over their useful lives.

7. What does "Retained Earnings" represent on a balance sheet?

Correct Answer: b) Profits reinvested into the company after paying dividends.
Retained earnings reflect cumulative profits that are reinvested into the business rather than distributed as dividends.

8. Which of the following is an example of a capital expenditure?

b) Purchasing a new production facility.
Capital expenditures involve acquiring or improving long-term assets that provide future benefits.

9. What happens when a company repurchases its stock?

Correct Answer: b) Cash decreases, and treasury stock is recorded.
Stock buybacks reduce cash and are recorded as treasury stock, a contra-equity account.

10. Why is free cash flow (FCF) important?

b) It represents the cash available after necessary expenditures, helping with investment and financial decisions.
Free cash flow indicates how much cash remains after capital expenditures and dividends, useful for investment decisions.

CHAPTER 6

MANAGERIAL ACCOUNTING

"In God we trust; all others bring data."

– W. Edwards Deming,
composer and economist

Managerial accounting takes accounting principles beyond mere numbers, transforming them into tools for better decision-making. It's not just about what happened last quarter, it's about understanding the "why" behind the numbers and using that knowledge to improve future outcomes. Imagine a small coffee shop owner, Sarah, who notices her profits fluctuating. Is it due to her rent, the price of coffee beans, or the timing of her sales? Managerial accounting provides the answers she needs to make informed changes.

The Purpose of Managerial Accounting

Unlike financial accounting, which primarily focuses on creating reports for external stakeholders such as investors, lenders, or regulators, managerial accounting is designed for **internal decision-making**. It's the backstage crew of accounting, quietly ensuring that every department and manager has the insights they need to steer the ship.

For example, let's say Leo, from our earlier chapters, is considering expanding his pet supply store. Should he relocate to a larger space or open a second location? Managerial accounting tools can help Leo analyze the costs, risks, and potential profits associated with each option.

One major distinction is that financial accounting adheres to strict **standards like GAAP** (Generally Accepted Accounting Principles), while managerial accounting is more flexible. It's **customized**, evolving with the company's needs.

Take Sarah's coffee shop again. She decides to analyze which pastries contribute the most to her overall profits. Financial accounting might report her total food revenue, but managerial accounting dives deeper, tracking each croissant and muffin to determine which items are worth stocking.

Managerial accounting isn't static—it evolves with the business. It requires continuous evaluation and recalibration. Consider a bakery that tracks which types of bread sell best in the winter versus the summer. The owner might discover that sourdough peaks in winter while brioche dominates in spring. Armed with this knowledge, she adjusts her inventory to minimize waste and maximize sales.

Similarly, imagine Leo, our pet supply store owner, tracking customer purchases over the year. If he finds that cat toys sell more during the holiday season, he can stock up accordingly and plan promotional campaigns.

Continuous Improvement with Managerial Accounting

The beauty of managerial accounting lies in its flexibility and focus on improvement. Businesses can fine-tune their operations, often with minimal investment, just by analyzing their own data. For example:

> ▸ A restaurant finds that delivery orders generate higher margins than dine-in service and decides to focus on growing delivery.
>
> ▸ A manufacturing company realizes that its energy costs spike in summer and switches to night shifts to reduce cooling costs.

These insights wouldn't be possible without managerial accounting tools.

Cost-Volume-Profit (CVP) Analysis

Understanding how costs influence profits is at the heart of **managerial accounting**, and one of the most powerful tools in this realm is **Cost-Volume-Profit (CVP) Analysis**. This method helps business owners answer critical questions:

> ▸ How many units must I sell to cover my costs?
>
> ▸ What happens to my profit if I lower prices or increase production?
>
> ▸ Which of my products generates the most return?

Despite its importance, many small business owners skip this crucial analysis, potentially leaving valuable insights undiscovered.

To perform a CVP analysis, it's vital to understand **variable costs** and **fixed costs**:

> ▸ **Variable Costs** are expenses that fluctuate with production or sales volume. For example, a florist's cost of flowers increases with the number of bouquets sold.
>
> ▸ **Fixed Costs**, on the other hand, remain constant regardless of production or sales. The florist's shop rent and electricity bill, for example, stay the same whether they sell 10 bouquets or 100.

The **contribution margin** is what's left of the sales revenue after subtracting variable costs. It's the money available to cover fixed costs and generate profit.

The **break-even point** tells how many sales are needed to cover the business's variable and fixed costs up until that unit. Every additional unit sold afterward results in net profit. This is calculated using the formula:

$$\text{Break-Even Point (units)} = \frac{\text{Fixed Costs}}{\text{Contribution Margin per Unit}}$$

Leo's Example

To better understand the concepts of variable costs, fixed costs, and contribution margin, let's apply them to **Leo and his pet supply shop**.

Leo sells **premium dog treats** for **$5 each**. Here's how his costs break down:

> ▸ **Variable Costs**: Each treat costs Leo **$2** to produce. This includes ingredients, packaging, and labor. These costs increase with the number of treats sold. For example:
>
>   ▸ Selling **1 treat** incurs a total variable cost of **$2**.
>
>   ▸ Selling **100 treats** incurs a total variable cost of **$200**.
>
>   ▸ Selling **1,000 treats** incurs a total variable cost of **$2,000**.

Fixed Costs: These are the costs that stay the same no matter how many treats Leo sells. For example:

> ▸ Rent for his shop = $1,500/month
>
> ▸ Internet and utilities = $1,000/month
>
> ▸ Insurance = $500/month

Together, Leo's fixed costs are $3,000/month. Whether Leo sells 10 treats or 1,000 treats, he still pays the same $3,000.

Now, let's calculate the **contribution margin** for each treat Leo sells. The contribution margin is the amount left over after covering variable costs, which contributes to paying off fixed costs.

> - **Selling Price per Treat**: $5
> - **Variable Cost per Treat**: $2
> - **Contribution Margin per Treat**: $5 - $2 = $3

For every treat Leo sells, **$3** contributes to his fixed costs.

To find Leo's break-even point—the number of treats he needs to sell to cover his variable and fixed costs until the point his business breaks even—where there's no profit or loss—we use the formula:

$$\text{Break-even Point} = \frac{\text{Fixed Costs}}{\text{Contribution Margin per Treat}}$$

Plugging in the numbers:

$$\text{Break-even Point} = \frac{\$3,000}{\$3} = 1,000 \text{ treats}$$

This means:

> - If Leo sells **exactly 1,000 treats**, he breaks even. He covers all his costs but doesn't make any profit.
> - If Leo sells **more than 1,000 treats**, he starts making a profit.
> - If Leo sells **less than 1,000 treats**, he's operating at a loss.

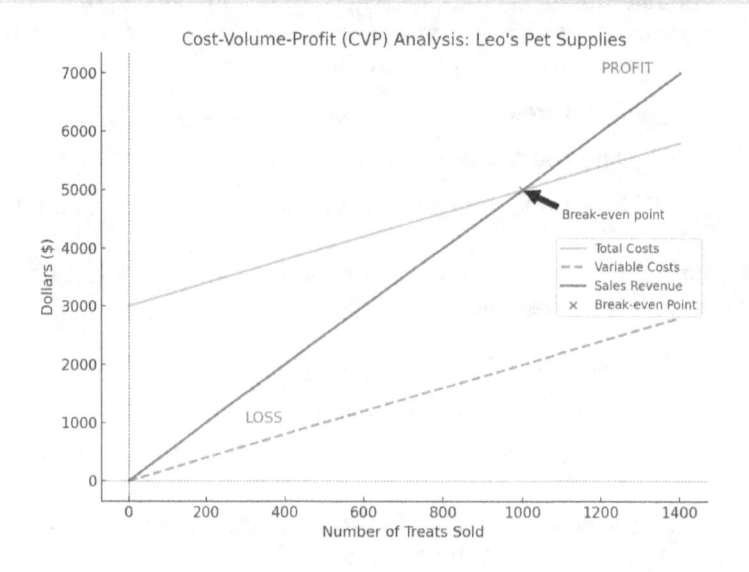

Once Leo sells more than **1,000 treats**, the contribution margin from each additional treat becomes **pure profit**. For instance:

- Selling **1,200 treats** generates:
  - Revenue: **1,200 × $5 = $6,000**
  - Variable Costs: **1,200 × $2 = $2,400**
  - Contribution Margin: **$6,000 - $2,400 = $3,600**
  - Profit (after fixed costs): **$3,600 - $3,000 = $600**

That's why CVP is a powerful decision-making tool:

1. **Pricing Strategy**: Leo could decide to increase the price of his treats to $6. But if sales drop because of the price increase, would his profit still grow? CVP analysis can help him forecast the impact.

2. **Cost Control**: If Leo negotiates with suppliers and reduces his variable cost to $1.50 per treat, his contribution margin increases, and he needs fewer sales to break even.

3. **Product Focus**: By comparing contribution margins across product lines, Leo can identify his most profitable items and allocate resources accordingly.

Product Costs and Period Costs

We discussed how variable and fixed costs shape decisions and help calculate break-even points. But let's dig a little deeper—how do businesses categorize their costs for even greater clarity? This is where the distinction between **product costs** and **period costs** becomes invaluable.

While CVP analysis highlights how costs interact with revenue, understanding the nature of these costs—whether tied to specific products or tied to time—adds another layer of precision to managerial accounting. Think of it like refining a recipe: by knowing exactly which ingredients (costs) contribute to each dish (product) and which are simply part of running the kitchen (overhead), you can make better decisions about pricing, investments, and operations.

Product Costs: Product costs are expenses directly tied to the production of a good or the delivery of a service. These costs are often referred to as **"inventoriable costs"** or **"direct labor costs"** because they can be directly traced back to specific products. For example:

- **Raw Materials:** In a small bakery, the flour, eggs, and sugar used to make cakes are product costs.

- **Direct Labor:** The wages paid to bakers for crafting those cakes.
- **Factory Overheads:** If the bakery rents an industrial kitchen exclusively for baking, the rental expense could also be considered a product cost.

Here's why product costs are important: They are treated as part of the **inventory value** on the balance sheet until the product is sold. Only when a product is sold does the associated product cost become an **expense** on the income statement. This approach helps businesses align costs with revenues.

Example: Leo's Pet Supplies Expands

Imagine Leo decides to add custom-designed pet collars to his product line. He pays $20 per collar to a local artisan who handcrafts each piece. If Leo also spends $5 per collar on packaging, the total product cost per collar is $25.

- Until sold, these collars are treated as **assets** (inventory).
- Once sold, their cost moves to **Cost of Goods Sold (COGS)** on the income statement.

Period Costs: Period costs, in contrast, are expenses that are tied to a **specific time period** rather than a specific product. They are recorded immediately on the income statement as expenses. Common examples include:

- Rent for a storefront
- Utility bills
- Advertising expenses
- General supplies
- Insurance

These costs don't fluctuate based on production volume and are considered **time-bound operational expenses.**

Example:

Let's revisit **Leo's Pet Supplies** to explore these concepts further. Leo's product costs for a bag of premium dog treats include:

- **$1,50 for ingredients** (variable cost, product cost)
- **$0,50 for packaging** (variable cost, product cost)
- $2,00 total product cost per bag

Leo's period costs, however, are more predictable and fixed over time:

- $3,000 for monthly rent
- $300 for internet services
- $200 for advertising

While product costs only appear as expenses when a product is sold, period costs are always expensed as they occur.

Understanding the difference between product and period costs is essential for making better financial decisions. Here's why:

- **Product costs affect inventory value and gross profit.** If inventory costs are inaccurate, it can distort a business's financial health.
- **Period costs impact net income.** Properly categorizing these costs ensures businesses understand their true operational efficiency.

For example, if Leo misclassifies his artisan collar costs as a period cost instead of a product cost, his profits may appear lower than they actually are. This could mislead potential investors or affect pricing decisions.

A Note on Customization in Managerial Accounting

While product and period costs are common classifications, businesses have the flexibility to tailor their accounting methods to suit their needs. For instance:

- A manufacturing company might use detailed **cost-per-unit systems** to track factory overhead.
- A service business might emphasize **time-tracking systems** to associate costs with specific projects or clients.

No matter the method, the goal remains the same: **Provide clear and actionable insights to guide decisions.**

Making Managerial Accounting Work for You

Let's face it: **managerial accounting can feel overwhelming**, especially when compared to the more structured world of financial accounting. Where financial accounting offers clear rules and standards, managerial accounting presents a wide-open landscape of possibilities. With so much room for customization, it's no wonder students (and even business owners) can feel a bit lost.

But here's the good news: **managerial accounting doesn't have to be complicated.** At its core, it's all about providing information that helps businesses make better decisions. The trick is to focus on the basics—those foundational principles that give you clarity and control over your operations. If the amount of information is feeling overwhelming, a good place to start is to zoom out to the big picture and compare numbers year over year at a summary level. That will often prompt you to find unexpected changes, and to then seek out details of specific changes, providing better guidance on what to analyze.

So, where does managerial accounting shine? It helps answer key questions, like:

> - Which products or services should you focus on?
> - What prices should you set?
> - How can you maximize your profits while keeping costs under control?

In the previous section, we explored the concept of **Cost-Volume-Profit (CVP) analysis**, which is one of the most powerful tools in managerial accounting. Now, let's simplify it even further by looking at the underlying equation:

Sales Revenue − Variable Costs − Fixed Costs = Profit

If this looks intimidating at first glance, don't worry, we can break it down into something more practical. Let's unpack each component:

> 1. **Sales Revenue**: Think of this as the number of units sold multiplied by the price of each unit.
> 2. **Variable Costs**: These are the costs that change with each unit sold, like materials or production costs. You can express this as units sold multiplied by the cost per unit.
> 3. **Fixed Costs**: These remain constant regardless of how many units you sell, things like rent, utilities, or salaries.

To bring this equation to life, let's use a real-world example:

Example: Cozy Coffee Corner

Cozy Coffee Corner is a charming neighborhood café where coffee lovers gather for their daily fix. The café sells its cups of coffee for **$4 each**. The **variable cost** (the cost of coffee beans, milk, and disposable cups) is **$1.50 per cup**. Meanwhile, the shop incurs **fixed monthly expenses** of **$2,000**, which cover rent, utilities, and staff wages.

Here's the breakdown:

> - **Sales Revenue** = Cups sold × price per cup
> - **Variable Costs** = Cups sold × cost per cup

> **Fixed Costs** = Total monthly expenses that don't change with sales volume

Let's assume Cozy Coffee Corner sells **1,200 cups of coffee** in a month. Here's how the numbers look:

> **Sales Revenue** = 1,200 × $4 = $4,800
>
> **Variable Costs** = 1,200 × $1.50 = $1,800
>
> **Fixed Costs** = $2,000

Now, plug these into the equation:
Profit = Sales Revenue − Variable Costs − Fixed Costs
Profit = $4,800 − $1,800 − $2,000
Profit = $1,000

From this example, Cozy Coffee Corner has a clear understanding of its financial health. They know that selling 1,200 cups of coffee in a month results in a $1,000 profit. If the owner wants to increase profits, they could explore:

> **Boosting sales volume**: Selling more cups of coffee by offering promotions or attracting new customers.
>
> **Raising prices**: If customers are loyal and not price-sensitive, a small increase (e.g., $4.25 per cup) could increase revenue without losing sales.
>
> **Reducing variable costs**: Negotiating better prices for coffee beans or switching to reusable cups to save on packaging costs.
>
> **Cutting fixed costs**: Finding ways to save on rent or utilities without compromising quality.

But this is not enough: the owner of Cozy Coffee Corner wants to calculate how many cups of coffee need to be sold to reach the **break-even point**, where the café's total revenue equals its total costs, resulting in zero profit. Even though he is currently in profit, he wants to know exactly how many cups of coffee he needs to sell to break even to see if he should raise prices or not.

Break-Even Formula

The break-even point is calculated using the **Cost-Volume-Profit (CVP) formula**:

Profit = (Price × Units Sold) − (Variable Cost × Units Sold) − Fixed Costs

At the break-even point, **Profit = $0**, so:

$0 = (\$4 \times \text{Units Sold}) - (\$1.50 \times \text{Units Sold}) - \$2,000$

Step-by-Step Calculation:

1. **Calculate the Contribution Margin**:
   The contribution margin per unit is the amount left after subtracting the variable cost from the selling price:
   Contribution Margin = $4 − $1.50 = $2.50 per cup

2. **Set Up the Equation**:
   Substitute the contribution margin into the formula:
   $0 = ($2.50 × Units Sold) − $2,000

3. **Solve for Units Sold**:
   Rearrange the equation to isolate the number of units:
   $2.50 × Units Sold = $2,000
   Units Sold = $2,000 ÷ $2.50 = 800 cups

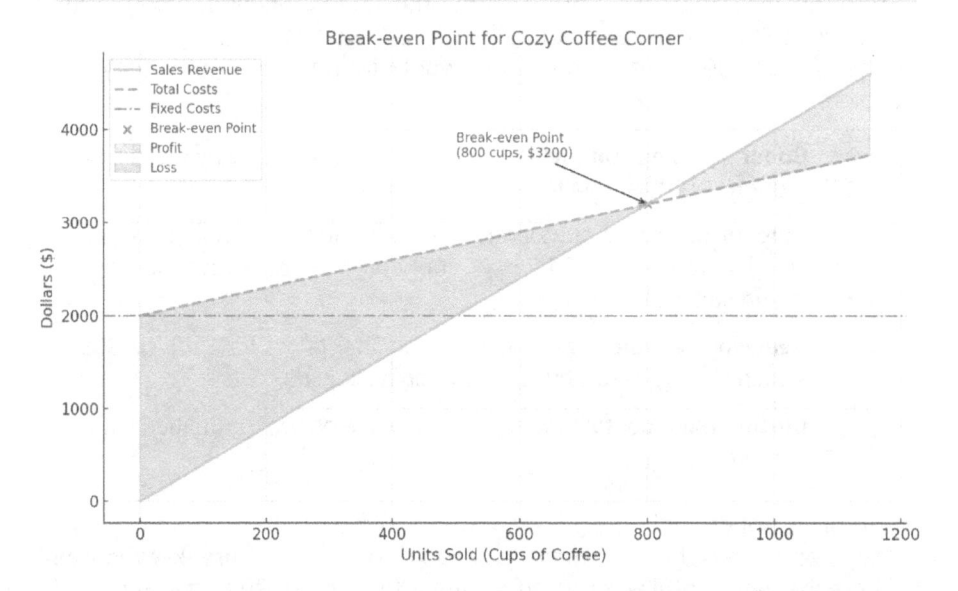

Break-even Point for Cozy Coffee Corner

To break even, Cozy Coffee Corner must sell **800 cups of coffee** in a month. At this point, the café's total revenue will cover both its variable and fixed costs, resulting in zero profit.

Pro tip: if you know how many cups of coffee you sell in a month, and what your breakeven number of cups is, you can calculate on which day of the month you become profitable. I.e. if a business sells 1200 cups in a month, and breaks even at 800, they become profitable around the 20th day of the month. 800/1200=67%. 67% of 30 days in a month is day 20.

Key Figures:

- **Contribution Margin per Cup**:
  Each cup contributes **$2.50** toward covering fixed costs and, eventually, profit.

- **Break-Even Revenue**:
  Multiply the break-even units by the price per cup:
  800 cups × $4 = $3,200 in revenue

What This Means for Cozy Coffee Corner

By calculating the break-even point, the café's owner gains crucial insights into the business's performance:

1. **Target Sales**: The owner knows that selling 800 cups in a month is the minimum target to avoid losses.

2. **Decision-Making Tool**: If costs change (e.g., rent increases or the café switches to more expensive beans), the break-even point must be recalculated to maintain financial clarity.

3. **Profit Forecasting**: Beyond the break-even point, every additional sale directly boosts profit by **$2.50 per cup**.

Setting Target Income Goals

Managerial accounting can also help business owners establish and achieve **target income goals**, which are the profits they aim to generate to meet their financial objectives. For a small business owner like Leo of "Leo's Pet Supplies," target income might be the funds needed to cover personal expenses, reinvest in the business, or achieve a specific milestone—such as opening a second location. For larger companies, target income could be based on **shareholder expectations**, **debt repayment plans**, or **dividend targets**.

Leo's Target: Expanding His Business

Leo dreams of opening a second store in a nearby neighborhood. To make this happen, he estimates he'll need **$50,000** for upfront costs like rent, shelving, and initial inventory. He decides he wants to raise this amount within the next 10 months. This sets Leo's monthly **target income** at **$5,000** above his current operating needs.

Using the formula for target income, we calculate how many units Leo needs to sell:

Target Income Formula:

Target Income = (Price per Unit * u) − (Variable Cost per Unit * u) − Fixed Costs

Where "u" is the number of units sold.

For Leo:

> ▹ **Price per Unit:** $5
> ▹ **Variable Cost per Unit:** $2
> ▹ **Fixed Costs:** $3,000/month

Plugging in Leo's target income goal:

$$5{,}000 = (5u) - (2u) - 3{,}000$$
$$5{,}000 = 3u - 3{,}000$$
$$8{,}000 = 3u$$
$$u = 2{,}667$$

Leo needs to sell **2,667 dog treats per month** to meet his goal. Currently, he sells around **1,800 treats monthly**, meaning he must significantly boost sales to reach his target.

Strategizing for Growth

Like any savvy business owner, Leo explores several strategies to close the gap:

Increasing Sales Volume: Leo could **launch a new marketing campaign** to attract more customers. Perhaps a "Buy One, Get One Free" promotion or partnerships with local dog trainers and veterinarians could help boost traffic to his store.

Adjusting Prices: By increasing the price of his dog treats slightly, say to **$5.50**, Leo can increase his **contribution margin**. Let's see how this adjustment impacts his goal:

New formula:

$$5{,}000 = (5.50u) - (2u) - 3{,}000$$
$$5{,}000 = 3.50u - 3{,}000$$
$$8{,}000 = 3.50u$$
$$u = 2{,}286$$

By raising his price to $5.50, Leo reduces the required sales volume to **2,286 treats**, a much more manageable target.

Lowering Costs: Leo negotiates with his supplier to lower the cost of ingredients from $2 to **$1.75**. With this reduction, the required sales volume decreases further:

New formula:

$$5{,}000 = (5.50u) - (1.75u) - 3{,}000$$
$$5{,}000 = 3.75u - 3{,}000$$
$$8{,}000 = 3.75u$$
$$u = 2{,}133$$

Now, Leo only needs to sell **2,133 treats per month**, a goal that feels within reach with the right strategy.

This example demonstrates how **target income analysis** can empower business owners to plan effectively. By experimenting with multiple variables—like price, costs, and sales volume, Leo gains control over his financial future.

Managerial accountants often employ similar strategies to help businesses of all sizes optimize profits. They evaluate the **contribution margin** of each product, adjust pricing strategies, and look for ways to reduce costs while maintaining quality.

Other method using CVP

To determine how many units you must sell to reach your target profit, you can use the following formula:

$$\text{Required Sales Units} = \frac{\text{Fixed Costs} + \text{Target Profit}}{\text{Contribution Margin per Unit}}$$

Returning to Leo's Pet Supplies, let's put this into practice. Suppose Leo has monthly fixed costs of $3,000, and each premium dog treat generates a contribution margin of $3. If Leo sets a target profit of $1,200, how many treats does he need to sell?

$$\frac{\$3{,}000 \text{ (Fixed Costs)} + \$1{,}200 \text{ (Target Profit)}}{\$3 \text{ (Contribution Margin per Unit)}} = 1{,}400 \text{ treats}$$

This means Leo must sell 1,400 treats per month to reach his desired profit of $1,200.

But sometimes, businesses prefer thinking in terms of sales revenue rather than units. To determine the total sales revenue required to achieve a target profit, use this formula instead:

$$\text{Required Sales Revenue} = \frac{\text{Fixed Costs} + \text{Target Profit}}{\text{Contribution Margin Ratio}}$$

Recall that the Contribution Margin Ratio indicates the portion of each dollar of sales that's available to cover fixed costs and profits. The formula for this ratio is:

$$\text{Contribution Margin Ratio} = \frac{\text{Sale Price per Unit} - \text{Variable Cost per Unit}}{\text{Sale Price per Unit}}$$

For example, if Leo's treats sell at $5 each with a variable cost of $2, his Contribution Margin Ratio would be:

$$\frac{\$5 - \$2}{\$5} = 0.60 \text{ or } 60\%$$

Using the earlier scenario, Leo's required sales revenue to reach the $1,200 target profit is:

$$\frac{\$3,000 \text{ (Fixed Costs)} + \$1,200 \text{ (Target Profit)}}{0.60 \text{ (Contribution Margin Ratio)}} = \$7,000$$

This means Leo needs $7,000 in monthly revenue to hit his profit goal.

By clearly defining how much you need to sell, CVP analysis enables smarter pricing, marketing, and production decisions, turning your business dreams into practical objectives.

Marginal Costing vs. Absorption Costing

When running a business, understanding costs is crucial. Every company needs to know how much it truly costs to make its products and whether it's making a profit. But there's more than one way to calculate profit, and the method used can change how financial statements look.

Two of the most common methods for handling costs are **marginal costing** and **absorption costing**.

Marginal costing focuses on how much each unit contributes to covering fixed costs and generating profit. It separates **variable costs**, which change with production levels, from **fixed costs**, which stay the same no matter how much is produced. This method is useful for decision-making because it helps businesses understand the impact of producing and selling one more unit.

Absorption costing, on the other hand, includes **all** production costs—both variable and fixed, when calculating the cost of each unit sold. This method is required for **external financial reporting** because it provides a complete picture of total production costs. Since fixed costs are spread across all units produced, profit calculations can fluctuate depending on how many units are made and sold in a given period.

To see how these two methods work in practice, let's look at an example.

Example:

Sarah runs a pottery shop and sells ceramic mugs. Each mug sells for **$25**. The cost to make each mug includes **$10 in clay, glaze, and labor**, which are variable costs because they change with the number of mugs made.

In addition to these costs, Sarah has **$4,000 in fixed costs per month** for rent, utilities, and equipment maintenance. These costs stay the same whether she makes 10 mugs or 1,000 mugs.

Let's assume Sarah **produces and sells 500 mugs** in one month.

In marginal costing, only variable costs are deducted from sales to calculate **contribution margin**. Fixed costs are then subtracted separately.

Sales Revenue (500 * $25)	$12,500
Variable Costs (500 * $10)	($5,000)
Contribution Margin	$7,500
Fixed Costs	($4,000)
Operating Profit	$3,500

In this case, Sarah's **contribution margin is $7,500**, meaning that after covering variable costs, she has $7,500 left to cover fixed costs and make a profit. Once fixed costs of **$4,000** are deducted, the final operating profit is **$3,500**.

With absorption costing, fixed costs are included in the cost of each unit produced. Since Sarah produces 500 mugs, she allocates her $4,000 fixed costs across all mugs, which adds $8 of fixed cost per mug ($4,000 ÷ 500 mugs).

This means the total cost per mug is:

- Variable cost per mug = $10
- Fixed cost per mug = $8
- Total production cost per mug = $18

Now, let's look at the income statement:

Sales Revenue (500 * $25)	$12,500
Cost of Goods Sold (COGS):	

- Variable Costs (500 * $10)	($5,000)
- Fixed Costs Allocated (500 * $8)	($4,000)
Gross Profit	**$3,500**
Other Fixed Costs (Non-Manufacturing)	($0)
Operating Profit	**$3,500**

The profit is the same ($3,500) in both cases, but the way costs are allocated is different.

In marginal costing, **fixed costs are deducted separately**, making it easier to see how much each sale contributes to covering fixed costs. This is useful for decision-making, especially when analyzing pricing or evaluating whether to accept a special order at a lower price.

In absorption costing, **fixed costs are included in the cost of each unit**, which is required for financial reporting. However, this method can sometimes make it harder to see the impact of producing or selling additional units.

Marginal costing helps businesses understand their break-even point and make short-term decisions. It highlights how much profit each sale generates before fixed costs are considered.

Absorption costing ensures that all costs are accounted for in financial statements. The problem is it can sometimes make profits look different depending on how much inventory is produced but not sold.

Both methods are valuable, and businesses often use marginal costing for internal decision-making while following absorption costing for official external reports.

Now that we've seen the differences in action, we can explore how these methods affect pricing, break-even analysis, and strategic decision-making.

Multi-Product Analysis

In real-world scenarios, businesses often juggle multiple products, each contributing differently to revenue and profits. While conducting **Cost-Volume-Profit (CVP)** analysis for a single product is straightforward, incorporating multiple products into the equation requires understanding their **sales mix** and **contribution margins**.

Revisiting Leo's Pet Supplies

Let's apply this concept to **Leo's Pet Supplies**, where Leo offers three product categories:

1. **Premium Dog Treats** ($5 each with a $2 variable cost)
2. **Dog Chew Toys** ($10 each with a $4 variable cost)

3. **Grooming Kits** ($20 each with a $10 variable cost)

Step 1: Analyze the Sales Mix

The **sales mix** refers to the proportion of total sales revenue generated by each product. Over the past month, Leo recorded:

- **800 Dog Treats** sold, contributing $4,000 in revenue.
- **500 Chew Toys** sold, contributing $5,000 in revenue.
- **200 Grooming Kits** sold, contributing $4,000 in revenue.

The total revenue is **$13,000**. The sales mix for each product is calculated as:

- **Dog Treats:** $4,000 ÷ $13,000 ≈ 30.8%
- **Chew Toys:** $5,000 ÷ $13,000 ≈ 38.5%
- **Grooming Kits:** $4,000 ÷ $13,000 ≈ 30.8%

Step 2: Determine Contribution Margins

The **contribution margin** for each product is calculated by subtracting variable costs from the sales price:

- **Dog Treats:** $5 - $2 = $3 contribution margin.
- **Chew Toys:** $10 - $4 = $6 contribution margin.
- **Grooming Kits:** $20 - $10 = $10 contribution margin.

We can also express these as percentages of the selling price:

- **Dog Treats:** $3 ÷ $5 = 60%.
- **Chew Toys:** $6 ÷ $10 = 60%.
- **Grooming Kits:** $10 ÷ $20 = 50%.

Step 3: Weighted Contribution Margin

To combine the products into a single CVP model, we calculate a **weighted contribution margin** based on their sales mix:

- Dog Treats: $3 × 30.8% = $0.92
- Chew Toys: $6 × 38.5% = $2.31
- Grooming Kits: $10 × 30.8% = $3.08

The weighted contribution margin is approximately **$6.31 per unit**.

Step 4: Applying CVP to Multi-Product Analysis

Leo's monthly fixed costs remain $3,000. To calculate the **break-even sales in dollars**, we divide fixed costs by the weighted contribution margin ratio:

$$\text{Break-Even Sales} = \frac{\text{Fixed Costs}}{\text{Weighted Contribution Margin Ratio}}$$

The weighted contribution margin ratio is:

$$\frac{\text{Total Weighted Contribution Margin}}{\text{Total Revenue}} = \frac{6.31}{13} \approx 48.5\%$$

Break-even sales:

$$\text{Break-Even Sales} = \frac{3,000}{0.485} \approx 6,186.6 \text{ dollars.}$$

In units: If Leo maintains the sales mix proportions, he needs to sell:

- **30.8% Dog Treats:** ≈ 1,907 units
- **38.5% Chew Toys:** ≈ 2,380 units
- **30.8% Grooming Kits:** ≈ 1,907 units

Strategic Decisions

By understanding his sales mix and contribution margins, Leo can identify which products generate the most profit relative to their sales.

From a managerial accountant's perspective, Leo faces a challenge in his **sales mix**. Most of his revenue stems from his **chew toys**, which have a **lower contribution margin per unit as** compared to his grooming kits. While chew toys bring in significant revenue, they contribute less profit per dollar earned compared to other products

Leo's Product Sales & Contribution Margins

Product	Units Sold	Price/Unit	Revenue	Variable Cost/Unit
Dog Treats	800	$5	$4,000	$2
Chew Toys	500	$10	$5,000	$4
Grooming Kits	200	$20	$4,000	$10
			$13,000	

Total Variable Costs	CM/Unit	Total CM	CM %	Sales Mix %
$1,600	$3	$2,400	60%	30.8%
$2,000	$6	$3,000	60%	38.5%
$2,000	$10	$2,000	50%	30.8%
$5,600		**$7,400**		**100%**

From the **sales revenue** column, it's evident that chew toys dominate Leo's sales mix. However, their **40% contribution margin** means only **40 cents of every dollar** earned from chew toys contributes to covering fixed costs or generating profit. Compare this to dog treats and grooming kits, both of which offer a **60% contribution margin**.

If Leo aims to boost his profitability, he might consider:

1. **Increasing Grooming Kit Sales**
   Grooming kits are tied with dog treats for the highest contribution margin percentage. However, their **total sales revenue** is the lowest among all products. Investing in marketing or bundling promotions for grooming kits could help increase their share in the sales mix.

2. **Maximizing Dog Treat Revenue**
   Dog treats already generate significant profits. Encouraging customers to buy more dog treats, perhaps through loyalty programs—could enhance profitability without introducing new costs.

3. **Improving Chew Toy Margins**
   Leo might consider negotiating better prices with suppliers or increasing the retail price of chew toys. This would help improve the **per-unit contribution margin** while maintaining chew toys as a cornerstone of his sales mix.

Variance Analysis

Running your business involves setting expectations for sales, costs, and profits every month. But when the month ends, and you close the books, the results are often different than what you forecasted. Maybe you spent more on materials than planned, or perhaps you sold fewer products than anticipated. These differences between what you expected (the budget) and what happened (the results) are called **variances**, and understanding them is key to improving business performance.

Variance analysis is the process of examining these differences to understand why they occurred. It helps answer important questions: **Are we spending too much? Are we using resources efficiently? Are we selling at the right price?**

By identifying where things went better or worse than planned, a business can make adjustments to improve efficiency and profitability.

Let's take a simple example. Imagine you own a bakery, and you budgeted **$2,000** for flour in a month, assuming flour costs **$2 per kg** and that you would need **1,000 kg**. At the end of the month, you check your expenses and see that you actually spent **$2,400**. This means you have a **negative variance** of **$400**, you spent more than expected. Now, the key question is: **why?**

To find the answer, you break down the variance into two parts:

> - **Price Variance** – Did the cost per kg of flour increase?
> - **Efficiency Variance** – Did you use more flour than expected?

First, you check the price you paid. If the supplier increased the price to **$2.20 per kg**, then part of your extra cost comes from this change. The price variance is calculated as:

$$(\text{Actual Price} - \text{Budgeted Price}) * \text{Quantity Purchased}$$
$$(2.20 - 2.00) * 1{,}000 = 0.20 * 1{,}000 = \$200$$

This means $200 of the extra cost came from the price increase.

Next, you check how much flour you actually used. If you expected to use **1,000 kg** but ended up using **1,100 kg**, then the efficiency variance is calculated as:

$$(\text{Actual Quantity Used} - \text{Budgeted Quantity}) * \text{Budgeted Price}$$
$$(1{,}100 - 1{,}000) * 2.00 = 100 * 2.00 = \$200$$

So, the other **$200 came from using more flour than expected**. Maybe there was waste, or maybe more cakes were made than planned.

Now, you understand that your total **negative variance of $400** was caused half by a price increase ($200**)** and half by inefficient use of materials ($200). With this information, you can take action, perhaps negotiate a better price with the supplier or find ways to reduce waste in production.

Variance analysis isn't just about costs. It can also be used to **analyze sales performance**. Suppose you expected to sell **500 cakes** at **$10 each**, generating $5,000 in revenue, but you actually sold only 450 cakes at $9 each, making $4,050. The difference is a sales variance of $950 less than expected. Again, breaking it down helps: was the problem the lower price, or simply selling fewer cakes?

$$(\text{Actual Price} - \text{Budgeted Price}) * \text{Actual Quantity Sold}$$
$$(9\ 10) \times 450 = -1 * \$450 = -\$450$$

So, **€450 of the loss came from lowering the price**.

$$(\text{Actual Quantity Sold} - \text{Budgeted Quantity}) * \text{Budgeted Price}$$
$$(450 - 500) * 10 = -50 * 10 = -\$500$$

And $500 came from selling fewer cakes than planned.

By breaking down the variance into clear causes, you can make better decisions. Maybe you realize that lowering the price didn't increase sales enough to be worthwhile. Or maybe you decide to improve marketing to sell more cakes next month.

Variance analysis is a powerful tool because it doesn't just show that something went wrong, it shows **why** it happened. With this knowledge, a business can adjust strategies, control costs, and ultimately improve profitability.

Inventory Accounting

Accounting for inventory is a crucial aspect of **managerial accounting**, ensuring that the **cost of goods sold (COGS)** aligns with the period in which the inventory is sold. Let's revisit **Leo's Pet Supplies** to explain how inventory transactions are recorded and how these affect financial statements.

Receiving Inventory

Leo orders **50 bags of premium dog treats** at a wholesale price of **$10 each**, totaling **$500**. Here's how the journal entry would look:

> **Debit**: Inventory (Asset Account) $500
>
> **Credit**: Accounts Payable (Liability Account) $500

Account	Debit	Credit
Inventory	$500	
Accounts Payable		$500

This entry ensures that the inventory value is accurately reflected as an asset until it is sold. If Leo pays immediately, the **Cash** account is credited instead of **Accounts Payable**.

Returning Defective Goods

On inspection, Leo finds **5 bags of defective treats**. He negotiates a return with his supplier, reducing his payable by **$50 (5 bags × $10)**. Here's the adjustment:

> **Credit**: Inventory (Asset Account) $50
>
> **Debit**: Accounts Payable (Liability Account) $50

Returning Defective Goods

ACCOUNT	DEBIT ($)	CREDIT ($)
Inventory (Asset)		50
Accounts Payable (Liability)	50	

This process, known as a **purchase return**, ensures that the defective goods are removed from inventory and the payable is reduced accordingly.

Handling Purchase Allowances

Sometimes, rather than returning defective inventory, a business negotiates a price reduction. If the supplier offers Leo a **$20 discount** for keeping the defective bags, the journal entry adjusts as follows:

- **Credit**: Inventory (Asset Account) $20
- **Debit**: Accounts Payable (Liability Account) $20

Handling Purchase Allowances

ACCOUNT	DEBIT ($)	CREDIT ($)
Inventory (Asset)		20
Accounts Payable (Liability)	20	

Selling the Inventory

Leo sells **10 bags of dog treats** at **$20 each**, generating **$200 in revenue**. Each bag costs him **$10** (COGS), so the journal entries would be:

1. **Recording the Sale**:
   - **Debit**: Cash or Accounts Receivable (Asset Account) $200
   - **Credit**: Revenue (Equity Account) $200

2. **Recording the Cost of Goods Sold (COGS)**:
   - **Debit**: COGS (Expense Account) $100
   - **Credit**: Inventory (Asset Account) $100

This two-step process ensures the revenue and the associated expense are correctly matched in the income statement.

1. Recording the Sale

ACCOUNT	DEBIT ($)	CREDIT ($)
Cash or Accounts Receivable (Asset)	200	
Revenue (Equity)		200

ACCOUNT	DEBIT ($)	CREDIT ($)
Cost of Goods Sold (*Expense or Equity*)	100	
Inventory (*Asset*)		100

Accounting for Shipping Costs

Shipping costs incurred to receive inventory are added to the **inventory value**. If Leo pays **$25** for shipping the 50 bags of treats, the total inventory cost becomes **$525 ($500 + $25)**. The journal entry looks like this:

- **Debit**: Inventory (Asset Account) $25
- **Credit**: Cash (Asset Account) $25

1. Recording the Shipping Costs

ACCOUNT	DEBIT ($)	CREDIT ($)
Inventory (Asset)	25	
Cash (Asset)		25

When selling the inventory, the **shipping costs** are distributed proportionally. For example, if Leo sells **10 bags**, the shipping cost per bag is **$0.50 (25/50)**. The **COGS for 10 bags** is:

- **(10 bags × $10 per bag) + (10 bags × $0.50 shipping) = $105**

The journal entry updates as follows:

- **Debit**: COGS (Expense Account) $105
- **Credit**: Inventory (Asset Account) $105

2. **Recording the Cost of Goods Sold (COGS)**

ACCOUNT	DEBIT ($)	CREDIT ($)
Cost of Goods Sold (Expense)	105	
Inventory (Asset)		105

Freight Out Costs

If Leo decides to offer **free shipping** to his customers, the **shipping cost** becomes his expense. For example, if Leo spends **$10 on shipping** for a customer's order, he records it as follows:

> **Debit**: Freight Out (Expense Account) $10
>
> **Credit**: Cash (Asset Account) $10

Freight Out Costs

ACCOUNT	DEBIT ($)	CREDIT ($)
Freight Out (Expense)	10	
Cash (Asset)		10

Key Takeaways

1. **Inventory transactions** reflect the costs incurred and ensure accurate matching with revenue.
2. **Purchase returns** and **allowances** adjust inventory and payables efficiently.
3. **Shipping costs** are integrated into inventory costs or recorded as expenses, depending on their purpose.
4. Proper accounting for inventory helps businesses track profitability and maintain accurate financial statements.

Inventory Management

Imagine you own a small bookstore. Every day, customers walk in looking for the latest bestsellers, classic novels, and school textbooks. If you don't have what they want, they might leave and buy from a competitor. But if you stock too many books, you risk having unsold inventory taking up space and tying up your money. In accounting, inventory is one of the most important assets a business owns. It represents products that are waiting to be sold, and its management directly affects financial statements, cash flow, and profitability. A company that **holds too much inventory** risks tying up capital, increasing storage costs, and dealing with potential losses due to damage or obsolescence. On the other hand, having **too little inventory** can lead to missed sales, customer dissatisfaction, and operational disruptions.

Proper inventory management helps businesses maintain the right balance between supply and demand while controlling costs. Inefficient inventory management can lead to **overstated or understated profits**, cash flow problems, and misallocation of resources.

To optimize inventory and minimize costs, businesses use key accounting tools and formulas, including Economic Order Quantity (EOQ), Reorder Level, Safety Stock, Maximum and Minimum Inventory Levels, Lead Time, and Stock Out Costs. Each of these plays a critical role in determining when and how much to order, ensuring that inventory is available without unnecessary financial strain.

Let's now explore these inventories management concepts with simple explanations and practical examples.

Economic Order Quantity (EOQ): How to Minimize Inventory Costs

One of the biggest challenges in inventory management is deciding how much stock to order at a time. If a company places too many orders in small quantities, it faces high ordering costs, such as administrative expenses and delivery charges. But if it **orders too much at once**, it risks higher storage costs and tying up cash in unsold goods. The solution is to find the **optimal order quantity**, the amount that minimizes both ordering and holding costs.

This is where the **Economic Order Quantity (EOQ)** formula comes in. EOQ helps businesses determine the ideal order size that balances these costs, ensuring they are neither overstocking nor understocking.

$$EOQ = \sqrt{\frac{2DS}{H}}$$

Where:

- **D** = Demand (units per year)
- **S** = Ordering cost per order
- **H** = Holding cost per unit per year

This formula helps determine the most cost-effective quantity to order each time inventory needs replenishing.

Example

Imagine you manage a bookstore that sells **notebooks**. You need to determine the best order size to keep costs under control.

> ▸ **Annual demand (D):** 10,000 notebooks
>
> ▸ **Ordering cost per order (S):** $50 (administrative expenses, delivery fees)
>
> ▸ **Holding cost per notebook per year (H):** $2 (storage, insurance, potential obsolescence)

Plugging these values into the EOQ formula:

$$EOQ = \sqrt{\frac{2 \times 10,000 \times 50}{2}}$$

$$EOQ = \sqrt{\frac{1,000,000}{2}} = \sqrt{500,000} \approx 707 \text{ units}$$

This means that the most cost-efficient way to manage inventory is to order **707 notebooks per order**. Ordering this amount minimizes total costs by balancing the frequency of orders with the cost of storing inventory.

From an accounting perspective, EOQ helps businesses control **inventory-related costs**, which impact both the **income statement and balance sheet**, can **improve financial efficiency**, reduce waste, and make more informed purchasing decisions.

Next, we'll look at **Reorder Level**, which determines when an order should be placed to prevent stockouts.

Reorder Level: Knowing When to Place an Order

While Economic Order Quantity (EOQ) helps determine **how much** inventory to order, businesses also need to know **when** to place an order to avoid running out of stock. This is where the **Reorder Level** comes in.

The **Reorder Level** is the point at which a new order must be placed to ensure that inventory never runs out before new stock arrives. Ordering too late can lead to stockouts, missed sales, and unhappy customers, while ordering too early increases storage costs and ties up capital.

The reorder level is calculated using the following formula:

Reorder Level = Daily Demand * Lead Time

Where:

> ▸ **Daily Demand** = The number of units sold or used per day
>
> ▸ **Lead Time** = The number of days it takes for a new order to arrive

Example

Imagine a clothing store sells **50 t-shirts per day**, and when the owner places an order, the supplier takes **10 days** to deliver. Using the formula:

Reorder Level = 50 * 10 = 500

This means that when the inventory level **drops to 500 t-shirts**, the store should immediately place a new order. This ensures that by the time the order arrives, there are still enough t-shirts to meet customer demand.

Properly setting a reorder level helps businesses operate efficiently while keeping inventory costs under control.

Next, we'll explore **Safety Stock**, which acts as a buffer in case of unexpected demand or supply delays.

Safety Stock: A Buffer Against Uncertainty

Even with a well-calculated reorder level, businesses can still face unexpected situations. What if demand suddenly increases? What if a supplier delays delivery? Without a backup plan, a company might run out of inventory, leading to lost sales and frustrated customers. To prevent this, businesses keep an extra quantity of stock called **Safety Stock**, a reserve that acts as a cushion against uncertainty.

Safety stock ensures that even if demand is higher than expected or deliveries are delayed, the company can continue operations smoothly. However, keeping too much safety stock can lead to high storage costs, while keeping too little increases the risk of stockouts.

Safety stock is calculated using the following formula:

Safety Stock = (Maximum Daily Usage * Maximum Lead Time)
    − (Average Daily Usage * Average Lead Time)

Where:

- **Maximum Daily Usage** = The highest number of units sold or used in a single day
- **Maximum Lead Time** = The longest time a supplier has taken to deliver stock
- **Average Daily Usage** = The usual number of units sold or used per day
- **Average Lead Time** = The typical time it takes for new stock to arrive

Example:

A grocery store sells bottled water and usually sells 100 bottles per day, with suppliers typically delivering within 5 days. However, on some hot days, demand increases to 150 bottles per day, and suppliers sometimes take up to 8 days to deliver.

Using the formula:

$$\text{Safety Stock} = (150 * 8) - (100 * 5)$$
$$\text{Safety Stock} = 1{,}200 - 500 = 700 \text{ bottles}$$

This means the store should keep 700 extra bottles in stock to cover unexpected demand or supplier delays.

By carefully calculating safety stock, businesses can strike the right balance between **minimizing costs and ensuring uninterrupted operations**.

Next, we'll explore **Maximum and Minimum Inventory Levels**, which help businesses maintain the right amount of stock at all times.

Maximum and Minimum Inventory Levels: Keeping Stock Under Control

Every business needs to maintain a careful balance when managing inventory. Ordering too much stock ties up cash, increases storage costs, and risks spoilage or obsolescence. On the other hand, keeping too little stock increases the risk of stockouts, leading to lost sales and dissatisfied customers. To manage this balance effectively, companies use **Maximum and Minimum Inventory Levels** to set clear limits on how much inventory they should hold at any given time.

The **Maximum Inventory Level** is the highest amount of stock a business should hold at any time. Keeping inventory below this limit prevents excessive holding costs and ensures efficient use of warehouse space.

The formula for calculating the **Maximum Inventory Level** is:

Maximum Inventory Level = Reorder Level + EOQ - Minimum Usage * Minimum Lead Time

Where:

> - **Reorder Level** = The stock level at which a new order is placed
> - **EOQ (Economic Order Quantity)** = The optimal order quantity to minimize costs
> - **Minimum Usage** = The lowest daily consumption of stock
> - **Minimum Lead Time** = The shortest time required for a supplier to deliver new stock

Example: Imagine a warehouse that stores cleaning supplies. The Reorder Level is 500 units, the **EOQ** is 1,000 units, and on slower days, only **20 units per day** are used. The **minimum supplier lead time** is 5 days.

Maximum Inventory Level = 500 + 1,000 − (20 * 5)
= 500 + 1,000 - 100 = 1,400 units

This means the warehouse should **never hold more than 1,400 units** to avoid unnecessary storage costs and inefficiencies.

The **Minimum Inventory Level**, sometimes called the **Buffer Stock Level**, is the lowest amount of stock that a company should have on hand before it risks running out completely. This level ensures that even if demand is slightly higher than expected or deliveries are delayed, there is still enough stock available.

The formula for calculating the **Minimum Inventory Level** is:

Minimum Inventory Level = Reorder Level - (Average Usage * Average Lead Time)

Where:

- **Reorder Level** = The point at which a new order is placed
- **Average Usage** = The typical number of units used per day
- **Average Lead Time** = The usual time required for a supplier to deliver

Example: A manufacturer uses 50 raw material units per day, the Reorder Level is 500, and the average lead time for deliveries is 6 days.

Minimum Inventory Level = 500 - (50 * 6) = 500 - 300 = 200 units

This means the manufacturer should **never allow stock to fall below 200 units** to avoid production stoppages.

By using **Maximum and Minimum Inventory Levels**, businesses can efficiently manage their stock, keeping costs low while ensuring they always have what they need to meet demand.

Next, we'll look at **Lead Time**, which affects when businesses should reorder stock.

Lead Time: The Key to Ordering at the Right Moment

In inventory management, knowing **when** to reorder stock is just as important as knowing **how much** to order. A business can't afford to wait until it completely runs out of stock before placing a new order. This is why understanding **lead time** is crucial.

Lead time refers to the amount of time it takes for an order to arrive after it has been placed. If a business does not account for lead time properly, it risks stockouts, production delays, and lost sales.

Several factors can influence how long it takes for inventory to arrive:

> - **Supplier processing time** – How quickly the supplier can prepare and ship the order.
> - **Shipping and transportation** – The time required to move goods from the supplier to the business.
> - **Customs or regulatory delays** – If importing goods, customs clearance can slow down deliveries.
> - **Seasonal demand fluctuations** – High-demand periods may cause suppliers to take longer to fulfill orders.

A business should always monitor its lead times and adjust its reorder levels accordingly.

To ensure stock never runs out while waiting for new inventory, businesses must calculate **Lead Time Demand**, which is the amount of stock needed during the waiting period.

The formula is:

Lead Time Demand = Average Daily Usage * Lead Time

Example: A hardware store sells 30 hammers per day on average, and it takes 7 days for a supplier to deliver new stock.

Lead Time Demand = 30 * 7 = 210 hammers

This means the store needs at least 210 hammers in stock when placing a new order to avoid running out before the new shipment arrives.

From an accounting perspective, lead time impacts cash flow, inventory turnover, and operational efficiency, by properly managing lead time, businesses can ensure that inventory arrives exactly when needed, **not too early, not too late**, keeping operations smooth and costs under control.

Next, we'll discuss **Stock Out Cost**, which explains the financial impact of running out of inventory.

Stock Out Cost: The Price of Running Out of Inventory

Every business relies on inventory to meet customer demand. But what happens when a business runs out of stock? This situation, called a **stockout**, can have serious financial consequences. **Stock Out Cost** refers to the losses a business incurs when it doesn't have enough inventory to fulfill orders.

When a business runs out of stock, the financial impact goes beyond just missing a sale. The most immediate consequence is **lost revenue and profit**, as potential customers who cannot find the product they need may **turn to competitors instead**. Since fixed costs remain the same regardless of sales volume, every lost transaction reduces overall profitability. Beyond direct financial losses, frequent stockouts can severely damage customer **trust and brand reputation**. If a business consistently fails to meet demand, customers may stop relying on it altogether, opting for competitors that can guarantee product availability. Over time, this can lead to the permanent loss of loyal customers, which is far more costly than a single missed sale.

To recover quickly from stockouts, companies often resort to **emergency restocking**, which typically involves placing urgent orders at **higher costs** or paying for expedited shipping. These additional expenses reduce profit margins and make inventory management less efficient. In manufacturing, the consequences of stockouts can be even more severe. A shortage of raw materials can halt production entirely, leading to missed deadlines, increased labor costs as workers remain idle, and potential penalties for failing to meet contractual obligations. The combined effects of lost sales, increased costs, and operational disruptions highlight why businesses must carefully manage their inventory to avoid stockouts and ensure a stable, efficient supply chain.

Stock out cost is not always easy to measure, but a common way to estimate it is:

$$\text{Stock Out Cost} = (\text{Lost Sales} \times \text{Profit per Unit}) + \text{Emergency Restocking Costs}$$

Example: A bicycle shop normally sells 20 bikes per day at a price of $500 each, with a profit of $100 per bike. Due to a stockout, the shop goes **5 days without bikes** to sell.

> - **Lost Sales:** 20×5=100 bikes
> - **Lost Profit:** 100×100=$10,000
> - **Emergency Restocking Costs:** $2,000 for express shipping

Total Stock Out Cost = 10,000 + 2,000 = $12,000

In this case, a single stockout results in a **$12,000 loss**, making it clear why avoiding stockouts is essential.

By understanding stock out costs, businesses can improve inventory planning, optimize reorder levels, and maintain customer satisfaction, all of which contribute to better financial performance and stability.

Budgeting

Few words strike fear into the heart of even the most organized manager like: *"It's time to prepare a budget."* The task can feel overwhelming, whether you're running a small family business or managing a mid-sized operation. However, a comprehensive and thorough budget is far from just a bureaucratic exercise, it's the key to **taking control of your financial future**.

Think of a budget as the compass guiding your business. Without it, you're navigating financial waters blindfolded. A good budget helps you:

> **Anticipate future needs** by predicting costs and income.
>
> **Align your goals with resources**, ensuring you're on track to achieve long-term plans.
>
> **Evaluate past performance**, offering insights into what's working and what needs adjusting.

Far from just a planning tool, budgeting also allows you to identify inefficiencies and areas for improvement. I recall working with a boutique retailer who avoided budgeting entirely, relying instead on "gut feelings." When we finally mapped out her expenses and revenues, she discovered a surplus of unsold inventory worth thousands. That simple exercise turned wasted resources into profit.

For budgeting to succeed, **everyone involved must be on board**—from the owners to the employees executing daily operations. A disorganized or uninterested leadership team can doom even the best intentions. To make it work, start with clear communication about the purpose and benefits of the budget.

Businesses often use one of two approaches to create a budget:

1. The Top-Down Approach

This method is especially popular in smaller businesses. Here, upper management drafts the budget based on their broad understanding of the company's needs and then incorporates input from relevant employees. It's quick and efficient, but it requires top-level leaders to have a firm grasp of the details.

2. The Bottom-Up Approach

Larger organizations tend to favor this collaborative model. Department managers prepare detailed resource requests that are then reviewed and approved by higher management. This creates a sense of ownership among team members but can be time-consuming.

If you're new to budgeting, don't overcomplicate it. Start by tracking your major sources of income and expenses over a few months. Use that data to create simple projections and identify patterns. Before you know it, you'll have a clearer view of your financial landscape—and a powerful tool to steer your business toward success.

Types of Budgets

Budgets are the glue that holds a business's financial strategy together, at the center of this process lies the **master budget**, which acts as the comprehensive blueprint for a company's financial planning. Think of the master budget as the umbrella under which all other specific budgets come together, each contributing insights into operating, investing, and financing activities.

The master budget is typically prepared annually or quarterly, depending on the needs of the business. Its creation involves a combination of detailed budgets that reflect the business's day-to-day operations and long-term goals. Let's break down the key components of these budgets.

Operating Budgets

Operating budgets are where the action happens. These budgets focus on the **core business activities** that keep operations running smoothly, including:

- **Sales Budgets**: Projections of revenue from selling goods or services.
- **Production Budgets**: Plans for how much product needs to be manufactured to meet sales targets.
- **Direct Materials and Labor Budgets**: Estimates of the resources, both raw materials and workforce, required for production.
- **Overhead Budgets**: Anticipated costs for supporting operations, like utilities and maintenance.

Each operating budget feeds into the overall financial picture, providing essential data for the **master budget**.

Financial Budgets

Financial budgets take a step back to look at the bigger picture. They offer a **projection of the company's financial future**, often in the form of "pro forma" financial statements, which rely on assumptions and estimates rather than confirmed data. The most common types include:

1. Budgeted Income Statement

This is essentially an income statement populated with **projections**. It's a tool to estimate revenue, expenses, and profit margins, allowing managers to anticipate how their decisions will impact the bottom line. Keeping the budgeted income statement aligned with the actual income statement format makes it easier to compare planned versus actual performance.

2. Budgeted Balance Sheet

This document projects what the company's assets, liabilities, and equity will look like at the end of a given period if the business follows its plan. The budgeted balance sheet often comes after other budgets, as it relies on their data for accuracy.

Leo Pet Supplies – Projected Budgeted Balance Sheet For Q4 2025

	ACCOUNT	AMOUNT ($)
1	ASSETS (Projected for 04 2025)	
2	Cash	12,000
3	Accounts Receivable	8,000
4	Inventory	10,000
5	Total Current Assets	30,000
6	Fixed Assets (Net of Depreciation)	50,000
7	TOTAL ASSETS	80,000
8	LIABILITIES AND EQUITY (Projected for Q4 2025)	
9	Accounts Payable	7,000
10	Short-term Loans	5,000
11	Total Current Liabilities	12,000
12	Long-term Debt	20,000
13	TOTAL LIABILITIES	32,000
14	Equity	
15	Retained Earnings	48,000
16	Total Equity	48,000
17	TOTAL LIABILITIES AND EQUITY	80,000

3. Cash Budget

The cash budget is a simplified version of the **statement of cash flows**. It projects cash inflows and outflows over a given period, helping the business ensure it has enough liquidity to meet its needs. Unlike formal cash flow statements, cash budgets are less rigid and more tailored for internal decision-making. For example, a small business might use a cash budget to track expected rent payments and income from seasonal sales in a straightforward table format.

Leo Pet Supplies Annual Marketing Budget

	Category	Annual Budget ($)
1	Online Advertising	24000
2	In-Store Promotions	14400
3	Social Media Campaigns	18000
4	Flyers and Brochures	9600
5	Local Events Sponsorship	12000
6	Radio Ads	7200
7	Community Workshops	4800
8	Other Print Media	8400

4. Marketing and Administrative Budgets: Allocations for promotion, customer outreach, and office management.

Pro Forma Financial Statements

Pro forma financial statements go beyond simple budgeting. They're used to explore "what if" scenarios, such as evaluating the financial outcomes of different growth strategies. For instance:

> - A company might create separate pro forma statements to analyze the effects of expanding into a new market versus investing in product development.
> - These statements allow business leaders to **visualize potential outcomes**, compare alternatives, and make informed decisions.

Here is an example of an Annual Marketing Budget for Leo Pet Supplies. This budget outlines the estimated yearly expenses allocated to various marketing activities, such as online advertising, in-store promotions, and local events sponsorship.

Specialized Budgets

Businesses often face situations that require more specific types of budgets to track and manage expenses effectively. While the **master budget** serves as the overarching financial plan, certain initiatives or investments demand focused budgeting tools tailored to the task. Below are some of these specialized budget types:

Capital Expenditure Budget

This budget is used to plan and manage spending on **capital assets** such as equipment, facilities, or long-term projects. For businesses making regular, significant investments, like a real estate developer purchasing land—it's essential to track these expenses over multiple years. A **capital expenditure budget** helps businesses forecast and prioritize their investments for maximum return.

For example, a veterinary clinic planning to expand its facility might use a capital expenditure budget to project costs over the next two years, including renovations, medical equipment, and new technology.

Program Budget

A **program budget** tracks expenses related to specific programs or initiatives within a company. This could be anything from employee training to a sustainability project.

Example:

Imagine a pet supply chain launching a customer service improvement initiative after receiving negative feedback from a survey. The program budget would include costs for training materials, workshops, and external consultants hired to improve staff skills. This ensures that all costs related to the initiative are consolidated and tracked efficiently.

Strategic Budget

The **strategic budget** is designed for long-term projects that align with a business's overarching goals. Unlike annual budgets, this type often spans multiple years to support **strategic initiatives** like launching a new product, entering a new market, or restructuring operations.

Example

A company planning to introduce a new line of eco-friendly pet toys could use a strategic budget to map out marketing, production, and distribution costs over three years. This would allow the business to evaluate the profitability and feasibility of its expansion plans.

Add-On Budget

An **add-on budget** builds upon the previous term's budget, modifying it to account for current changes without a full overhaul. Adjustments might include:

- Inflation
- Wage increases
- New compliance regulations

Example:

If Leo Pet Supplies sees a modest 3% increase in costs due to rising supplier prices, the existing budget can simply be updated to reflect these changes rather than being recreated from scratch. This approach saves time while ensuring the budget remains relevant.

Top Budgeting Software for Small and Medium Businesses

Selecting the appropriate budgeting software is crucial for small and medium-sized businesses (SMB) aiming to streamline financial planning and maintain fiscal health. Below is a curated list of top budgeting software options, along with their respective advantages and disadvantages (*from NerdWallet.com*):

1. QuickBooks Online

QuickBooks Online is a widely recognized accounting solution among SMBs in the United States. It offers comprehensive budgeting tools, including income and expense tracking, customizable financial reports, and integration with various financial institutions. The platform's user-friendly interface and scalability make it suitable for businesses of varying sizes. However, some users have reported that advanced features can be complex to navigate, and the cost may increase with the addition of premium functionalities.

2. X.ero

Xero is a cloud-based accounting software that provides robust budgeting and forecasting capabilities. It allows for real-time financial tracking, seamless bank reconciliation, and offers a wide range of third-party app integrations. Xero's intuitive design is particularly appealing to users without extensive accounting backgrounds. On the downside, certain advanced features may require additional fees, and customer support response times have been noted as an area for improvement.

3. Zoho Books

Zoho Books is part of the Zoho suite of business applications, offering a cost-effective solution for budgeting and financial management. It includes features such as automated workflows, multi-currency handling, and detailed financial reporting. The integration with other Zoho products enhances its utility for businesses already using the Zoho ecosystem. However, some users may find the initial setup process time-consuming, and certain advanced functionalities might be limited compared to other platforms.

4. PlanGuru

PlanGuru specializes in budgeting, forecasting, and performance review, making it a strong choice for businesses seeking in-depth financial analysis tools. It supports multi-year forecasting and offers over 20 standard forecasting methods. While PlanGuru provides powerful features, it may present a steeper learning curve for new users, and its pricing is on the higher end, which could be a consideration for smaller businesses.

5. Float

Float focuses on cash flow forecasting and management, integrating seamlessly with accounting software like QuickBooks and Xero. It provides real-time insights into cash flow, helping businesses make informed financial decisions. The platform's visual dashboards are user-friendly, but its functionality is primarily centered on cash flow, which may necessitate supplementary tools for comprehensive budgeting needs.

6. Odoo

Odoo is an open-source suite of business applications offering a comprehensive accounting and budgeting solution, particularly appealing due to its free access to essential accounting tools such as journal entries, ledgers, trial balances, and financial statements. While basic accounting features are free, advanced modules and specialized support in Odoo can incur extra costs, similar to Xero and QuickBooks. Overall, Odoo represents an excellent choice for SMBs willing to invest some initial setup time to benefit from its cost-effective, customizable approach to financial management.

More on Managerial Accounting: Tools and Techniques for Precision

Managerial accounting is a vast and versatile discipline, deeply shaped by the specific needs of different industries. Its lack of standardization offers flexibility but also means that it cannot be fully captured in a single textbook or guide. Below is an overview of additional key concepts and techniques in managerial accounting that are often encountered in practice.

Standard Costing

Standard costing is a method that uses **estimated costs** for tracking expenses such as cost of goods sold and gross profit. These estimates, often derived from historical data or projections, simplify the budgeting process and allow businesses to spot inefficiencies through the calculation of variances. For instance:

> ▸ An **unfavorable variance** occurs when actual costs exceed estimates.
>
> ▸ A **favorable variance** occurs when actual costs are lower than anticipated.

For example, a furniture manufacturer might estimate the cost of producing a table at $100. If the actual cost rises to $110, the variance is unfavorable, highlighting areas to investigate, such as higher material or labor costs.

Normal Costing

In contrast to standard costing, normal costing relies on **actual costs** for materials, labor, and overhead during production or service delivery. Variances can still occur, but the approach strives for more precision by using real-time data. When the variances are significant, adjustments must also be made to inventory accounts, not just cost of goods sold.

Activity-Based Costing (ABC)

Activity-based costing (ABC) takes a deeper dive into the costs of overhead. Unlike traditional costing methods that assign overhead based on broad measures like labor hours or machine time, ABC looks at all activities driving costs. This method is particularly useful in manufacturing.

For instance, a company producing standard air filters and customized specialty filters would recognize that specialty filters demand extra consultation, reconfiguration of machines, and custom packaging, all of which add to their actual cost. ABC ensures these costs are accounted for, offering more accurate pricing strategies.

Job Order Costing

Job order costing is used when products or services are highly customized, making it important to track costs by individual job or project. A construction firm building houses would allocate lumber, labor, and other expenses separately for each house. Similarly, law firms and accounting firms track billable hours and resources used for each client independently. This granular approach ensures precise billing and better cost control.

Work in Process (WIP) Accounting

In manufacturing, inventory isn't just raw materials or finished goods; there's often a middle ground called **Work in Process (WIP).** WIP accounting captures the value of partially completed products in the production cycle. This is essential for maintaining accurate inventory records and providing an up-to-date picture of production costs.

For instance, a car manufacturer might have 500 vehicles in production at various stages. WIP accounting ensures these semi-complete units are valued correctly in financial statements, reflecting their actual progress toward completion.

Make or Buy Analysis

Businesses frequently face the decision to either **make a product in-house** or **buy it from a supplier.** This process, called a make-or-buy analysis, evaluates costs but also considers factors such as control, quality, and strategic alignment.

For example, a retailer like Walmart may negotiate with suppliers, leveraging its scale to drive down prices. If a supplier's pricing is too high, Walmart might decide it's more cost-effective to produce the product itself. The decision often depends not only on financial factors but also on long-term strategic benefits.

Creativity in Managerial Accounting

Managerial accounting isn't just about applying formulas; it often requires **creativity and adaptability.** Each business, department, or project may present unique challenges requiring innovative solutions. Successful managerial accountants blend their technical knowledge with creative problem-solving to develop strategies that make a tangible impact.

For instance, a tech startup operating on a tight budget might implement a hybrid costing system combining elements of standard costing and activity-based costing to optimize their operations without overspending.

Decision-Making Scenarios

Now that you've gained a solid understanding of managerial accounting concepts like fixed costs, variable costs, and contribution margins, let's see how these principles actually help businesses make crucial financial decisions. In the following scenarios, you'll step into the shoes of real business owners facing everyday challenges, from deciding whether to manufacture products in-house or outsource them, to evaluating product profitability or pricing strategies.

Scenario 1: The Make-or-Buy Decision

Imagine you own a small, popular Italian restaurant known for its fresh pasta dishes. You've built a loyal customer base who love your authentic handmade pasta, but recently you're considering whether to continue making pasta in-house or buy ready-made pasta from an external supplier. This type of decision, known as a **make-or-buy decision**, is a common and crucial choice many businesses face.

To decide wisely, you need to clearly analyze your costs and benefits, applying the managerial accounting tools you've learned, particularly the distinction between fixed and variable costs, and the concept of contribution margins.

Currently, your monthly costs for producing fresh pasta internally are:

> **Variable Costs:**
>
> > Ingredients (flour, eggs): **$500**
> >
> > Direct labor (staff wages specifically for pasta making): **$300**

> **Fixed Costs (allocated to pasta production):**
>
> > Equipment rental (specialized pasta-making machine): **$200**
> >
> > Utilities (electricity, water used specifically for pasta-making): **$250**

Now, a local supplier offers to deliver freshly-made pasta directly to your restaurant for a fixed price of **$700 per month**. To make a clear comparison, let's summarize both alternatives into a simple statement:

Cost Comparison	Make Pasta (Internal)	Buy Pasta (External)
Variable Costs (ingredients, labor)	$500 + $300 = **$800**	Included in price
Fixed Costs (equipment, utilities)	$200 + $250 = **$450**	$0 (Not applicable)
Total Monthly Costs	$1,250	$700
Difference		Save $550 per month

This cost-comparison clearly illustrates the financial benefit of **purchasing externally.** However, let's briefly consider non-financial aspects too:

> **Quality & Branding:** If customers specifically come to your restaurant for homemade pasta, outsourcing might affect your brand image or customer loyalty negatively.

> **Control & Flexibility:** Making pasta internally gives you better control over quality and availability, whereas external purchasing depends on supplier reliability.

After considering both financial and non-financial aspects, your analysis using managerial accounting principles strongly suggests that, strictly from a financial standpoint, buying pasta externally is significantly more cost-effective (saving $550 monthly). Unless the potential negative impact on your restaurant's brand outweighs this financial advantage, outsourcing pasta production would be the wiser decision.

Scenario 2: Should You Keep or Replace a Declining Product?

Let's imagine you own a small gourmet coffee shop that's popular for its premium pastries and beverages. Over the past few years, one particular pastry, a special almond croissant, has been your top seller. However, lately you've noticed that demand is decreasing, profits from this pastry are declining, and you're considering whether to continue offering it or replace it with a new, trendy pastry that customers have requested.

To make an informed decision using managerial accounting principles, you'll analyze both options based on cost, revenue, and profitability.

First, let's look at your current almond croissant:

> - **Selling Price:** $4 per croissant
> - **Variable Cost:** $2.50 per croissant (ingredients, packaging, labor)
> - **Monthly Sales:** 500 croissants (previously 800, but sales have declined)
> - **Fixed Costs Allocated (like special baking equipment depreciation):** $400 per month

Your current contribution margin per croissant (selling price minus variable cost) is $1.50 ($4.00 − $2.50). With current monthly sales of 500 units, your total contribution margin is $1,250 (500 × $2.50 profit per croissant). After subtracting the $400 fixed cost, your net monthly profit from almond croissants is $850.

Now, let's say you have an opportunity to replace this almond croissant with a new pastry, a specialty cheesecake. You estimate monthly cheesecake sales at around 700 units. Here's the breakdown:

> - **Selling Price:** $5.00 per cheesecake slice
> - **Variable Cost:** $2.80 per slice (higher-quality ingredients, packaging, labor)

- **Monthly Sales (estimated):** 700 slices
- **Additional Fixed Costs Allocated (e.g., new refrigeration equipment):** $400 per month (same as almond croissants, because you'd use the same baking area and display case)

Using managerial accounting, let's compare clearly:

Product Profit Comparison

Item	Make Pasta (Internal)	Buy Pasta (External)
Monthly Sales Units	500 units	700 units
Selling Price per Unit	$4.00	$5.00
Variable Cost per Unit	$2.50	$2.00
Contribution Margin per Unit	$2.50	$3.00
Total Contribution Margin	$1,250 (500 * $2.50)	**$2,100 (700 * $3.00)**
Fixed Costs	$400	$400
Net Monthly Profit	**$850**	**$1,700**

From a pure cost-volume-profit standpoint, switching from almond croissants to cheesecakes clearly increases your monthly profit by $8,500.

But, there's more to consider than just the numbers. While cheesecake promises better profits, you must also weigh intangible factors. For example, loyal customers may associate your coffee shop with the almond croissant and might be disappointed to see it removed from your menu. Alternatively, adding the cheesecake may attract new customers, increasing overall foot traffic.

Scenario 3: Lease or Buy

Imagine you're opening a boutique clothing store in a prime spot downtown. The landlord presents you two tempting options: lease the store space for $3,200 monthly or buy the property with a mortgage, paying $2,500 per month plus $400 for maintenance and insurance, and an additional $400 monthly for property taxes, totaling $3,300 monthly.

At first glance, leasing seems slightly cheaper at $3,200 versus buying at $3,300 per month. However, let's thoroughly examine this scenario from a managerial accounting perspective, considering the long-term impacts, hidden costs, and strategic implications.

Detailed 5-Year Cost Analysis:

> **Leasing**: At $3,200 per month, over five years, you pay $192,000. Once this lease ends, you own nothing, and the landlord could significantly increase rent or not renew the lease.
>
> **Buying:** Over five years, mortgage payments total $150,000 ($2,500 × 60 months), maintenance/insurance costs $24,000, and property taxes cost $24,000. Thus, total buying costs amount to $198,000 over five years.

Although buying initially costs $6,000 more over five years, you must also consider the bigger picture:

With buying, each mortgage payment builds equity, making the property a valuable business asset. Owning provides long-term cost stability because mortgage payments remain constant. Additionally, buying offers significant tax advantages: you can deduct mortgage interest and depreciation expenses, lowering your taxable income and partially offsetting the higher initial costs.

However, buying also introduces important considerations related to flexibility and risk. If business slows down or you want to relocate, owning the property can limit your ability to adapt quickly. Selling the property in a hurry may force you to accept a lower price, potentially incurring financial losses. Conversely, leasing offers the advantage of flexibility—if your business circumstances change or you want to move to a better location, you can easily end your lease agreement without significant financial risk.

Here's a side-by-side comparison of these additional factors clearly outlined:

Factor	Leasing Option	Buying Option
Monthly Cost	Slightly lower ($3,200)	Slightly higher ($3,300)
Equity Building	None	Builds ownership equity
Tax Benefits	Lower	Higher (depreciation & interest)
Flexibility	Higher flexibility (easy to move)	Lower flexibility (long-term commitment)
Risk of Property Value Loss	None	Potential risk if market value declines
Long-Term Cost Stability	Lower (potential rent increases)	Higher (mortgage fixed)

In summary, leasing grants you the freedom to adapt quickly if market conditions change or your location no longer fits your needs. Buying, while potentially beneficial in building long-term value and gaining significant tax advantages, ties you financially and strategically to a specific property.

Scenario 4: Invest in New Machinery or Stick with Existing Equipment?

Imagine you own a small printing company specializing in promotional materials. Over the years, your trusted printing machine has reliably served your business, but lately, it's starting to show its age, maintenance costs keep climbing, energy bills are rising, and occasional machine failures slow down production. Now you're at a crossroads: **should you continue using your current machine, or is it time to invest in new, more efficient equipment?**

Your existing printer is still functioning, but its costs are starting to add up. Each month, you're paying:

- **Maintenance and Repairs:** $250 per month ($3,000 per year)
- **Energy Consumption:** $220 per month ($2,640 per year)
- **Lost Revenue Due to Inefficiency:** $100 per month ($1,200 per year)

Total Annual Cost of Keeping Your Old Machine: $6,840

At first glance, sticking with your current machine seems straightforward, no new investment needed. But let's see how it compares to buying new equipment.

A modern printing machine costs **$25,000**, which is definitely a significant upfront investment. However, it offers noticeable ongoing benefits:

- **Lower Maintenance Costs:** $100 per month ($1,200 per year)
- **Reduced Energy Consumption:** $180 per month ($2,160 per year)
- **Recovered Revenue from Efficiency (no delays):** $1,200 annually

Excluding depreciation, this new machine reduces your total annual operating costs to **$4,560** (1,200 + 2,160 + 1,200).

Because this equipment is a significant investment, you'll spread its cost over its useful life through **depreciation**. Assuming a useful life of 10 years and no salvage value, you use the straight-line depreciation method:

Annual Depreciation: $2,500 per year
Total Annual Cost Including Depreciation: $7,060

Depreciation itself isn't a cash expense, it's an accounting measure that helps spread the machine's cost across its useful life. Although it reduces your taxable income, it doesn't involve actual cash leaving your business.

Break-Even Analysis: let's look at how quickly you'll recover your initial $25,000 investment from the savings generated by the new equipment. First, calculate annual savings clearly:

Annual Savings = Cost of Old Machine - Cost of New Machine (excluding depreciation)

$6,840-$4,560=$2,280

With a **25% tax rate**, your annual tax savings (the tax shield) from depreciation would be:

$2,500×25%=$625 annually

This means that beyond your initial cost savings of $2,280 per year, you have an extra tax benefit of $625, bringing the total annual financial advantage to:

$2,280+$625=$2,905

Now, let's find out how long it takes to recoup your investment:

$$\text{Payback Period} = \frac{\text{Initial Investment}}{\text{Adjusted Annual Savings}} = \frac{\$25,000}{\$2,905} \approx 8.6 \text{ years}$$

This means you'll fully recover your initial investment in about **8.6 years**, after which you'll start benefiting fully from the savings each year.

Your final decision depends greatly on your business strategy and financial health. If you're planning to operate for at least another 10 years, investing in new equipment makes sense. The initial cost may feel significant, but the reduced operating expenses, improved efficiency, and tax benefits clearly pay off over time.

If your current cash position isn't strong, delaying the investment or exploring financing options (like leasing or loans) might be more prudent. These alternatives allow you to maintain healthier cash flow while still investing in your business's future.

Scenario 5: Offer Discounts to Boost Sales Volume or Maintain Regular Pricing?

Imagine you own a cozy clothing boutique that has recently noticed declining sales. You're faced with a decision: should you offer discounts to attract more customers, or is it wiser to maintain regular pricing and protect your profit margins?

This type of decision is exactly where managerial accounting shines. Let's clearly analyze this scenario, step-by-step, with easy-to-follow examples and friendly explanations.

Currently, your signature jackets sell for **$100 each**, and you typically sell about **50 jackets per month**. Each jacket costs you **$50** to produce, leaving you with a profit (or **contribution margin**) of $50 per jacket.

This scenario generates:

> - **Monthly revenue:** 50 jackets × $100 each = **$5,000**
> - **Cost of goods sold:** 50 jackets × $50 each = **$2,500**
> - **Gross profit:** $5,000 − $2,500 = **$2,500**

Now, let's evaluate what happens if you offer a 20% discount to boost your sales volume.

Suppose you introduce a 20% discount, bringing the price down from **$100 to $80 per jacket**. You estimate this lower price will boost monthly sales from **50 to 80 jackets**. Let's clearly see what happens financially:

> - **Monthly revenue:** 80 jackets × $80 each = **$6,400**
> - **Cost of goods sold:** 80 jackets × $50 each = **$4,000**
> - **Gross profit:** $6,400 − $4,000 = **$2,400**

Interestingly, although your total revenue increased, your gross profit actually **decreased** slightly by **$100** ($2,500 → $2,400). You're selling more jackets, but earning less per sale.

To understand this situation better, let's apply a break-even analysis to determine how many jackets you must sell at the discounted price to match your original gross profit ($2,500):

Contribution margin per jacket (regular price):

$$\text{Selling Price} - \text{Variable Cost} = \$100 - \$50 = \$50$$

$$\text{Break-Even Quantity} = \frac{\text{Fixed Costs}}{\text{Contribution Margin per Unit}}$$

$$\frac{\$1{,}500}{\$50} = 30 \text{ jackets}$$

Contribution margin per jacket (discounted price):

$$\$80 - \$50 = \$30$$

$$\frac{\$1{,}500}{\$30} = 50 \text{ jackets}$$

This clearly shows that if you offer the discount, you need to sell about **84 jackets** each month, 34 more than your original 50, to maintain the same profitability.

Offering discounts can seem attractive because you see immediate increases in sales volume. But when we apply what we've learned and do the calculation, we realize that the answer is more nuanced than we originally thought.

> **Cash Flow & Inventory Turnover:**
> Discounts can speed up inventory turnover, freeing up cash and reducing inventory holding costs. However, if the increased sales don't meet expectations (for example, less than 84 jackets), you risk reducing your overall profitability.
>
> **Customer Expectations & Brand Value:**
> Regular discounts can condition customers to wait for price cuts, potentially harming your brand's reputation and long-term pricing power. Customers might perceive your boutique as less premium, leading to future difficulties in maintaining higher prices.
>
> **Alternative Strategies:**
> Instead of a broad discount, consider targeted promotions, such as special sales events or limited-time promotions. These often boost sales without permanently impacting customer expectations or significantly harming profit margins.

Chapter 6 Assessment Test

1. **What is the primary focus of managerial accounting?**

    a. To generate reports for external stakeholders.

    b. To provide information for internal decision-making.

    c. To ensure compliance with financial reporting standards.

2. **Which of the following is an example of a fixed cost?**

    a. Wages paid to hourly workers.

    b. Rent for a warehouse.

    c. Cost of raw materials.

3. **What does the contribution margin represent?**

    a. The total revenue left after all costs are deducted.

    b. The portion of sales revenue available after covering variable costs.

    c. Fixed costs divided by total sales revenue.

4. **In Cost-Volume-Profit (CVP) analysis, what happens at the break-even point?**

    a. The company starts making a profit.

    b. Total revenue equals total costs.

    c. Fixed costs exceed total revenue.

5. **Which of the following is classified as a period cost?**

    a. Direct labor used in production.

    b. Rent for a company's headquarters.

    c. Cost of goods manufactured.

6. **What is the key distinction between product costs and period costs?**

    a. Product costs are directly tied to inventory, while period costs are expensed as incurred.

    b. Product costs fluctuate, whereas period costs remain constant.

c. Product costs apply to financial accounting, while period costs apply only to managerial accounting.

7. **In a multi-product CVP analysis, what is the sales mix?**
   a. The proportion of total revenue generated by each product.
   b. The ratio of variable costs to total sales revenue.
   c. The difference between sales volume and break-even sales.

8. **Which costing method assigns overhead costs based on actual activities rather than broad cost drivers like direct labor hours?**
   a. Job Order Costing.
   b. Activity-Based Costing (ABC).
   c. Absorption Costing.

9. **What formula is used to calculate the break-even point in units?**
   a. Fixed Costs ÷ Contribution Margin per Unit.
   b. Total Revenue ÷ Total Costs.
   c. Variable Costs ÷ Contribution Margin Ratio.

10. **What tool helps businesses decide whether to manufacture a product in-house or outsource production to a supplier?**
    a. Make-or-Buy Analysis.
    b. Job Order Costing.
    c. Standard Costing.

Answers

1. Correct Answer: b) To provide information for internal decision-making.
Managerial accounting focuses on helping business owners and managers make informed operational decisions rather than reporting to external stakeholders.

2. Correct Answer: b) Rent for a warehouse.
Fixed costs, like rent, do not fluctuate with production levels, whereas wages for hourly workers and raw materials are variable costs.

3. Correct Answer: b) The portion of sales revenue available after covering variable costs.
The contribution margin helps determine how much revenue is left to cover fixed costs and generate profit.

4. Correct Answer: b) Total revenue equals total costs.
At the break-even point, a company covers all fixed and variable costs but does not yet earn a profit.

5. Correct Answer: b) Rent for a company's headquarters.
Period costs are expensed immediately and are not directly tied to the production of inventory, unlike direct labor and manufacturing costs.

6. Correct Answer: a) Product costs are directly tied to inventory, while period costs are expensed as incurred.
Product costs include direct materials, labor, and overhead, while period costs (e.g., rent, advertising) are treated as expenses in the period they occur.

7. Correct Answer: a) The proportion of total revenue generated by each product.
Sales mix represents how much each product contributes to total revenue and is crucial in multi-product CVP analysis.

8. Correct Answer: b) Activity-Based Costing (ABC).
ABC assigns costs based on actual business activities, improving cost accuracy compared to traditional methods.

9. Correct Answer: a) Fixed Costs ÷ Contribution Margin per Unit.
This formula calculates the break-even point, the sales volume at which total revenue covers all costs.

10. Correct Answer: a) Make-or-Buy Analysis.
This tool helps businesses evaluate whether producing a product in-house or outsourcing is more cost-effective.

CHAPTER 7

Income Tax Accounting

> *The hardest thing in the world to understand is the income tax.*
>
> — *Albert Einstein,*
> *Nobel Prize-winning physicist*

Income tax accounting is a vital branch of accounting that ensures individuals, businesses, and even nonprofits comply with tax regulations while optimizing their financial position. The goal of tax accounting is simple: pay the least amount of money, while still remaining compliant according to the law.

It's often said that taxes are one of life's only certainties, which perhaps speaks to the enduring necessity of the tax-accounting profession. Every year, individuals file their tax returns, businesses calculate their tax liabilities, and even nonprofits report their financial activities to regulatory agencies like the **Internal Revenue Service (IRS)**. This ensures that taxes owed are paid and that exemptions, deductions, and credits are applied accurately.

For businesses, good tax accounting practices are about more than just compliance. They can also serve as a strategic tool. For example, small businesses can defer certain expenses or take advantage of tax credits to reduce their liability, allowing them to reinvest in growth.

Even organizations that don't pay taxes, such as charities, must engage in tax-related accounting. **Annual information returns** are often required to disclose how funds are raised and spent, ensuring transparency and accountability. For example:

> A nonprofit might need to show how much of its revenue goes toward program activities versus administrative costs.
>
> Donors often rely on these filings to confirm that their contributions are being used effectively.

In such cases, professional accountants ensure that these reports are accurate and comply with federal and state requirements.

Income tax accounting professionals must stay updated on ever-changing tax laws and regulations. They help individuals and businesses:

> File accurate returns.
>
> Identify potential deductions and credits.
>
> Plan strategies for reducing future tax burdens.

Whether it's a tax professional working with a family during tax season or a team of accountants handling the complex filings of a Fortune 500 company, the demand for this expertise is enormous. This demand also highlights why accounting remains one of the most stable and in-demand professions.

Marginal Tax Rate versus Average Tax Rate

For entrepreneurs and business owners, understanding the distinction between **marginal tax rate** and **average tax rate** is crucial when planning tax strategies and filing their returns. Both concepts are central to how income is taxed, especially in a **progressive tax system** like the one used for income taxes in most countries.

Marginal Tax Rate

The **marginal tax rate** refers to the rate of taxation applied to the next dollar earned within a given tax year. As income increases, the marginal tax rate changes, moving progressively higher as more income falls into higher brackets. This structure helps ensure that lower-income earners pay less tax on their essential income, while higher earners pay proportionally more on their additional income.

For example, let's imagine a small consulting business:

> The first $5,000 of income might be taxed at **0%**.
>
> The next $5,000 at **15%**.
>
> Any income over $10,000 at **20%**.

If the business earns $13,000, the first $5,000 is tax-free, the next $5,000 incurs $750 in taxes, and the final $3,000 incurs $600 in taxes. The **total tax owed is $1,350.**

A frequent misconception is that when income moves into a higher tax bracket, the entire amount earned is taxed at the higher rate, but this is not the case. Only the income within the higher bracket is taxed at the new rate, while income in lower brackets remains taxed at their respective rates.

Using our example, the $13,000 business earning does not retroactively tax the initial $5,000 at 20% when it enters the highest bracket. This misunderstanding can create unnecessary anxiety about earning more income. In reality, the **marginal tax rate encourages incremental income growth** by ensuring only the additional dollars are taxed at higher rates.

Average Tax Rate

The **average tax rate** reflects the proportion of total income paid in taxes. It is calculated by dividing total taxes owed by total income. In our example:

- $5,000 taxed at 0% = $0
- $5,000 taxed at 15% = $750
- $3,000 taxed at 20% = $600

The total tax of $1,350 divided by $13,000 of income results in an **average tax rate of 10.4%.**

Unlike the marginal tax rate, which escalates with income, the average tax rate gives a cumulative view of how much of total earnings are lost to taxes.

The Progressive Tax System

This system of increasing marginal tax rates is known as a **progressive tax system**, where higher earners pay a greater proportion of their income in taxes. It's designed to balance fairness, ensuring that individuals with lower incomes retain more of their money for essential needs.

For instance, someone earning $5,000 annually may see their income taxed at a lower rate, or not taxed at all, because that money is vital for basic survival. Conversely, someone earning $5,000,000 can afford to pay a higher marginal tax rate on additional income without sacrificing necessities.

A **regressive tax system** works in the opposite way, taking a larger percentage of income from low earners. Sales tax is a good example.

- A person earning $5,000 annually who spends $2,500 on goods at a 10% sales tax rate pays $250 in taxes, which is **5% of their total income.**

> A person earning $5,000,000 who spends the same amount also pays $250, but this represents only **0.005% of their income.**

Regressive systems disproportionately burden lower-income individuals, making them less equitable compared to progressive systems.

Accrual or Cash Accounting for Income Tax Purposes?

When it comes to income tax reporting, businesses must decide whether to use **accrual basis accounting** or **cash basis accounting**, depending on their revenue levels and the nature of their operations. This decision can significantly impact how and when income and expenses are recognized, ultimately influencing taxable income.

Cash Basis Accounting: Simplicity for Small Businesses

Cash basis accounting is often the go-to method for small businesses, particularly those earning less than $25 million over previous 3 yrs. Under this approach:

> - **Revenue** is recognized when cash is received.
> - **Expenses** are deducted only when they are paid.

For example, let's consider a small bakery. If it invoices $5,000 for catering services in December but doesn't receive payment until January, that $5,000 isn't taxed until the next fiscal year. Similarly, the bakery can't deduct the cost of flour purchased on credit until it actually pays the supplier.

This simplicity makes cash accounting appealing for businesses with straightforward operations and minimal inventory. It aligns with cash flow, making it easier for business owners to understand their financial position at any given time.

Accrual Basis Accounting: A Requirement for Larger Businesses

Businesses earning more than $10 million annually (on average) over the previous three years are required by the **IRS** to use **accrual basis accounting**. Under this method:

> - **Revenue** is recognized when goods are delivered or services performed, even if payment hasn't been received.
> - **Expenses** are deducted when incurred, even if they haven't been paid.

For example, a tech consulting firm that completes a $50,000 project in December must report that income for the current year, even if the client doesn't pay until February. Similarly, it can deduct the $10,000 cost of subcontracted work in December, even if it hasn't yet paid the subcontractor.

The accrual method provides a more accurate picture of profitability, especially for businesses with delayed cash inflows or outflows. However, it requires careful tracking of accounts receivable and payable, which can add complexity.

Inventory and Mixed Methods

Businesses that maintain inventory, like retailers or manufacturers, are generally required to use **accrual accounting** for inventory-related expenses, regardless of their revenue levels. The **IRS mandates** that inventory expenses align closely with revenue from inventory sales.

For instance, a bicycle shop selling 50 bikes from its inventory must deduct the cost of those bikes as they are sold, not when the bikes were purchased. This ensures that profit calculations reflect actual sales activity.

Interestingly, businesses may still use cash accounting for non-inventory expenses, creating a **hybrid approach** that combines simplicity with compliance.

FIFO and LIFO Inventory Methods

When accounting for inventory, businesses can choose between **FIFO (First-In, First-Out)** and **LIFO (Last-In, First-Out)** methods:

- **FIFO:** Assumes the oldest inventory is sold first. This method generally results in higher net profits during inflationary periods because older, lower-cost inventory is matched with revenue.
- **LIFO:** Assumes the newest inventory is sold first. This reduces net profit during inflationary periods because higher-cost inventory is deducted, lowering taxable income.

For example:

- A tire retailer buys 1,000 tires at $40 each, then another 1,000 at $42 each.
- Under FIFO, the cost of goods sold for the first 1,000 tires is $40 per tire.
- Under LIFO, the cost of goods sold for the same 1,000 tires is $42 per tire.

LIFO is better suited for businesses in inflation-prone industries like fuel or manufacturing, where inventory costs rise significantly over time. It helps reduce tax liabilities and improve cash flow.

FIFO works best for businesses handling perishable or time-sensitive goods, ensuring that older stock is sold first and the balance sheet aligns with real-world inventory practices.

Example: Using LIFO (Last-In, First-Out)

Business: A Retail Gas Station Chain

Scenario:

A gas station purchases fuel at fluctuating prices due to volatile oil markets. In January, it buys 10,000 gallons at $3.00 per gallon, and in February, it buys 10,000 more gallons at $3.50 per gallon. Fuel prices are expected to rise steadily.

Reason for Using LIFO:

The gas station opts for the LIFO method to reduce its taxable income. By assuming that the most recent, higher-cost inventory is sold first, the cost of goods sold (COGS) reflects the $3.50 per gallon price, which increases expenses and lowers reported profit.

Benefit:

- **Tax Reduction:** During inflationary periods, LIFO minimizes net profit on paper, reducing the amount of taxes owed.
- **Cash Flow Preservation:** The business retains more cash to reinvest, such as upgrading pumps or expanding to new locations.

Limitation:

For public financial reporting, LIFO may show lower profitability, which might deter investors if the business is publicly traded.

Example: Using FIFO (First-In, First-Out)

Business: A Fresh Produce Distributor

Scenario:

A distributor sells perishable items like fruits and vegetables. In January, it buys 1,000 crates of apples at $20 per crate, and in February, it buys another 1,000 crates at $25 per crate. Inventory turnover is rapid because produce has a short shelf life.

Reason for Using FIFO:

The distributor uses FIFO because it assumes the oldest inventory (January's $20 crates) is sold first. This method aligns with the physical flow of goods, ensuring that the first crates to enter storage are also the first to leave, minimizing spoilage.

Benefit:

> - **Accurate Profit Representation:** FIFO aligns with actual inventory movement and shows higher profits when prices are rising, appealing to investors.
> - **Simplicity:** For perishable goods, FIFO reflects the natural order in which items are sold.

Limitation:

FIFO can lead to higher taxable income during inflationary periods, increasing the tax burden. However, for this distributor, the benefits of accurate representation and reduced spoilage likely outweigh this disadvantage.

Balancing IRS Rules and GAAP

Income tax reporting is governed by the **IRS**, while financial reporting for public or investor purposes is governed by **GAAP**. This distinction means that businesses may present their finances differently depending on the audience. For example, a company might use LIFO for tax purposes to reduce taxable income and FIFO for public reporting to appeal to investors.

This flexibility allows businesses to optimize their strategies, but it also requires a strong understanding of both regulatory frameworks. Accountants must navigate these rules carefully to ensure compliance while maximizing financial benefits.

Tax Deductions vs. Tax Credits

When it comes to managing taxes, it's crucial to distinguish between **tax deductions** and **tax credits**. Both can significantly lower the amount of taxes owed, but they function in very different ways.

Tax Deductions

A **tax deduction** reduces your taxable income, which in turn lowers the amount of tax you owe based on your applicable marginal tax rate. For businesses, common tax deductions include:

- Operating expenses like **supplies, advertising, and rent**.
- Contributions to employee benefit plans such as health and retirement programs.
- Payments for professional services, including accounting or legal advice.

Example:

Imagine a shoeshine business with $9,000 in income under a marginal tax system:

- The first $5,000 is taxed at 0%, and the remaining $4,000 is taxed at 15%, resulting in a $600 tax liability.
- If the business qualifies for a $1,000 deduction, its taxable income drops to $8,000. Now, only $3,000 is taxed at 15%, reducing the tax owed to $450—a savings of $150.

It's important to note that **tax deductions are not a dollar-for-dollar reduction in taxes owed**. They merely reduce the portion of income subject to taxation. For example, a $1,000 deduction in a 15% tax bracket saves only $150 in taxes. This common misunderstanding can lead to overestimating the value of a deduction.

Tax Credits

A **tax credit**, on the other hand, provides a **dollar-for-dollar reduction** in the total tax bill. Tax credits are particularly valuable because they reduce taxes owed directly, regardless of the taxpayer's income or marginal tax rate.

Example:

If our shoeshine business receives a $500 tax credit instead of a $1,000 deduction:

- Its original tax liability of $600 drops directly to $100, resulting in a $500 savings.
- By contrast, the $1,000 deduction only reduced the tax bill from $600 to $450, illustrating the greater impact of a credit.

Tax credits are often used as incentives to promote specific behaviors or investments that benefit society, such as renewable energy or employee benefits.

Examples of Common Tax Credits

The government frequently offers tax credits to encourage activities it deems beneficial. Some examples include:

> **Renewable Energy Credits:** For businesses or individuals investing in solar panels or other green energy technologies.
>
> **Small Business Health Insurance Credit:** For businesses covering at least 50% of employees' health insurance costs.
>
> **Accessibility Improvement Credits:** For making business sites accessible to individuals with disabilities.
>
> **Research and Development Credits:** For businesses investing in innovation and new technologies.

Key Differences at a Glance

Tax Deductions	Tax Credits
Reduces taxable income.	Directly reduces the tax bill.
Value depends on the marginal tax rate.	Value is a dollar-for-dollar savings.
Example: A $1,000 deduction saves $150 in a 15% tax bracket.	Example: A $1,000 credit saves $1,000 in taxes owed.
Common deductions include operating expenses and employee benefits.	Common credits encourage specific investments, like renewable energy or employee healthcare.

Long-Term Capital Gains vs. Ordinary Income

When it comes to reducing tax liabilities, the distinction between **long-term capital gains** and **ordinary income** plays a pivotal role. For individuals and businesses, understanding these categories can lead to significant tax savings and smarter financial decisions.

Ordinary Income

Ordinary income is what most of us are familiar with, it's the money earned from regular work or services. This includes wages, salaries, tips, commissions, and bonuses. Ordinary income is taxed at the **marginal tax rate**, which can climb significantly as income increases.

For example, a friend of mine who runs a small catering business earns $60,000 annually in wages. She also collects a commission for managing event bookings. All of this is taxed as ordinary income at progressively higher rates as her earnings grow. While rewarding, her business success also comes with a hefty tax bill.

Long-Term Capital Gains

Capital gains refer to profits from selling investments like stocks, bonds, or real estate at a higher price than their purchase cost. For these gains to qualify as **long-term**, the investment must be held for at least **one year** before being sold.

Here's the advantage: Long-term capital gains are taxed at **lower rates** than ordinary income. For example, if that same friend from the catering business decided to invest $10,000 in stocks and sold them two years later for $15,000, the $5,000 profit would be taxed at the lower long-term capital gains rate, not her ordinary income tax rate.

Why this discrepancy? The government encourages **capital investment** because it fuels economic growth and job creation. By offering a lower tax rate on long-term gains, they incentivize individuals and businesses to invest.

Comparing Tax Rates

The difference in tax rates between ordinary income and long-term capital gains can be substantial. For example:

> - Ordinary income for high earners might be taxed at rates as high as **37%**.
> - Long-term capital gains for the same group might be taxed at **20% or less**.

This gap represents a major opportunity for tax savings. A large corporation or wealthy individual can save millions by strategically classifying income as capital gains rather than ordinary income.

Many accountants and businesses actively look for ways to convert ordinary income into capital gains to take advantage of these lower rates. Some common strategies include:

> 1. **Real Estate Investments:** Selling property held for more than a year allows businesses and individuals to classify the profit as long-term capital gains. For example, a property development company I know strategically holds its properties for over a year to qualify for lower tax rates when selling.
> 2. **Selling Depreciable Assets:** Businesses can sell equipment or assets they no longer need and, in some cases, classify part of the proceeds as capital gains. For instance, a construction company might

> sell an old bulldozer, recognizing some of the profit as a capital gain rather than ordinary income.
> 3. **Stock Investments:** Holding onto stocks or mutual funds for over a year before selling ensures the gains qualify for long-term rates. This approach encourages patience and long-term financial planning.
> 4. **Capital Loss Carryovers:** If an investor incurs a capital loss in one year, they can carry it forward to offset future gains, reducing overall tax liability.

Why the Government Encourages Capital Gains

The lower tax rates on long-term capital gains reflect the government's desire to promote **economic growth**. By rewarding investment, the policy aims to:

> - Stimulate job creation.
> - Drive innovation.
> - Expand the economy.

However, this disparity in rates also fuels a robust industry of accountants and financial advisors who specialize in finding creative, **legal ways to reclassify income.**

Why Business Entity Type Matters: A Tax Perspective

The choice of **business entity type** has a profound impact on how a business is taxed, and understanding these differences is essential for business owners seeking to optimize their tax liability. Each entity type—from sole proprietorships to LLCs and corporations—comes with unique tax implications that can influence how much income is retained and how much is owed to the government.

Pass-Through Taxation

Most small business entities, such as **sole proprietorships, partnerships, LLCs, and S corporations**, are typically subject to **pass-through taxation**. This means that the profits (or losses) of the business are not taxed at the business level. Instead, they "pass through" to the owners and are reported on their personal income tax returns.

For example, imagine a **single-owner LLC** that earns $100,000 in net income. The LLC itself doesn't pay taxes on this amount. Instead, the owner includes the $100,000 as personal income on their tax return and pays income tax according to their personal tax bracket. This can be advantageous for avoiding **corporate taxes** but may result in higher taxes for the individual if their business income pushes them into a higher bracket.

I once worked with a friend who operated a small bakery as an LLC. At the end of her first year, she was surprised to learn that even though her business didn't directly pay taxes, she owed a significant amount because her $70,000 profit increased her personal taxable income. This underscores the importance of understanding how **pass-through taxation** works.

C Corporations: The Double Taxation Dilemma

C corporations operate differently. Unlike pass-through entities, the C corporation is taxed as a **separate entity**. When a C corporation earns $100,000 in net income:

1. The corporation pays corporate taxes on its income, typically at a lower rate than personal income taxes.
2. If the remaining profits are distributed as **dividends** to shareholders, those dividends are taxed again on the shareholder's personal tax return.

This phenomenon, known as **double taxation**, often deters small business owners from choosing a C corporation structure. However, C corporations have their benefits:

- Retained earnings can remain in the business without incurring additional taxes, which is ideal for companies planning to reinvest in growth.
- Corporate tax rates are often lower than personal rates, making this structure appealing for larger companies with high profits.

For instance, a tech startup earning $500,000 might prefer to operate as a C corporation to take advantage of lower corporate tax rates, reinvest the bulk of its profits, and minimize dividend payouts.

S Corporations: A Hybrid Approach

S corporations offer a middle ground. They are treated as **pass-through entities** for tax purposes, meaning profits are taxed on the owners' personal returns, similar to an LLC. However, they come with certain restrictions:

- Owners must pay themselves a "reasonable salary," which is subject to payroll taxes.
- Shareholder numbers are capped, and ownership is limited to U.S. citizens or residents.

An S corporation can be advantageous for small businesses with multiple shareholders, as it avoids double taxation while still offering flexibility in profit distribution.

Comparing Tax Implications

Here's how $100,000 in net income might be taxed under three different structures (based on general U.S. tax principles):

Entity Type	Tax Level	Tax Implications
LLC (Single – Owner)	Pass-through to owner	$100/000 taxed as personal income; no corporate tax.
S Corporation	Pass-through to owner(s)	Profit divided among owners; personal income tax applies.
C Corporation	Entity level + dividends	Corporate tax on $100000; dividends taxed separately if distributed.

For example:

> - An LLC owner reports the $100,000 as personal income, paying taxes at their marginal rate.
> - An S corporation owner splits income between a salary and dividends, with the latter taxed at lower rates.
> - A C corporation pays corporate taxes on the $100,000, and if dividends are issued, those are taxed again.

Choosing the right business entity involves more than just tax considerations. It depends on:

> - **Business goals:** Are you reinvesting profits or prioritizing personal income?
> - **Ownership structure:** How many owners are involved, and what level of liability protection is needed?
> - **Growth plans:** Do you expect to attract investors or keep operations small?

For a small coffee shop with steady earnings, an LLC might provide the simplicity and flexibility needed. Conversely, a manufacturing firm planning to scale operations might benefit from the reinvestment opportunities offered by a C corporation.

By understanding the tax implications of different structures, business owners can make informed decisions that align with their financial goals and minimize unnecessary tax burdens.

Chapter 7 Assessment Test

1. **What is the primary purpose of income tax accounting?**

   a. To prepare financial statements for external stakeholders.

   b. To ensure compliance with tax regulations while optimizing tax obligations.

   c. To maximize profits by avoiding taxes.

2. **What is the marginal tax rate?**

   a. The average rate of tax paid on total income.

   b. The rate applied to the next dollar earned.

   c. The total tax divided by total income.

3. **In a progressive tax system, which of the following is true?**

   a. Higher earners pay a greater percentage of their income in taxes.

   b. All earners pay the same percentage of their income.

   c. Lower earners pay a higher percentage of their income in taxes.

4. **What is the difference between accrual basis accounting and cash basis accounting?**

   a. Accrual basis records income and expenses when cash is received or paid; cash basis records them when earned or incurred.

   b. Accrual basis records income and expenses when earned or incurred; cash basis records them when cash is received or paid.

   c. There is no difference; both methods record transactions the same way.

5. **Which inventory accounting method matches older inventory costs with revenue?**

   a. LIFO (Last-In, First-Out)

   b. FIFO (First-In, First-Out)

   c. Weighted Average Cost

6. What is a major advantage of the LIFO inventory method during inflationary periods?

   a. It minimizes taxable income.
   b. It maximizes net income.
   c. It simplifies inventory tracking.

7. What is the primary difference between tax deductions and tax credits?

   a. Deductions reduce taxable income; credits reduce taxes owed directly.
   b. Deductions reduce taxes owed directly; credits reduce taxable income.
   c. Both have the same effect on taxes owed.

8. Which of the following income types is taxed at a lower rate?

   a. Ordinary income.
   b. Short-term capital gains.
   c. Long-term capital gains.

9. How are profits taxed in a pass-through entity like an LLC?

   a. At the business level only.
   b. At both the business and personal levels (double taxation).
   c. At the owner's personal income tax rate.

10. Why might a business choose a C corporation structure?

    a. To avoid corporate taxes entirely.
    b. To reinvest profits without incurring additional taxes.
    c. To simplify tax filing processes.

Answers

1. What is the primary purpose of income tax accounting?

Correct Answer: b) To ensure compliance with tax regulations while optimizing tax obligations.
Income tax accounting focuses on compliance with tax laws and finding ways to reduce tax liabilities within legal limits.

2. What is the marginal tax rate?

Correct Answer: b) The rate applied to the next dollar earned.
The marginal tax rate applies to the next dollar of income, reflecting the progressive nature of the tax system.

3. In a progressive tax system, which of the following is true?

Correct Answer: a) Higher earners pay a greater percentage of their income in taxes.
Progressive tax systems ensure higher income earners pay more, promoting fairness by taxing additional income at higher rates.

4. What is the difference between accrual basis accounting and cash basis accounting?

Correct Answer: b) Accrual basis records income and expenses when earned or incurred; cash basis records them when cash is received or paid.
Accrual accounting aligns income and expenses with the period they occur, while cash basis focuses on actual cash transactions.

5. Which inventory accounting method matches older inventory costs with revenue?

Correct Answer: b) FIFO (First-In, First-Out)
FIFO assumes the oldest inventory is sold first, aligning with actual inventory flow in many businesses.

6. What is a major advantage of the LIFO inventory method during inflationary periods?

Correct Answer: a) It minimizes taxable income.
By matching higher-cost inventory with revenue, LIFO reduces net income and lowers tax liabilities during inflation.

7. What is the primary difference between tax deductions and tax credits?

Correct Answer: a) Deductions reduce taxable income; credits reduce taxes owed directly.
Deductions lower taxable income, while credits directly lower the amount of tax owed, making credits more valuable.

8. Which of the following income types is taxed at a lower rate?

Correct Answer: c) Long-term capital gains.
Long-term capital gains are taxed at a lower rate to encourage long-term investments.

9. How are profits taxed in a pass-through entity like an LLC?

Correct Answer: c) At the owner's personal income tax rate.
Pass-through entities don't pay taxes at the business level; instead, profits are taxed on the owner's personal return.

10. Why might a business choose a C corporation structure?

Correct Answer: b) To reinvest profits without incurring additional taxes.
C corporations can retain earnings for reinvestment without being taxed again, unlike pass-through entities where profits are taxed immediately.

CHAPTER 8

ACCOUNTING FOR INVESTORS

"*Price is what you pay.
Value is what you get.*"

— *Warren Buffett,
Investor and Philanthropist*

Previously, we looked at accounting through the lens of a small business owner, someone deeply involved in the daily grind of decision-making. Now, we're stepping into the shoes of an **outside investor**, someone focused on evaluating opportunities to buy into a business, property, or other assets without being tied to the day-to-day operations.

Through financial statements and reports, accounting tells the story of a company's health, potential, and risks. Questions such as "Can this business sustain its profitability?" or "Does it have enough liquidity to weather tough times?" can be answered through sound financial reporting.

But to make sense of this information, investors need a common language, and that's where **GAAP**—the Generally Accepted Accounting Principles—comes in.

GAAP

GAAP (Generally Accepted Accounting Principles) serves as the foundation of financial reporting in the United States. It was established to ensure consistency, transparency, and fairness in the way businesses present their financial information. For investors, accountants, and regulators alike, GAAP provides the "rules of the game," making financial data comparable across companies and industries.

The Importance of Standardization

Investors rely on financial statements to make informed decisions, and **consistency** is key. Without uniform rules, companies could manipulate their reports, broadening definitions of income or narrowing expenses, to make their financial health appear better than it is. Imagine trying to compare two companies, one counting non-operational revenue as income while the other does not. It would be like comparing apples to oranges, making informed investment decisions nearly impossible.

GAAP ensures that businesses report income, expenses, and other financial metrics in a **standardized format**, creating **apples-to-apples comparisons**. This standardization is not only important for investors but also for tax authorities like the IRS. Without GAAP, auditors would waste time deciphering each company's unique methods, adding unnecessary complexity to the system.

To address this need for consistency, the **U.S. Securities and Exchange Commission (SEC)** requires publicly traded companies to adhere to GAAP. These rules establish a framework that:

1. Protects investors by ensuring reliable financial information.
2. Supports accountants by providing a clear, universal standard for their work.
3. Simplifies financial oversight by regulators and tax authorities.

For accountants, proficiency in GAAP makes them highly employable, as the demand for professionals skilled in these standards is widespread.

GAAP Hierarchy

The **GAAP hierarchy** serves as a framework that helps accountants determine which authoritative guidance to follow when preparing financial statements. While GAAP outlines the principles and rules for financial reporting, the hierarchy provides a structured **roadmap** for interpreting and applying these principles, ensuring consistency across businesses.

Introduced by the **Financial Accounting Standards Board (FASB)**, the GAAP hierarchy prioritizes different levels of guidance to ensure that accountants use the most reliable and applicable standards. It's essentially a ranking system for accounting rules, ensuring that businesses adhere to the most authoritative guidance available in any given situation.

The Levels of GAAP Hierarchy

1. **Level 1: Authoritative Guidance.** This is the most authoritative level, encompassing standards issued by governing bodies like FASB, the **Securities and Exchange Commission (SEC)** for public companies, and other official accounting boards. These include:
    - Statements of Financial Accounting Standards (SFAS)
    - Accounting Standards Updates (ASUs)
    - Interpretations, staff positions, and EITF (Emerging Issues Task Force) consensuses.
2. **Level 2: General Industry Practices.** If no authoritative guidance exists, accountants turn to established practices specific to their industry. For example, a hospital might rely on industry-specific recommendations for valuing medical equipment.
3. **Level 3: Interpretations and Recommendations.** In the absence of industry-specific rules, accountants consult widely accepted interpretations or recommendations from reliable accounting literature, such as:
    - Non-authoritative articles or white papers published by accounting professionals.
    - Standards proposed but not officially adopted.
4. **Level 4: Professional Judgment.** When no formal guidance exists, accountants use their professional expertise and ethical judgment to ensure that financial reporting remains fair, consistent, and transparent.

Smaller Businesses and GAAP

While smaller businesses may not need to follow every specific GAAP rule, they benefit from adhering to the broader principles of good accounting practice. These principles ensure accurate record-keeping, clear financial communication, and effective management of resources.

Small business owners should familiarize themselves with what is often referred to as **"The House of GAAP."** This metaphorical house is supported by:

1. **Four Principles:** These columns uphold the integrity of GAAP and include concepts like relevance and reliability in financial reporting.
2. **Four Assumptions:** These foundational ideas include accrual accounting and going concern, which form the base upon which financial statements are prepared.

3. **Two Constraints:** These act as stabilizers, ensuring the cost of reporting does not outweigh its benefits and that information is not overly complex or difficult to understand.

The Four Accounting Principles

1. The Measurement Principle

This principle defines how the value of an asset is recorded. GAAP relies on two primary methods:

- **Historical Cost Principle**: Assets are always recorded at their original purchase price. For instance, imagine a bakery purchasing an industrial oven for $20,000 after negotiating down from $22,000. Regardless of its sticker price or any future appreciation, the oven must be recorded at $20,000. Even if the oven's resale value climbs to $25,000 due to increased demand, the books reflect only its historical cost, ensuring consistency in reporting.

- **Fair Value Principle**: This method applies when an asset's market value is readily available. For example, a pet store investing in shares of a popular pet food company would report those stocks at their current market value, as this figure is easily accessible and reflects the true worth of the investment.

Adjustments: Depreciation is allowed under the measurement principle to reflect an asset's declining value over time. Imagine that bakery's industrial oven depreciating $2,000 annually due to wear and tear. However, assets like land are typically not adjusted upwards for appreciation, adhering to the conservative nature of GAAP.

2. The Revenue Recognition Principle

Revenue is recognized when it's **earned**, not necessarily when cash changes hands. This principle provides a clearer view of a business's financial activity.

Imagine a landscaping company completing $50,000 worth of projects in a month but only receiving $35,000 in payments by month's end. GAAP requires the full $50,000 to be recognized as revenue, with the unpaid $15,000 recorded as **accounts receivable**.

But what if some customers don't pay? Say $3,000 of that $15,000 is deemed uncollectible. The company would adjust its accounts receivable and record the loss as a "bad debt expense," ensuring its financial statements reflect the true state of its receivables.

This principle also recognizes revenue beyond cash, such as bartered goods or services. For example, a yoga studio offering free classes in exchange for cleaning services would record revenue equivalent to the market value of the classes provided.

3. The Expense Recognition Principle

Expenses must be reported in the same period as the revenues they help generate. This principle ties closely to the **matching principle**, creating logical, aligned income statements.

Consider a clothing retailer that spends $10,000 on advertising for a spring collection. The retailer's sales spike by $50,000 in April due to the campaign. Under GAAP, the $10,000 in advertising expenses must be reported in April, the same period the revenue was earned. This alignment ensures that the financial statements clearly show the connection between the expense and the benefit it generated.

Without this principle, businesses might distort their earnings by delaying expenses, making financial reports less meaningful for investors and stakeholders.

4. The Full Disclosure Principle

Transparency is the cornerstone of this principle. Businesses must disclose all relevant information that could impact how users interpret their financial statements.

For example, imagine a restaurant preparing its financials while negotiating a new lease. If the new lease will triple its rent, the restaurant must include this information as a **footnote** in its financial statements. This disclosure provides a clearer picture of the business's future financial obligations, which is critical for lenders or investors evaluating the restaurant's profitability.

Disclosures might also cover legal risks, changes in accounting policies, or significant upcoming expenditures. This principle builds trust and ensures no critical detail is hidden from stakeholders.

The Four Accounting Assumptions

The **Four Accounting Assumptions** act as the foundation for all financial reporting. They aren't just technical rules, they're the guiding principles that ensure financial statements are meaningful, standardized, and easy to interpret.

1. The Going Concern Assumption

This assumption is built on the idea that a business will continue to operate for the foreseeable future, rather than closing or being sold. It's a way of saying, "We expect this company to keep running, so we'll value its assets accordingly."

Here's a simple analogy: Imagine you're running a coffee shop. You've invested in a high-end espresso machine for $10,000. If your coffee shop is thriving, the machine is seen as an asset helping you generate revenue. But if you decide to close the shop tomorrow, the machine would likely need to be sold at a lower "liquidation" price. The **going concern assumption** allows accountants to avoid treating your business as if it's shutting down, keeping financial statements focused on growth and continuity.

If a business is struggling and might not survive, accountants are required to disclose this uncertainty. For instance, when a friend's family bakery faced declining sales during a tough year, their financial statements clearly mentioned that their ability to continue depended on securing additional funding. This transparency helped investors understand the risks.

2. The Monetary Unit Assumption

The monetary unit assumption ensures that all financial transactions are recorded in a stable, measurable unit—typically the currency of the country where the business operates. For businesses in the U.S., this means using U.S. dollars.

Imagine a small tech startup that's doing business in both the U.S. and Europe. While their European clients pay in euros, their accounting team converts everything into dollars for their financial reports. Why? Because it's impossible to add or compare different currencies directly without converting them. The **monetary unit assumption** ensures that all financial data is expressed in a common language that's easy to understand.

However, this assumption has its limits. It doesn't account for inflation or changes in purchasing power. For instance, a $10,000 investment made ten years ago would still be reported as $10,000 today, even though its real value might be different.

3. The Business Entity Assumption

One of the most critical assumptions, the business entity assumption, draws a clear line between personal and business finances. This is especially important for small business owners, who sometimes mix the two without realizing the trouble it can cause.

For example, I once helped a friend who owned a dog grooming business. She was using the business account to pay for personal expenses like her Netflix subscription and even groceries. When tax season arrived, her accountant had to untangle the mess to separate personal spending from legitimate business expenses. The **business entity assumption** demands that a business be treated as a completely separate "person" for financial purposes. This not only protects the business's financial integrity but also makes it easier to track performance and taxes.

4. The Time Period Assumption

The time period assumption breaks a company's operations into regular intervals—such as months, quarters, or years—for the purpose of reporting. This makes it easier for stakeholders to analyze the business's performance over time.

Imagine you're managing a small clothing boutique. You wouldn't wait five years to assess whether you're profitable; instead, you'd review monthly or quarterly reports. The **time period assumption** allows you to generate income statements, balance sheets, and cash flow reports for these specific periods.

For example, during the holiday season, your boutique might see a huge surge in sales. By reviewing quarterly reports, you can compare holiday performance with slower months like February and plan your inventory and marketing budget accordingly. This assumption ensures that financial activity is consistently monitored and assessed within specific, meaningful time frames.

The Two Accounting Constraints

While the **principles and assumptions** of accounting create a basic structure for financial reporting, the **constraints** provide important limits to prevent accounting from becoming unnecessarily complex. These two constraints ensure that accounting practices remain both practical and meaningful, especially for businesses with limited resources.

1. The Materiality Constraint

This constraint answers the question: *Does this transaction or piece of information really matter?* Businesses are only required to record and report financial details that could **influence the decisions of a reasonable person**.

Imagine this: A small coffee shop purchases a box of pens for $10. Technically, this is an expense, but would it really affect anyone's understanding of the shop's financial health? Probably not. According to the **materiality constraint**, this transaction is too insignificant to worry about, so the business doesn't need to go out of its way to document it in detail.

On the other hand, let's say that same coffee shop purchases a new espresso machine for $5,000. That's a material transaction, it impacts the shop's assets and profitability, and must be carefully recorded.

The materiality constraint ensures that accounting focuses on what **matters most**. For small businesses, this sometimes means ignoring details that are too insignificant compared to the big picture. For larger corporations, however, even smaller items might be considered material, as their scale means that small differences can have a big impact.

2. The Cost-Benefit Constraint

The cost-benefit constraint ensures that **the effort of creating financial disclosures is worth the value they provide.** Essentially, it's about weighing the costs of producing information against the benefits of having it available to users like investors, creditors, or managers.

For example, imagine a boutique clothing store is considering whether to track detailed customer demographic data alongside its sales figures. While this data could provide some insights, the cost of implementing and maintaining such a system might outweigh the value it offers to investors or management. According to the cost-benefit constraint, the store could skip this disclosure if the costs of collecting and reporting the data exceed its usefulness.

However, in a larger retail chain, the same demographic data might be invaluable for marketing and strategic planning. For a bigger company with more resources, the **benefits** of this disclosure could easily justify the cost of producing it.

This constraint highlights the practical side of accounting, the larger interests of business can often take precedence over unnecessary documentation.

What investors are really looking for

Once you've grasped the foundational principles, assumptions, and constraints of accounting, the next step is to understand what investors are really looking for in a company's financial statements. At its core, **an investor's primary concern is a company's ability to generate reliable, sustainable income**—income that not only reflects current profitability but also signals long-term stability and growth.

Investors don't just care about profits—they care about **where those profits come from.** A company's net income, while important, is just one piece of the puzzle. For example, a record company might suddenly generate $20 million in profits from the unexpected success of a breakout jazz album. While impressive, this windfall is likely a one-off event, not something the company can replicate every year. Contrast this with a similar $20 million profit earned by an industrial supply company through its regular operations—selling tools and equipment to construction firms.

The difference is **sustainable income**. This term refers to a business's ability to consistently generate income through its core activities, year after year. Sustainable income is more valuable to investors because it reflects the business's true earning potential, rather than being influenced by one-time gains or extraordinary circumstances.

When companies release their income statements, they often separate **operational revenue** (income generated by normal business activities) from **non-operational revenue** (income from activities outside the usual scope of business). This distinction is critical for investors evaluating a company's financial health.

Let's consider a small bakery. Its operational revenue comes from selling bread, pastries, and coffee. However, if the bakery sells an old delivery van for $15,000, that income is considered non-operational. While it boosts the bakery's total income for the year, it doesn't reflect the bakery's ability to generate revenue from its core business, baking and selling food. Investors rely on this distinction to understand which parts of a company's income are sustainable and which are not.

The **value of a company** in the eyes of investors is a combination of its market position, the quantity of its earnings, and the reliability of those earnings. Reliability hinges on how much of the income is sustainable. A company with high, stable operational income will likely attract more investor confidence than one with fluctuating or unpredictable earnings.

For example, a tech startup that regularly earns revenue from its software subscription service is more appealing to investors than a startup that posts large profits one year due to selling off patents but shows inconsistent income otherwise. Sustainable income serves as a litmus test for a company's long-term viability and resilience.

Annual Reports

The **annual report** is a comprehensive snapshot of the business's performance, strategies, and plans. This document serves two purposes: first, to provide transparency and compliance with accounting standards like GAAP, and second, to act as a **sales pitch** to current and potential investors.

The **annual report** contains the key financial statements: the income statement, balance sheet, retained earnings statement, and statement of cash flows. Together, these provide a detailed view of the company's financial health. But the value of the report goes beyond just the numbers.

One critical addition is the **management analysis section.** Here, the company's leadership discusses industry trends, anticipated challenges, and strategic opportunities for the upcoming year. For investors, this analysis provides context and insight into how the business is preparing to grow and overcome obstacles.

Accompanying the financial statements are **notes** that outline the accounting methods used. These are especially valuable to experienced accountants, as they offer a behind-the-scenes look at how the company arrived at its reported figures.

Finally, the annual report includes an **auditor's report**, prepared by a Certified Public Accountant (CPA). This third-party verification checks whether the company's financial statements comply with GAAP, providing an additional layer of trust for investors.

For investors, the annual report is akin to a **scorecard.** It reveals whether a company is performing well, adapting to market trends, and maintaining financial stability. The management analysis section is particularly important, offering a glimpse into leadership's vision and strategy.

Imagine you're considering investing in a tech company. The financial statements might show strong profits, but the management section reveals the company is heavily reliant on a single product line that's facing increased competition. This kind of insight helps you make more informed decisions about the long-term viability of the business.

Pro Forma Income

In addition to GAAP-compliant income statements, many companies provide **pro forma income reports**, which exclude unusual or non-recurring items. These reports aim to show what the company's earnings might look like under "normal" circumstances, making it easier for investors to focus on sustainable income.

For example, let's say a construction company incurs a one-time expense of $5 million to obtain a permit for a new project. While this cost must be included in the GAAP-compliant income statement, it might be excluded from the **pro forma income report** to reflect a more typical earnings scenario.

However, investors should approach pro forma reports with caution. Companies sometimes use these reports to present an overly optimistic picture of their profitability, excluding items that perhaps shouldn't be omitted. In extreme cases, the gap between GAAP income and pro forma income can be enormous, leading to accusations of **bad-faith reporting.**

The SEC has issued guidance to reduce misuse of pro forma reporting, but the responsibility often falls on investors—and trained accountants—to assess the integrity of these reports. A seasoned accountant, for instance, can critically evaluate whether the adjustments made in a pro forma report are reasonable or whether they're masking deeper financial issues.

Choosing Investments

By leveraging financial data presented under standardized frameworks like GAAP, investors can evaluate opportunities with confidence, ensuring a **level playing field** for comparisons.

The process begins by verifying the accuracy and consistency of financial reporting. Once satisfied, the investor can move on to a **side-by-side evaluation** of investment opportunities using established comparison methods and financial ratios.

When assessing investments, three primary methods help investors benchmark a company's performance:

1. **Intracompany Basis:** This involves comparing a company's current performance against its own past results. For example, if a local gym increased its annual revenue by 20% over the past three years but showed a decline of 5% this year, this trend might raise concerns about its future profitability. Investors use this method to identify whether the company is improving or struggling over time.

2. **Intercompany Basis:** This method compares one company's performance to that of its **direct competitors**. For instance, when evaluating two mid-sized car manufacturers, investors might compare revenue growth, debt ratios, and profit margins. By analyzing companies within the same industry, this approach helps investors assess **relative performance** in similar market conditions.

3. **Industry Average:** This comparison evaluates how a company stacks up against the **industry average**. For instance, if a restaurant chain has a profit margin of 12%, while the industry average is 18%, it may suggest the company is underperforming. This method helps investors gauge whether a company is aligned with, exceeding, or falling behind broader industry standards.

Financial Ratios

To dive deeper into financial analysis, investors rely on **financial ratios**. These ratios help quantify a company's financial health, growth potential, and ability to manage debt. Two of the most commonly used ratios are:

1. **Current Ratio**

The current ratio measures a company's ability to meet its short-term obligations using its short-term (or "current") assets.

> - **Formula**: Current Assets ÷ Current Liabilities
> - A **healthy company** typically has a current ratio of at least **1:1**, meaning it can cover its immediate debts. Ideally, a ratio closer to **2:1** provides greater assurance of liquidity.

For instance, if a bookstore has $200,000 in current assets and $100,000 in current liabilities, its current ratio would be **2:1**, indicating strong short-term financial stability. Conversely, a ratio below **1:1** might signal potential cash flow issues, which could deter risk-averse investors.

2. **Price-to-Earnings (P/E) Ratio**

The P/E ratio is a solvency ratio that evaluates a company's valuation relative to its earnings.

> - **Formula**: Market Price per Share ÷ Earnings per Share (EPS)

> A **high P/E ratio** often indicates the market expects significant future growth, even if current earnings are low. A **low P/E ratio**, on the other hand, may signal a stable company with modest growth potential, often seen as a "value stock."

For example, if a tech company has a P/E ratio of 40, it might indicate optimism about its future innovations. Meanwhile, a utility company with a P/E ratio of 10 might appeal to investors seeking consistent dividends and reliability.

How Investors Use These Tools

Investors combine the comparison methods with ratios to make well-rounded decisions. For example:

> - **Intracompany Analysis + Current Ratio:** Analyzing whether a company's liquidity has improved year over year.
> - **Intercompany Comparison + P/E Ratio:** Comparing a startup's valuation with its competitors to identify whether it's overvalued or undervalued.
> - **Industry Average + Current Ratio:** Determining if a company's liquidity aligns with industry norms.

Chapter 8 Assessment Test

1. **What is the main purpose of GAAP in financial reporting?**

   a. To help businesses reduce their tax liabilities.

   b. To standardize financial information for comparability.

   c. To allow companies flexibility in presenting financials.

2. **Which of the following is considered the most authoritative source in the GAAP hierarchy?**

   a. Industry best practices.

   b. Professional judgment.

   c. Statements issued by FASB or the SEC.

3. **Under the Measurement Principle, how should an industrial oven purchased for $20,000 be recorded?**

   a. At the discounted price of $20,000.

   b. At its market value of $25,000.

   c. At the original sticker price of $22,000.

4. **What does the Revenue Recognition Principle require?**

   a. Record revenue when payment is received.

   b. Record revenue when the sale is invoiced.

   c. Record revenue when it is earned, regardless of payment timing.

5. **According to the Full Disclosure Principle, what should a business disclose in its financial statements?**

   a. Only numerical data directly tied to revenue.

   b. All relevant information that could affect users' interpretation.

   c. Only information legally required by tax authorities.

6. **What does the Going Concern Assumption imply?**

   a. A business will likely shut down in the near future.

   b. A business will continue operating for the foreseeable future.

c. Assets should always be reported at liquidation value.

7. **Why is the Business Entity Assumption important in accounting?**

   a. It allows business owners to combine personal and business finances.

   b. It protects investors from taxation.

   c. It separates personal finances from business records.

8. **What is sustainable income?**

   a. Income from one-time gains like asset sales.

   b. Income generated consistently from core business operations.

   c. Estimated income adjusted for inflation.

9. **What is the role of the auditor's report in the annual report?**

   a. To explain the company's marketing strategy.

   b. To verify compliance with GAAP and enhance investor trust.

   c. To justify executive salaries and bonuses.

10. **What does the current ratio measure?**

    a. A company's profitability based on historical trends.

    b. A company's ability to meet short-term obligations.

    c. The relationship between debt and equity.

Answers

1. What is the main purpose of GAAP in financial reporting?

Correct Answer: b) To standardize financial information for comparability.
GAAP ensures consistency across financial statements, allowing investors to compare companies on a level playing field.

2. Which of the following is considered the most authoritative source in the GAAP hierarchy?

Correct Answer: c) Statements issued by FASB or the SEC.
These are Level 1 sources in the GAAP hierarchy and carry the highest level of authority.

3. Under the Measurement Principle, how should an industrial oven purchased for $20,000 be recorded?

Correct Answer: a) At the discounted price of $20,000.
The Historical Cost Principle within GAAP requires recording assets at their actual purchase price.

4. What does the Revenue Recognition Principle require?

Correct Answer: c) Record revenue when it is earned, regardless of payment timing.
This principle ensures revenue reflects actual business activity, not just cash inflows.

5. According to the Full Disclosure Principle, what should a business disclose in its financial statements?

Correct Answer: b) All relevant information that could affect users' interpretation.
Transparency is key, including details like future lease obligations or legal risks.

6. What does the Going Concern Assumption imply?

Correct Answer: b) A business will continue operating for the foreseeable future.
This assumption allows financial statements to reflect long-term operations rather than liquidation.

7. **Why is the Business Entity Assumption important in accounting?**

Correct Answer: c) It separates personal finances from business records.
Maintaining this boundary ensures accurate reporting and tax compliance.

8. **What is sustainable income?**

Correct Answer: b) Income generated consistently from core business operations.
Investors value sustainable income as a sign of long-term profitability and stability.

9. **What is the role of the auditor's report in the annual report?**

Correct Answer: b) To verify compliance with GAAP and enhance investor trust.
An auditor's report adds third-party credibility to the financial statements.

10. **What does the current ratio measure?**

Correct Answer: b) A company's ability to meet short-term obligations.
A ratio of 2:1 or higher generally indicates strong short-term financial health.

Conclusion

Congratulations on completing *Accounting for Beginners [All-in-One]!* By reading this book, you've already taken a significant step toward mastering the "language of business." Whether you're a student, a small business owner, or someone exploring accounting to enhance your career, you've built a foundation that will serve you well in both your professional and personal financial life.

Practice, Patience, and Progress

Accounting, like any other skill, improves with practice. The concepts you've learned—ranging from the basic principles to financial statement analysis—may feel complex at first, but they become second nature with consistent application. Treat every financial transaction or report as an opportunity to sharpen your understanding. Just as a chef refines their recipes over time or a musician perfects their craft through repetition, your fluency in accounting will grow as you immerse yourself in its practice.

Here's the good news: the tools and techniques you've studied are not just theoretical, they're practical. Here are a few steps to help you apply your new knowledge effectively:

Set Regular Review Periods: Whether monthly, quarterly, or annually, commit to reviewing your financial statements regularly. This discipline will keep you in tune with your finances and allow you to spot trends or issues before they become problems.

Stay Organized: Create a system for keeping track of receipts, invoices, and other records. Whether you prefer physical filing cabinets or digital tools, organization is the backbone of accurate accounting.

Leverage Technology: If you haven't already, explore accounting software to simplify your processes. Many platforms can automate tasks like invoicing, expense tracking, and financial reporting, freeing you up to focus on strategy and growth.

Seek Support When Needed: Don't hesitate to consult with professionals, whether it's for tax preparation, audits, or strategic planning. Temporary assistance from a CPA or bookkeeper can pay dividends. And give you long-term success in your accounting processes and systems.

Building Confidence and Making Informed Decisions

As you continue to apply these principles, you'll gain the confidence to make informed decisions, identify opportunities, and address challenges with clarity.

Whether you're evaluating a potential investment, preparing for tax season, or managing day-to-day operations, your growing knowledge will give you the tools to succeed.

Your Next Steps

Keep Learning: Stay curious and seek out additional resources. Accounting evolves, and staying updated on new practices, software, or regulations will help you remain effective.

Experiment and Analyze: Apply what you've learned to your personal or business finances. Track your progress and use your insights to improve.

Set Goals: Whether it's achieving better cash flow, growing your savings, or scaling your business, let your newfound accounting knowledge guide you toward your goals.

Accounting is more than a profession or a skill, it's a lens through which you can view and understand the financial world. By embracing this newfound knowledge, you've empowered yourself to take control of your finances and make wiser, more strategic decisions.

Thank you for taking this journey with us, and here's to your continued success!

Glossary

Accrual Accounting: A method of accounting where revenues and expenses are recorded when they are earned or incurred, not when cash is received or paid.

Amortization: The gradual write-off of an intangible asset's cost over its useful life, such as patents or trademarks.

Assets: Resources owned by a company that have economic value, including cash, inventory, buildings, and intellectual property.

Balance Sheet: A financial statement that provides a snapshot of a company's assets, liabilities, and equity at a specific point in time.

Capital Expenditures (CapEx): Funds used by a business to acquire, maintain, or improve physical assets like buildings or equipment.

Cash Flow: The movement of money into and out of a business during a specific period, used to assess liquidity.

Cost of Goods Sold (COGS): The direct costs of producing goods or services sold by a business, including materials and labor.

Current Assets: Assets that can be converted into cash within one year, such as accounts receivable and inventory.

Current Liabilities: Debts or obligations a business expects to settle within one year, such as accounts payable or short-term loans.

Depreciation: The allocation of the cost of a tangible asset over its useful life, reflecting wear and tear or obsolescence.

Dividends: A portion of a company's earnings distributed to shareholders, typically in the form of cash or additional shares.

Equity: The residual interest in the assets of a company after deducting liabilities, representing ownership interest.

Expenses: Costs incurred by a business in the process of earning revenue, such as salaries, rent, and utilities.

FIFO (First-In, First-Out): An inventory valuation method where the oldest inventory costs are used to calculate the cost of goods sold.

Fixed Costs: Expenses that remain constant regardless of production levels, such as rent or insurance.

GAAP (Generally Accepted Accounting Principles): A set of standardized accounting rules and guidelines used in the U.S. to ensure consistency and transparency in financial reporting.

Income Statement: A financial statement that summarizes a company's revenues, expenses, and profits over a specific period.

Inventory: Goods available for sale or raw materials used in production.

Liabilities: Financial obligations or debts owed by a company to creditors, such as loans, accounts payable, and mortgages.

LIFO (Last-In, First-Out): An inventory valuation method where the newest inventory costs are used to calculate the cost of goods sold.

Liquidity: The ability of a business to meet its short-term financial obligations, often measured by ratios like the current ratio.

Net Income: The amount of profit remaining after all expenses, taxes, and costs have been deducted from total revenue.

Non-Operating Revenue: Income derived from activities outside a company's primary operations, such as the sale of assets.

Operating Expenses: Costs directly related to the day-to-day operations of a business, such as wages, rent, and marketing.

Profit Margin: A financial ratio that shows the percentage of revenue remaining as profit after expenses.

Revenue: Income generated from normal business activities, such as the sale of goods or services.

Retained Earnings: The cumulative amount of net income that a company retains for reinvestment rather than distributing as dividends.

Trial Balance: A worksheet listing all ledger account balances to check that total debits equal total credits in the accounting system.

Variable Costs: Costs that vary in proportion to production levels, such as raw materials and shipping expenses.

Working Capital: The difference between current assets and current liabilities, indicating the company's short-term financial health.

Bonus Chapter and Tools

As an added bonus, with your purchase of *Accounting for Beginners*, you gain access to an **exclusive extra chapter: Chapter |9| dedicated to detecting and preventing financial fraud.** This bonus chapter provides invaluable insights into protecting your business from potential risks and maintaining ethical financial practices.

THE FRAUD TRIANGLE

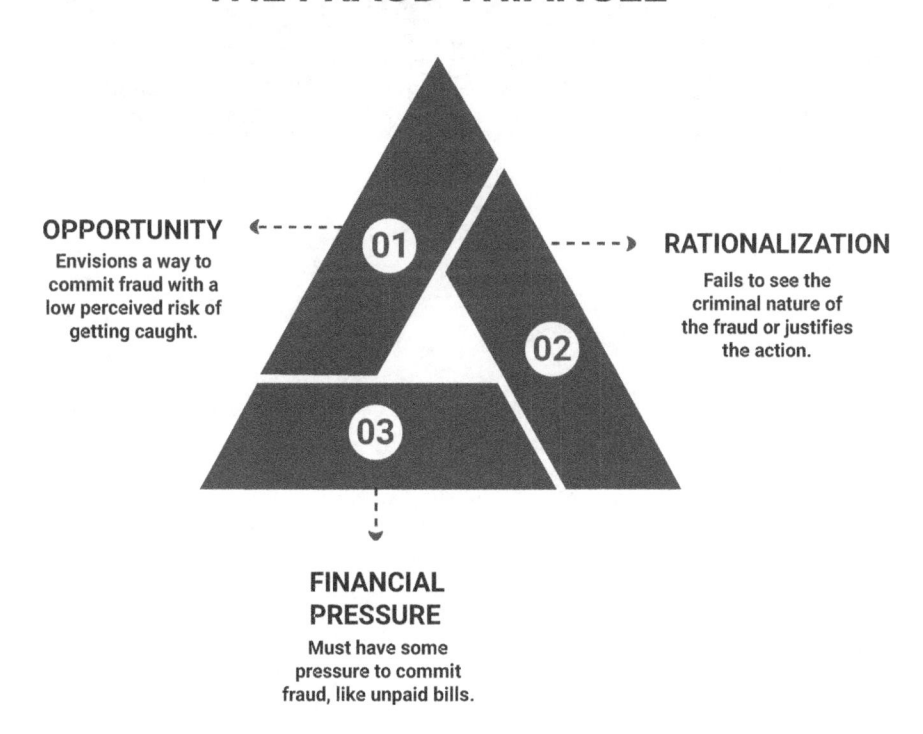

OPPORTUNITY ← 01
Envisions a way to commit fraud with a low perceived risk of getting caught.

RATIONALIZATION →
Fails to see the criminal nature of the fraud or justifies the action.

02

03

FINANCIAL PRESSURE
Must have some pressure to commit fraud, like unpaid bills.

In addition, you gain access to **ten accounting templates** to help you manage your business and personal finances with ease. These include templates for **customer income and expense tracking**, **profit and loss statements (monthly and yearly)**, and **receivable and payable management**. You'll also find **inventory management sheets**, a **personal finance dashboard**, and a **simple budget tracker**. Whether you're monitoring expenses, analyzing profitability, or optimizing cash flow, these Excel templates provide a structured and efficient way to stay on top of your finances. While you may eventually transition to more advanced tools like **QuickBooks Online** or **Xero**, these files serve as an excellent resource for beginners. They'll help you get comfortable with fundamental accounting concepts and calculations, allowing you to organize your finances clearly, simply, and effectively.

Download your Bonus here (or click on the link if you are on Kindle:

https://financeknightspublications.aweb.page/p/f797b918-e718-4241-b45f-e16e5db8b3c9

About Us

FINANCE KNIGHTS
PUBLICATIONS

Finance Knights Publications is an expert-driven publishing house specializing in business, investment, and accounting books designed to equip entrepreneurs and professionals with the knowledge they need to succeed.

Over the past year, we've helped numerous business owners, both beginners and seasoned professionals, establish LLCs, S Corps, and other structures, while also guiding them through essential topics like tax optimization, compliance, and sustainable growth.

Our bestselling titles, such as **Dummies Guide to Starting Your Own Business, QuickBooks Online for Beginners Bible Edition 2 Books in 1, and LLC Beginner's Step-by-Step Guide,** have become essential resources for individuals looking to navigate the complexities of business ownership and financial management. These books stand out for their clarity, depth, and actionable advice, making even the most complicated concepts accessible.

At the core of Finance Knights Publications' success is its commitment to collaborating with the foremost experts in the industry. This approach ensures that each book is not only a repository of knowledge but also a tool for real-world application, providing readers with concrete strategies and methods to achieve their goals.

My name is Carmelo, founder of Finance Knights Publications. After 16 years of service in the Armed Forces, I decided to pursue my passion for business and personal finance, leaving behind a life of discipline and duty to create something meaningful. My mission is to empower individuals with the knowledge to achieve financial freedom.

This book is the result of extensive research, drawing on the expertise of leading professionals in business, tax, and law, to provide you with the tools needed for success.

At *Finance Knights Publications*, I'm fortunate to work alongside my partner and a team of dedicated collaborators from around the world. Together, we strive to deliver the very best in every book we produce, sharing practical insights and strategies to help others break free from financial constraints and live the life they've always dreamed of.

My goal is to make a real difference in the lives of those who seek the same freedom I once pursued. I hope this book inspires you to take that leap and create the life you truly deserve. Thank you for taking the time to read my work, I'm deeply grateful and honored to be part of your journey.

Could you do us a favor?

If you've made it this far, I want to thank you for sticking with us, it means so much!

At this point, I'd love to hear your thoughts.

If you haven't already done so, will you please take a moment to leave an honest review on Amazon?

As you know, many people judge a book by its cover, and, more importantly, by its reviews.

Your feedback can help other budding business owners find the guidance they need to start on the right foot.

It **costs you nothing** and **takes less than a minute**, and could help other people just like you, improve themselves so they can live a life of independence.

Remember, you can include a photo of the cover, a quick comment, a friendly encouragement, anything you'd like.

Scan the QR code or click the link (if you're on Kindle):

https://www.amazon.com/review/create-review/?ie=UTF8&channel=glance-detail&asin=B0DRTNJ419

Again, all of this is *completely optional*, there's no obligation whatsoever, but if you do decide to post:

Pat yourself on the back for making a positive difference in someone else's life. Remember, what goes around comes around.

Thank you from the bottom of our hearts for your support. It truly means so much to us.

If you spotted any issues or have ideas to improve this book, send us a note at **info@financeknightspublications.com**. We greatly appreciate your input, and if we integrate your suggestions, we'll gladly email you our updated digital copy as a small token of thanks.

Best regards, **Finance Knights Publications**

Made in United States
Cleveland, OH
25 August 2025